UK FINANCIAL INSTITUTIONS AND MARKETS

UK FINANCIAL INSTITUTIONS AND MARKETS

MICHAEL PAWLEY
DAVID WINSTONE
PATRICK BENTLEY

MACMILLAN

First published in 1991 by
MACMILLAN EDUCATION LTD
Houndmills, Basingstoke, Hampshire RG21 2XS
and London
Companies and representatives
throughout the world

ISBN 0–333–55535–X hardcover
ISBN 0–333–55536–8 paperback

A catalogue record for this book is available
from the British Library.

Typeset and illustrated by
TecSet Ltd, Wallington, Surrey.

Printed in Great Britain by
Billing & Sons Ltd, Worcester

For our parents

CONTENTS

LIST OF FIGURES

LIST OF TABLES

CHAPTER 1

INTRODUCTION

This book provides a broad framework of the UK financial system within which the nature and operations of the respective financial institutions and markets are then analysed. The emphasis is on institutions and markets as dynamic entities which react to their environment, the major elements of which are *competition, regulation and market structure*. The text is thus analytical rather than descriptive, to reflect the reactive and proactive nature of UK financial institutions and markets.

Some knowledge of elementary economics is assumed, particularly in terms of flows of funds in the economy, the definition and role of money, and basic macroeconomic concepts. There are no specific chapters on the operation of monetary policy, although several chapters (notably on the banks, the building societies and the Sterling money markets) place emphasis on the importance of how monetary policy operations affect the competitive market environment and hence strategy and operations of the financial institutions.

Chapters 2 and 3 introduce fundamental concepts that are of major importance to all financial institutions – financial intermediation and interest rates. The crucial nature of financial intermediation and hence of financial institutions and markets to the efficient working of the economy is detailed in terms of the benefits available to ultimate lenders (surplus units) and ultimate borrowers (deficit units). The main elements of financial intermediation are set out – maturity transformation of funds, aggregation of savings, pooling of financial risk and reductions in transactions costs – and are examined in terms of their importance and relationship to the various groups of financial institutions. Disintermediation is described, and examples provided as to the effects on groups of financial institutions.

In Chapter 3 the classical loanable funds approach and the Keynesian liquidity preference approach to interest rate determination are explained. These apparently contradictory viewpoints are resolved by looking at the similarities in the theories once both the short term and the long term are taken into consideration. The term structure of interest rates is explained, and the fundamental factors underlying the shape of the yield curve – risk, liquidity preference and expectations – are examined, and examples of yield curves shown.

In Chapter 4 a summary is given of the number and types of banks in the UK – retail, clearing, merchant, other British, American, Japanese and overseas. Details are provided as to their main areas of activity, size and importance. Competition between themselves and other lending institutions is examined. The need for a regulatory regime and supervision is explained within the provisions of the 1987 Banking Act and the Basle Agreement. Reference is made to the nature of risk and LDC debt provision as well as the necessity to handle risk incurred through new financial instruments and off-balance-sheet activities. Finally profitability is reviewed, and diversification/conglomeration considered.

In Chapter 5 an aggregate balance sheet of the building societies is used to show their activities and the relative importance of the different assets and liabilities held. The effects of the building societies' cartel on societies' interest rates, the supply of mortgage loans, and the mix of price and non-price competition amongst building societies are analysed. Competition with the retail banks for personal sector balances and mortgage loans is examined in terms of the markedly changed conditions in the 1980s compared with the 1970s (and a regulatory matrix is used to stress this point). Financial innovation by building societies is noted, and trends in the industry's share of personal sector business are set out. Recent changes in the attitude towards profitability are pointed out, and the constraints of the capital adequacy and liquidity regulations are outlined.

Chapter 6 examines the primary role of the various sectors of the insurance industry in providing risk transfer mechanisms, and the important secondary role as large institutional investors in the financial markets. In terms of the former, the scope of the chapter covers the concept of risk management and insurance as a risk transfer mechanism through a consideration of the classification of insurance business, market size and profitability, competition and solvency, underwriting, and finally costs. With regard to the secondary role, the size and components of insurance company investments are examined, and maturity matching is considered.

The functions of the various specialist non-bank financial intermediaries are dealt with in Chapter 7. The operations, size and growth of unit trusts are specified and compared, and contrasted with the operations and growth of investment trusts. The importance of pension funds to the operation of the financial system is emphasised with reference to their market size, and their functions are considered. National Savings, venture capital funds and finance houses are all examined in terms of their activities and roles in the financial system.

Chapter 8 deals with the role and function of the Bank of England, including sample balance sheets, and the early sections are devoted to analysing the Bank's main responsibilities – regulation, supervision, banking, lender of last resort, national debt management, exchange market intervention and the operation of monetary policy. The manner in which the Bank's regulatory role has changed in recent years with the advent of the Securities and Investments Board and the various Self Regulatory Organisations is stressed. Speculation as to the possibility of a European Central Bank is outlined, and the implications for the role of the Bank of England in any such future system are examined.

Chapter 9 deals with the Sterling money markets. The main participants are identified, with reasons for their participation. Instruments are listed and a detailed examination is made of the price/yield relationship and also the relevance of time to maturity in relation to liquidity, using Treasury Bills as an example. The role of the Discount and parallel markets is explained, introducing the lender of last resort function of the Bank of England. From this follows an analysis of bank base rate determination. Following this chapter it should be possible for the reader to interpret a Financial Times money market report.

Chapter 10 considers the Eurocurrency markets. There is a discussion of definitions to facilitate understanding of the nature of such markets. A distinction is made between Euromarkets and the International Banking Market. Participants and reasons for participation are identified and size and growth of the markets is illustrated and explained. Interest rate comparisons are made with domestic rates and how the relationship has changed over time. Finally an explanation is given of the way in which interest rate differentials between Euro rates of different currencies determine forward margins/rates in the forward foreign exchange market.

The role of the capital market is analysed in Chapter 11, with special attention given to the primary and secondary markets of the Stock Exchange. The implications of Big Bang for institutional and personal investors, and for the members of the Stock Exchange themselves are detailed. The problem of competition from overseas stock markets is highlighted with reference to the changes in the Stock Exchange. Recent topical areas of concern such as insider dealing – what it is, how it is patrolled – and the October 1987 crash, why it happened, whether computers were at fault, and the implications for market efficiency are investigated.

The changing regulatory framework for UK financial institutions and markets is set out in chart form in Chapter 12, and the activities and responsibilities of the main regulatory bodies – The Department of Trade and Industry, The Securities and Investments Board, the Bank of England, and the various Self Regulatory Organisations – are examined. The need for regulation of financial institutions is emphasised with reference to recent institutional frauds (e.g. Barlow Clowes, Posgate), and given the interdependence of institutions, the problems of 'Domino' effects are stressed. Recognition is given however to the need for a level playing field amongst financial institutions to prevent non-neutral competitive conditions, and the question of whether or not financial institutions and markets are over-regulated compared with other sectors of the economy is discussed. The attitude and response of financial institutions to compliance and polarisation rules are laid out.

A synthesis of recent changes in the structure of the financial system, how those changes have affected financial institutions and markets, and how the institutions have in turn reacted is provided in the final chapter. This brings together in a coherent manner the major trends occuring in the UK financial system that affect all financial institutions and that have been referred to in earlier chapters. The tendency for mergers to occur is rationalised, and the effects of mergers that at times produce large conglomerates on the degree of competition in the financial system are investigated, as are the conflicts of interest that arise. The impact of deregulation and re-regulation on the degree of competition in financial markets is pointed out, and the response of institutions in the form of financial innovation is detailed. The effects of financial markets becoming increasingly internationalised and the approach of 1992 are discussed with reference to the threats and opportunities for UK financial institutions. The reasons behind the growth of securitisation and off-balance-sheet business are also examined.

CHAPTER 2

FINANCIAL INTERMEDIATION

2.0   INTRODUCTION

An analysis is made of the nature of financial intermediation with particular emphasis in this chapter on the main aspects of financial intermediation – maturity transformation, risk pooling, aggregation of savings, and reduction in transactions costs. Financial intermediation is contrasted with trends in the 1980s and 1990s for disintermediation to occur in some sectors. Flow of funds tables for the main sectors of the economy are used to show the pattern of intermediation activities in recent years.

2.1   FINANCIAL INTERMEDIATION

Financial institutions perform the financial intermediation role of transferring funds from ultimate lenders (surplus units) to ultimate borrowers (deficit units). It is conventional to use the term 'ultimate' to differentiate these lenders and borrowers from the financial institutions themselves, which will also be lending and borrowing. A person with savings (a surplus unit) might for example place them in a bank deposit account, and would therefore be an ultimate lender. The bank would then on-lend those funds to an ultimate borrower (a deficit unit).

Financial intermediaries channel funds that might otherwise be 'idle' by their financial intermediation function.

The ultimate lender will have a financial claim against the financial intermediary, which represents a claim for money (e.g. a depositor has a claim against the bank for the money deposit to be paid back). Conversely, a financial intermediary will hold a claim on an ultimate borrower to pay back the money. Funds originally held by ultimate lenders may thus turn into two financial claims during the intermediation process. The ultimate lender has a claim (asset) against the financial institution (a liability to the institution), which in turn on-lends the money and has a financial claim (asset) against the ultimate borrower (whose loan represents a liability). A financial claim represents the holder's right to payment of a sum of money or stream of income some time in the future. The broad term 'financial claim' can be narrowed down to specific 'financial instruments' such as building society accounts, bank accounts, equities, bonds etc.

All financial claims have the same characteristics which tend only to differ by degree rather than substance. All claims will have a degree of liquidity, for instance, which is the ability to change the claim into cash quickly and without capital loss. The ability to do so without taking a capital loss is important because a 20 year gilt could be sold relatively quickly, for example, but that does not necessarily mean it is liquid because it is possible that it might only be sold with a capital loss. Each financial claim will also possess a degree of risk, in the form of default risk (particularly possible when lending to an ultimate borrower, but less likely when 'lending' to a financial institution), capital risk (high for equities, but low for bank and building society deposits), and income risk, which is the risk of being locked in at fixed rates of interest when interest rates in general rise.

Financial claims also embody a yield, in the form of interest payments, dividends, and any gain/loss in the capital value of the asset. The yield on a share for example, will consist of the dividends paid plus increases in the value of the share. Yields are generally related to liquidity and maturity (see Chapter 3 for an explanation of the term structure of interest rates) and particularly to the level of risk involved. Figure 2.2 shows that the greater the

Figure 2.1 *Financial Intermediation*

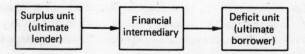

Figure 2.2   *The Risk/Return Trade-off*

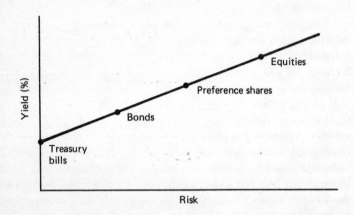

level of risk of a financial instrument, the greater the required yield by investors.

Investors will in general attempt to maximise returns for a given level of risk, or minimise risk for a given level of return.

Some claims, such as bonds and equities, will be marketable, whilst others, such as savings accounts and life assurance policies, are not. Similarly, some financial claims have a specific maturity, such as bonds or gilts, whilst others will have no definite life span, such as equities and deposit accounts.

Ultimately, there is an asymmetry of information in that borrowers know more about the risk and return of their business than do ultimate lenders, such that financial institutions fill the gap that exists by acting as intermediaries.

Financial intermediation is influenced by four broad factors (Llewellyn, 1985): (i) changes in the volume of demand for financial intermediation, (ii) changing portfolio preferences of customers which determine the type and nature of instruments demanded, (iii) changes in the financial market environment, (iv) changes in financial institutions' own objectives, constraints and portfolio behaviour.

The combination of these forces leads to changes in the structure and operation of financial institutions and markets.

The UK financial institutions and markets are involved with the running of the payments system, the provision of funds for borrowers, the provision of instruments for lenders, the creation of financial assets and liabilities, and the supply of non-intermediation financial services. The role of the financial markets is the efficient allocation of resources amongst competing uses, the transfer of risk, and the supply of instruments for portfolio allocation.

It is important for the health of an economy that financial markets are efficient. Efficiency in this context has three main aspects. Markets need to be allocatively efficient, in other words to channel savings into the most profitable businesses; they need to be dynamically efficient, which means the ability to change and innovate in the face of evolving customer needs and changing market environment, and they need to be operationally efficient by providing services at the lowest possible cost.

One of the most important aspects of market failure is the externalities that arise from the failure of a financial institution, particularly in the form of loss of investors' funds, and on a wider scale in the loss of confidence in financial markets. It is generally argued that the exit of a financial institution through insolvency entails higher costs than that of an industrial company, and as such prudential regulations are far more important, as subsequent chapters will show.

The main functions of financial intermediaries are:-

(i) Maturity transformation of funds;
(ii) Risk pooling;
(iii) Aggregation of savings;
(iv) Reduction in transactions costs.

2.2 MATURITY TRANSFORMATION

In general, most financial institutions are able to use relatively short-term liabilities to finance long-term assets. The majority of building society liabilities for example are short-term deposits (up to six months) yet these are used to finance long term mortgages, typically for twenty-five years (although in practice homeowners move every seven years on average). They are able to carry out this maturity transformation of funds without having liquidity problems because of the law of large numbers. When the financial institution has a large number of depositors, it will know from experience that only a small proportion of depositors' funds will be withdrawn on any one day. The institution therefore only has to maintain sufficient cash or liquid assets to meet those withdrawals, and can then lend to borrowers a further proportion or multiple of the deposits (leaving a desired amount in a variety of liquid forms), often for long periods of time.

Retail banks and building societies, as they tend to have large numbers of depositors, are able to carry out substantial maturity transformation, whereas merchant banks, with a smaller depositor base, tend to have a smaller ability to carry out maturity transformation.

2.3   RISK POOLING

Financial intermediaries carry the risk of defaults on the loans they grant and thus ultimate lenders who have used a financial intermediary do not have to face the risk of ultimate borrowers defaulting. For example, depositors can place their funds in a financial institution, and know that (except in very exceptional circumstances) their money will be returned when required. If financial institutions did not exist, then ultimate lenders would face the risk of lending to ultimate borrowers. In effect very little lending would be carried out because of the high risks involved for ultimate lenders (or if lending did occur, it would be at very high rates of interest to compensate for the risk). Financial institutions can accept the risk because they know that as a proportion of total funds lent, defaults are likely to represent only a small fraction (in effect the law of large numbers is again an important factor). Moreover, financial institutions will in practice set a spread between deposit and lending rates that takes account of likely defaults according to past experience.

2.4   AGGREGATION OF SAVINGS

Financial institutions carry out the service of collecting together all of the savings of individuals (many of which will be relatively small) and companies and bundling them up into larger loans. Financial intermediaries can thus provide loans for borrowers in the size required by aggregating savings. If financial intermediaries did not exist, borrowers would have to borrow directly from the many different savers, which would involve heavy transactions costs and be infeasible.

2.5 REDUCTION IN TRANSACTIONS COSTS

As financial institutions deal with a large number of clients they can operate on considerably smaller unit costs per transaction than the ultimate lender would face. Straightforward 'shoe-leather' or search costs can be reduced for both ultimate lenders and borrowers by financial intermediaries because of the presence in many cases of branch networks, and because of the power of advertising.

2.6 DISINTERMEDIATION

It is also possible for *disintermediation* to occur. This is where surplus units lend directly to deficit units without a financial institution providing the intermediation function.

In Figure 2.3 companies lend directly to each other on the inter company market (see Chapter 9) without any financial intermediation taking place. In Figure 2.4 financial institutions are merely acting as go-betweens, advising their clients, rather than acting specifically as intermediaries. With the changes introduced in Big Bang (see Chapter 11) the retail banks were able to move into the Stock Exchange and buy member firms, thus gaining fee-income from acting as an adviser to the issue, and so recapturing some of the business lost through disintermediation.(See Chapter 13.)

Figure 2.3   *Disintermediation – Inter Company Market*

Figure 2.4 *Disintermediation – Pre-Big Bang*

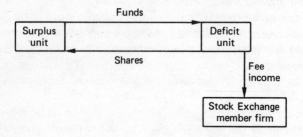

Figure 2.5 *Disintermediation – Post-Big Bang*

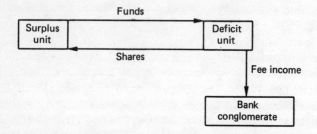

Figure 2.6 *Financial Intermediation and Flow of Funds*

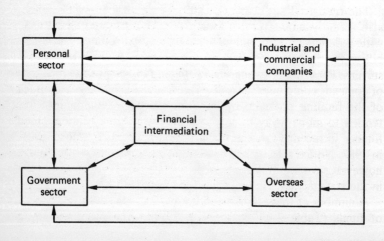

2.7 FLOW OF FUNDS

Financial intermediation can be seen in a flow of funds context. Within this flow of funds there will be many linkages, including of course intra-sector flows, (movement of funds within sectors), and it should be recognised that intermediation amongst financial institutions themselves is not shown here. The linkages can be shown by looking at the financial deficits and surpluses for the sectors.

Table 2.1 shows the financial transactions of the personal sector, and particularly the level of any financial surplus or deficit that exists. A surplus is when saving exceeds investment, and a deficit occurs when investment exceeds saving. From the table it is clear that the personal sector has moved into a position of financial deficit in recent years. A surplus of £8.8 billion in 1984 has been turned into a deficit of £5.9 billion in 1989, 1st half. (With a large deficit of £14.5 billion in 1988). Borrowing for house purchase has been particularly strong, especially from building societies as opposed to banks, but has eased to a large extent as a result of high interest rates in 1989. Holdings of UK company securities have fallen in the 1980's, but are mirrored by indirect holdings of securities through life assurance and pension funds, claims on which have grown steadily. Deposits with banks and building societies have grown fast, particularly with the stock market crash of 1987 when a lot of funds were withdrawn from the stock market and placed in deposit accounts, and with the attraction of relatively high interest rates in 1989.

The Industrial and Commercial Companies Sector (ICC's) has also recently moved into a financial deficit position (Table 2.2) with a deficit of £8.5 billion for the first half of 1989, and £6.2 billion for the whole of 1988, whereas previously the sector was in surplus. Particularly strong was borrowing to carry out acquisitions of domestic companies, as well as overseas investments, with much of the funding provided by bank borrowing as companies have tended to move away to some extent from Stock Market based finance in recent years, particularly since the Stock Market crash in 1987. Notice that there are large balancing items in the figures however, showing that there are considerable omissions and errors in the statistics for the financial transactions of ICC's.

A number of trends can be discerned from the sources and uses of funds (Table 2.3) of the rather heterogeneous grouping of

Table 2.1   *Personal Sector$^{(a)}$ Financial Transactions*

£ billions Increase in assets/decrease in liabilities +	1984	1985	1986	1987	1988	1989 H1
Financial Surplus/deficit of which:	+8.8	+7.5	+2.8	−6.5	−14.5	−5.9
Net claims on life assurance and pension funds	+18.5	+19.0	+19.5	+20.8	+21.8	+12.7
Deposits with building societies	+13.2	+13.3	+11.8	+13.6	+20.2	+8.6
Deposits with UK banks	+3.3	+5.1	+8.4	+8.4	+16.9	+9.3
Public sector debt	+4.3	+0.8	+4.4	+3.4	−0.3	−2.4
UK company securities	−5.6	−6.0	−3.1	+0.5	−2.0	−1.0
Borrowing for house purchase	−17.0	−18.5	−26.3	−29.1	−39.7	−15.8
Of which from building societies	−14.5	−14.1	−18.8	−14.6	−23.2	−10.8
Borrowing from UK banks$^{(b)}$	−4.2	−6.7	−5.2	−8.7	−12.9	−7.3

(a)   Includes individuals, private non-profit-making institutions and unincorporated businesses.
(b)   Other than for house purchase.

Source: Bank of England Quarterly Bulletin (February 1990)

intermediaries that make up the Other Financial Institutions (OFIs) sector. Liquid assets holdings have been increased in recent years, particularly since the Stock Market crash, and with the advent of high interest rates. Holdings of British government securities, by contrast, have tended to grow more slowly in 1988 and 1989. Withdrawals of funds from overseas equity markets can be clearly seen in 1987, with a subsequent reversal towards growth

Table 2.2 *Selected transactions of industrial and commercial companies*

£ billions	1984	1985	1986	1987	1988	1989 H1
	+6.3	+5.4	+1.8	+1.9	−6.2	−8.5
Selected financial transactions requiring financing (increase +)						
Trade investments mergers	+4.2	+3.8	+2.6	+2.5	+9.4	+3.6
Long-term investments overseas	+4.1	+4.7	+6.1	+13.8	+9.7	+6.8
Balancing item	−	+2.5	−0.2	+7.0	+16.7	+5.9
Net financing requirement (−)	−3.3	−6.1	−10.0	−23.6	−46.5	−24.3
Selected financial items (increase −)						
Bank and other borrowing	+7.4	+8.0	+10.0	+13.3	+33.3	+18.0
Capital issues	+1.7	+5.1	+7.8	+17.9	+9.1	+4.3
Investment from overseas	−2.7	−0.3	+3.0	+2.9	+3.6	+6.7
Bank deposits	−1.4	−4.8	−11.0	−8.5	−6.4	−7.2

Source: Bank of England Quarterly Bulletin (February 1990)

in overseas equities again in 1988 and 1989. With the public sector finances moving into surplus in 1988 and 1989 there has been a fall in government debt in existence, and a consequent fall in holdings by OFIs.

The overseas sector has invested heavily in UK securities in recent years (Table 2.4), with total overseas take-up of UK securities rising significantly since 1984, from £1.2 billion to over

Table 2.3   *Other financial institutions' sources and uses of funds*

£ billions	1984	1985	1986	1987	1988	1989 H1
Sources of funds						
Bank Borrowing	− 6.4	−4.2	−14.1	−16.6	−10.0	−11.8
Life assurance and pension funds	−17.8	−18.4	−18.8	−20.2	−20.9	−12.4
Unit trust units	−0.6	−1.1	−2.2	−3.5	0.5	−
Capital issues	−0.2	−0.6	−3.3	−3.6	−6.0	−4.3
Other sources	−0.7	−4.3	−2.9	−3.0	−2.6	−2.2
Total	−25.7	−28.5	−41.2	−47.0	−39.0	−30.7
Use of funds						
Liquid assets	+6.5	+4.9	+8.7	+18.7	+13.0	+11.6
British government securities	+5.5	+5.2	+3.2	+0.8	−1.7	−6.6
UK company securities	+5.0	+8.3	+9.3	+17.1	+12.4	+7.3
Overseas securities	+2.4	+7.0	+17.5	−7.6	+6.0	+9.3
Lending for house purchase	+0.7	+0.6	+2.8	+4.7	+5.8	+1.5
Other uses	+1.9	−0.1	+0.7	+3.9	+3.3	+1.8
Total	+21.9	+25.9	+42.1	+37.6	+38.8	+24.9
Net identified financial transactions	−3.9	−2.6	+1.0	−9.4	−0.1	−5.8

Source: Bank of England Quarterly Bulletin (February 1990)

Table 2.4 *Selected overseas sector financial transactions*

£ billions Increase in assets/decrease in liabilities +	1984	1985	1986	1987	1988	1989 H1
Net identified financial transactions [a] of which:	−7.9	−7.9	−9.9	−6.2	+4.2	−
UK direct investment in overseas securities	−2.7	−3.1	−6.1	−6.9	−5.8	−3.1
UK portfolio investment overseas	−9.9	−19.4	−23.1	−3.3	−9.9	−14.7
Total take-up of overseas securities [b]	−13.4	−23.2	−29.7	−3.7	−16.1	−18.0
Overseas direct investment in UK securities	+0.9	+5.5	+6.0	+7.6	+6.0	+2.5
Overseas portfolio investment in the United Kingdom	+0.3	+0.8	+1.5	+3.1	+3.3	+2.5
Total overseas take-up of UK securities [c]	+1.2	+6.3	+7.5	+10.7	+9.3	+5.1
Net deposits with UK banks [d]	+10.4	+7.4	+11.2	+1.5	+14.3	+6.6

[a] Line 39 Table F.
[b] Line 32 Table F.
[c] Line 31 Table F.
[d] Lines 21 + 24 Table F.
Source: Bank of England Quarterly Bulletin (February 1990)

£10 billion for the whole of 1989. Overseas deposits with UK banks have also remained strong, largely as the result of high interest rates in the UK relative to other countries. It can also be seen that total UK take-up of overseas securities has been extremely large in 1985 and 1986, with a heavy drop in 1987 after the crash, and that take-up of overseas securities in 1989 was again extremely large.

REFERENCES

Bain, A.D. (1981) *The Economics of the Financial System.*
Llewellyn, D.T. (1985) *The Evolution of the British Financial System*. Institute of Bankers.

CHAPTER 3

INTEREST RATES

3.0 INTRODUCTION

Interest rates are fundamental to an understanding of financial institutions and markets. This chapter presents an analysis of why there are so many different rates of interest in an economy (the 'spectrum' of interest rates), and examines the theoretical determination of the general level of interest rates through classical loanable funds theory and Keynesian liquidity preference theory. Finally, the term structure of interest rates and theories of the underlying term structure are explained.

3.1 THE SPECTRUM OF INTEREST RATES

Interest rates can be viewed simply as the price of money, the return that lenders require from borrowers. In the terms established in Chapter 2, borrowers (deficit units) will give lenders a supply of claims against themselves to be paid at a later date. Lenders, who have surplus funds available, provide the funds in return for the claims against the borrower which will be paid at a later date. The price at which claims are exchanged is the rate of interest, or price of money. Lenders will require a larger sum to be repaid in the future, i.e. the interest rate will generally be positive, to take account of default risk, to compensate for loss of liquidity, and for foregoing the chance of consumption now for consumption in the future.

There is a vast array of interest rates on the financial assets available in an economy, and differences in interest rates between different financial claims will be influenced by the factors below:-

(i) Risk

Financial institutions take great care in assessing the credit worthiness of prospective borrowers (often using credit scoring techniques). Those who are deemed to be high risk borrowers (i.e. a high chance of defaulting) will be required to pay a greater rate of interest. In practice, banks charge a percentage over the London Inter Bank Offer Rate (LIBOR) to corporate customers in accordance with the perceived risk. There will be instances, of course, when the risk is too high and cannot be compensated for by any level of interest rate, in which case the loan will be refused. The risk on different paper assets will also be reflected in the interest rate charged. For example, the discount rate (a form of interest rate) on eligible bank bills will be lower than on normal commercial bills because they have been accepted by an eligible bank which means that they are eligible for discount at the Bank of England and are therefore less risky.

(ii) Time to Maturity

The duration of the financial claim will be a factor in the rate of interest charged. In general, the larger the time to maturity of the loan, the greater will be the rate of interest required by the lender to compensate for both the loss of liquidity and the fact that uncertainty will increase with longer transactions (see the section below on the term structure of interest rates).

(iii) The Size of the Loan or Deposit

Wholesale (large) deposits will tend to attract a higher rate of interest than retail (small) deposits to reflect the lower unit transactions costs. With respect to loans, it would normally be expected that the greater the size of the loan then the greater would be the rate of interest charged to reflect the risk for the financial institution of increasing the concentration of its asset portfolio on a smaller number of large loans. In practice however, this may often not be the case as larger corporate wholesale borrowers may be extremely credit-worthy customers.

(iv) Competition between Institutions

The degree of competition between financial institutions and any market imperfections that might exist will tend to affect interest rates. For example, banks and building societies compete for deposits, which affects the interest rates across the whole spectrum of retail deposit facilities offered (in marked contrast to the 1970s when market imperfections such as the building societies' cartel influenced competition and hence interest rates – see Chapter 5). Competition will also tend to affect the interest rate on loans. The greater the level of competition, the lower interest rates would be. By contrast, the greater the degree of concentration in a market (i.e. the smaller the number of financial institutions in a specific market or the existence of institutions with a high proportion of market share) the lower would interest rates on deposits be, and the higher would be the rate on loans, other things being equal (i.e. the institutions would have the ability to increase their spreads).

(v) Marketability of the Financial Asset

The less marketable or liquid an asset is (the more difficult it is to buy or sell) the greater will be the rate of interest paid on it, and the more marketable, the lower the rate of interest.

(vi) The Need for Profits

Financial institutions need to take account of the required rate of return by their shareholders, their operational costs, and the possibility of defaults, and set their interest rates accordingly. It should also be noted however that financial institutions might have a policy of maximising growth, or maintaining customer loyalty, or might indulge in price cutting to increase market share, rather than necessarily aiming to maximise short-term profitability.

(vii) Inflation Expectations

The (nominal) interest rates charged by lenders will partly be a reflection of their perception of future inflation. As expectations amongst financial institutions will tend to vary to some degree, then their interest rates will tend to vary.

(viii)   Government policy

Many government actions can impinge upon the activities of financial institutions and their customers and hence on interest rates (see later chapters). Taxation policies, requirements for institutions to hold reserves, capital adequacy constraints, and monetary controls, amongst others, may all affect the pattern of interest rates.

3.2   NOMINAL AND REAL INTEREST RATES

A nominal rate of interest can be viewed as a simple money rate of interest. If the money rate paid on a £10,000 loan was £1,400 per annum, then the nominal rate of interest would be equal to 14 per cent. Real rates of interest take into account the effects of inflation. A simplified method of calculating a real rate of interest is to subtract the rate of inflation from the nominal rate of interest. So, for a nominal rate of interest of 14 per cent, and an inflation rate of 8 per cent, the real rate of interest would be 6 per cent. To be mathematically correct, however, the real rate of interest should be measured as:-

$$\frac{1 + \text{Nominal Interest Rate}}{1 + \text{Inflation Rate}} - 1$$

$$\text{i.e. } \frac{1.14}{1.08} - 1 = 5.55\%$$

3.3   THE GENERAL LEVEL OF INTEREST RATES

There are two main theories relating to the determination of the general level of interest rates.

(i) Classical Loanable Funds Theory

It is argued that the real rate of interest will tend to be determined by the supply and demand for loanable funds, the former being determined by the level of saving, and the latter by the desire for investment. Figure 3.1 shows how the interest rate r_1 is determined by the level of saving (supply of loanable funds) and the level of investment (demand for loanable funds). At an interest rate of r_2 (Figure 3.2) the supply of funds available will be larger than the demand for those funds (i.e. Q_2 as opposed to Q_3 as borrowers will regard the cost of borrowing as too high) and market forces will push interest rates down. As interest rates fall, saving will fall (arrow 1) and borrowing for investment will rise (arrow 2), until the equilibrium point is reached at an interest rate of r_1.

On the other hand, if interest rates are at r_3 (Figure 3.3) the demand for investment funds will be greater than the supply (i.e. Q_4 as opposed to Q_5). Borrowers want to borrow at this low rate of interest but savers find it relatively unattractive. The interest rate will be bid up as potential borrowers compete for the scarce supply of funds available. As interest rates rise, some of the demand will recede (arrow 3) as investment projects become unprofitable, and saving will increase as interest rates become more attractive, until an equilibrium is again reached at r_1Q_1.

Figure 3.1 *Loanable Funds*

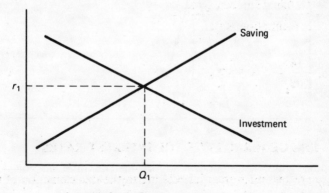

Loanable funds: Supply and demand

Figure 3.2   *Loanable Funds: Excess Supply*

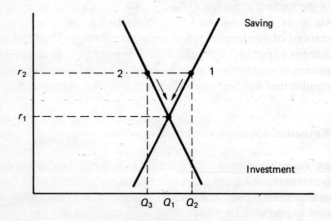

Loanable funds: Supply and demand

Figure 3.3   *Loanable Funds: Excess Demand*

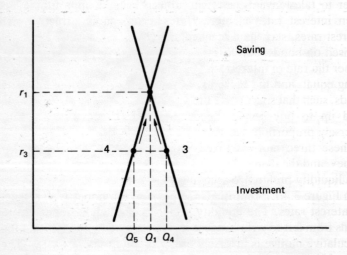

In this theory the money supply has no influence on real variables such as saving and investment, only on the level of prices, and hence has no influence on the real rate of interest. It is argued that changes in the general level of real interest rates will come about through changes in the savings and investment behaviour of the various sectors of the economy. Savings and investment behaviour in time can be affected by, *inter alia*, changes in expectations of future income, changes in expectations of inflation and changes in productivity of capital investment equipment. Such changes could lead to the supply and demand curves shifting, and a new equilibrium interest rate being attained.

(ii) Keynesian Liquidity Preference Theory

Keynes maintained that there are three motives for holding money: transactions, precautionary and speculative.

Transactions balances are held for day-to-day expenditure, and will tend to rise with increases in income, but will in general only be affected to a small degree by changes in interest rates. Precautionary balances are held for unexpected expenditure, such as the car breaking down, and will again be affected by income, but very little by interest rates. Speculative balances are held in order to take advantage of speculative gains on financial assets when interest rates change. Bond prices move inversely with interest rates, such that when interest rates fall, capital gains are realised on bonds, and losses made when interest rates rise. The higher the rate of interest, the more likely it is to fall, other things being equal, and the more likely are capital gains to be made on bonds, such that speculative balances will be low as they have been used up to buy bonds. Speculative money balances are thus inversely proportional to the rate of interest.

These three motives together can be called the demand for money, and the demand for money can be represented graphically as a liquidity preference schedule.

In Figure 3.4 *LP* represents the demand for money with respect to interest rates. The liquidity preference schedule slopes downwards from left to right because it is influenced by the fact that the speculative motive is inversely proportional to interest rates. The rate of interest r is determined by the supply of money and the demand for money as represented by the liquidity preference schedule. If the supply of money falls, e.g. to M_2 the rate of interest will rise to r_1 (Figure 3.5)

Figure 3.4   *Liquidity Preference Theory*

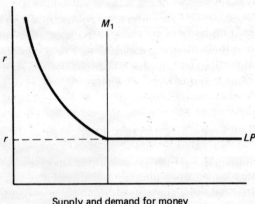

Supply and demand for money

Figure 3.5   *Liquidity Preference Theory: A fall in the supply of Money.*

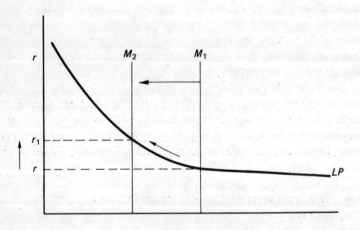

Supply of and demand for money

Although the Keynesian and classical theories appear to be contradictory they are in fact similar if both the short-run and long-run are considered. The Keynesian liquidity preference theory tends to agree that in the long run changes in the money supply will in fact be reflected in prices, whilst the classical school accepts that in the short run changes in the money supply can in fact have effects on real variables.

In practice, a number of factors will affect the general level of interest rates. Lenders will generally require a real rate of return, such that nominal interest rates should be sufficient to cover expected rates of inflation. If there is considerable uncertainty regarding expected inflation, a higher rate of return may be required. A weak currency may result in the government maintaining high interest rates to attract overseas capital into the country and prop up the value of the currency. A long term deficit on the current account of the balance of payments will have similar effects in terms of a depreciating currency, and again higher interest rates may be needed.

The government's stance on monetary policy can have considerable effects on the general level of interest rates, particularly if as in recent years it is trying to control the growth rate of the money supply and hence inflation through high interest rates. Short term money market rates are influenced by open market operations (see Chapter 9) which has a ripple effect to other longer term interest rates in the economy (although it should be recognised that the authorities cannot *control* interest rates, but only influence them, and an attempt to push interest rates above what financial markets and institutions think is sustainable will be unsuccessful). In relation to monetary policy, changes in the size of the Public Sector Borrowing Requirement (PSBR) will also tend to affect interest rates. A high PSBR will tend to lead to higher interest rates, other things being equal, as the need to sell a large volume of government debt will generally necessitate offering higher interest rates to encourage investors to take them up.

3.4 THE TERM STRUCTURE OF INTEREST RATES

The relationship between yield (interest payments and any capital gains or losses) and maturity on assets of the same type (e.g. gilts) is referred to as the term structure of interest rates. Figure 3.6 shows some typical yield curves for gilts.

The 'normal' yield curve will tend to slope upwards from left to right, because of the greater degree of risk in terms of inflation,

Figure 3.6   *Representative Yield Curves (Gilts)*

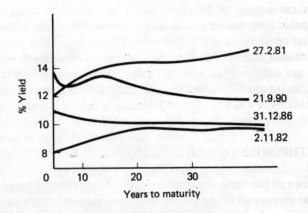

Figure 3.7   *Yield Curves and Expectations*

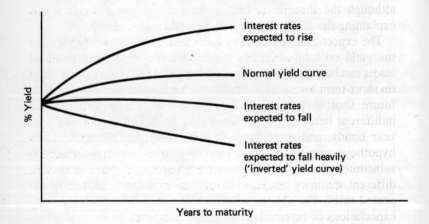

default risk and to compensate for loss of liquidity the greater the time to maturity.

If interest rates are expected to rise, the yield curve would be expected to become steeper, as lenders will not wish to lend long term now and be locked in at low interest rates when higher ones are on their way, but will instead want to lend short term. Borrowers, on the other hand, will want to borrow long term to lock into today's rates and so benefit when interest rates rise in the future but will not want to borrow short term. There will thus be an excess supply of funds at short maturities, but an excess demand at long maturities, holding down yields in the former, but pushing up yields in the latter.

If interest rates are expected to fall, the opposite will occur. If there are extremely strong expectations of a reduction in interest rates, an inverted or negative yield curve may develop, where the expecations of a fall in rates wipes out any risk or liquidity effects.

3.5 THEORIES OF THE TERM STRUCTURE

Theories of the term structure of interest rates ideally need to be able to explain all of the yield curves as represented in Figure 3.6. In practice, the individual theories cannot adequately explain the shape of the yield curve at any particular time, and market practitioners certainly view them with a degree of scepticism, although the theories in combination do go some way towards explaining the term structure of interest rates.

The expectations hypothesis states that the relationship between the yield on long-term financial assets and short-term financial assets can be explained by market expectations regarding the yield on short-term assets. It is maintained that all investors know what future short-term rates will be, and that an investor will be indifferent between buying a ten-year bond and buying ten one-year bonds, and there are no costs involved. The expectations hypothesis treats short-term and long-term securities as perfect substitutes such that investors take no account of uncertainty of different maturity assets, and forward rates are equated to expected rates. The shape of the yield curve is thus determined by expectations of future short-term interest rates.

In the liquidity preference hypothesis, ten one-year bonds are not a perfect subsitute for a ten-year bond, as the level of liquidity differs. Substitutability can be obtained, but at a price, and that price is the liquidity premium. In the liquidity preference hypothesis, investors require greater liquidity premiums the less liquid is a given asset. That is, investors have a preferred level of liquidity and require higher returns to be coaxed into a less liquid position. In an uncertain world, investors will prefer short-term assets over long-term assets because they are more liquid (can be turned quickly into cash and without capital loss), especially as short-term bond prices tend to be less volatile than long-term. The liquidity hypothesis thus stresses that the yield curve will normally slope upwards from left to right. The important aspect of the liquidity premium hypothesis that is not inherent in the expectations hypothesis is that investors are risk averse, and so will prefer more capital-certain short-term assets over longer term more volatile assets. This also tends to refute the expectations hypothesis that states that bonds of different maturities are perfect substitutes.

From the point of view of financial institutions, it should be noted that different types of institution have different preferences for the maturity of their assets. Pension funds and life funds prefer to hold long dated assets that they can match with their liabilities whilst building societies and banks may hold shorter maturities in general as they require a higher degree of liquidity. Financial institutions do not perceive these assets as being highly similar, but prefer certain maturities, and this may affect the term structure of interest rates. This is known as the segmented markets theory.

The segmented markets hypothesis maintains that the liquidity preference approach may well be correct for some investors, such as building societies which prefer certainty of capital over certainty of income, but for others, such as insurance companies, longer term securities will be preferred because of their income. As different investors have different preferences for specific bands of maturities, then interest rates will be determined by the supply and demand in each segment of the market. The yield curve may thus be a series of separate segmented markets, with the yield being determined by the supply and demand for that maturity of asset, and that maturity alone.

REFERENCES

Dodds, J.C. and Ford, J.L. (1974) *Expectations, Uncertainty and the Term Structure of Interest Rates*. Martin Robertson, London.
Llewellyn, D.T. and Tew, B. (1988) 'The Sterling Money Markets and the Determination of Interest Rates'. *National Westminster Bank Quarterly Review*, February.

CHAPTER 4

THE UK BANKING SECTOR

4.0 INTRODUCTION

At the end of February 1990 the UK Banking Sector (formerly the monetary sector) contained the institutions in Table 4.1.

Table 4.1 *The UK Banking Sector*

	No.
Retail Banks	21
Discount Houses	8
British Merchant Banks	31
Other British Banks	167
American Banks	44
Japanese Banks	29
Other Overseas Banks	290
Total	590

Source: Bank of England Quarterly Bulletin (February 1990)

With the exception of the Discount Houses, and by some classifications also the British Merchant Banks, they can all be classified as Commercial Banks.

In order to give an indication of the importance of each group of institutions within the UK banking sector, shown in Table 4.2 are the size of deposits in each group.

As can be readily seen from the table, it is the retail banks which hold the majority of sterling deposits, while Japanese and American banks hold the majority of foreign currency deposits, denoting their importance in the Euromarkets (see Chapter 10).

Table 4.2   *Deposit Balances end-June 1990 of Groups of Institutions within UK Banking Sector*

Deposits	Sterling		Other Currency	
	£b	% share	£b	% share
Retail Banks	284.842	54.7	61.421	9.8
Discount Houses	15.135	2.9	0.402	
British Merchant Banks	31.178	6.0	15.800	2.5
Other British Banks	41.944	8.1	10.078	1.6
American Banks	20.131	3.9	88.743	14.2
Japanese Banks	36.067	6.9	212.423	33.9
Other Overseas Banks	90.982	17.5	237.757	37.9
Total	520.279	100.0	626.624	100.0*

* Total not 100 per cent due to rounding

Source: data aggregated from *Bank of England Quarterly Bulletin* (August 1990).

4.1 RETAIL BANKS

Within the classification of Retail Banks are the Clearing Banks, so called because they handle the majority of the UK's cheque and credit clearing. That is, they handle the transfer of funds from one bank to another via balances at the Bank of England, necessary when payments are made between individuals or companies which bank with different banks.

The banks represented on the Committee of London and Scottish Bankers (CLSB) are:

Bank of Scotland	National Westminster
Barclays	Standard Chartered Bank
Lloyds	Royal Bank of Scotland
Midland	TSB Group

Table 4.3 *Retail Banks*

There are 21 banks classified as retail banks. They are:
  Abbey National plc
  Abbey National Trust Services plc
  Allied Irish Banks plc
  The Banking Department of the Bank of England
  The Bank of Ireland
  The Bank of Scotland
  Barclays Bank plc
  Clydesdale Bank plc
  Co-operative Bank plc
  Coutts & Co.
  Girobank plc
  Lloyds Bank plc
  Midland Bank plc
  National Westminster Bank plc
  Northern Bank plc
  The Royal Bank of Scotland plc
  TSB Bank Northern Ireland plc
  TSB Bank Scotland plc
  TSB Bank plc
  Ulster Bank Ltd.
  Yorkshire Bank plc

Source: *Bank of England Quarterly Bulletin*, banks listed as at 12.1.90.

A summary of the changes in their deposits is given on a monthly basis in a table published in the Financial Times on the third Wednesday of every month (except December, second Wednesday).

The principal function of the retail/clearing banks is to take retail deposits (£100 000 or less) and wholesale deposits (greater than £100 000) and on-lend them in the form of overdrafts and various types of loans. This business is with both the personal and corporate sectors. In addition to this, the banks provide a wide range of other services producing fee income.

These services include factoring, leasing, unit trusts, credit cards, executor and trustee, investment and tax advice, share

Table 4.4   *Balance Sheet (selected items)*
             Banks in the UK, end September 1990

£ millions	
Sterling liabilities	
sight deposits	155,753
time deposits	260,036
CDs and other short term paper	43,556
Total Sterling deposit liabilities	459,345
Capital and other funds	55,452
Total other currency deposit liabilities	685,275
Sterling assets	
till money	2,774
cash ratio deposit	1,342
loans to discount houses	8,706
inter bank loans	81,457
UK bank CDs	16,069
building society CDs and time deposits	1,813
treasury bills	3,713
eligible L.A. bills	120
eligible bank bills	9,864
total sterling advances	324,609
total sterling assets	531,003
total other currency assets	681,490
Total assets, sterling and other currency	1,212,493
Total sterling acceptances	17,420
of which by eligible banks	17,151
eligible liabilities	348,030

Source: *Bank of England Quarterly Bulletin*, selected items table 3.1

dealing and portfolio management, insurance and estate agency.
Of course, many of these services are provided by bank subsidiary
companies. This business diversification has been possible due to
deregulation in financial markets, allowing previously traditional
barriers between different types of financial services to be broken
down. In turn this has led to new competition for the banks,
principally from the building societies, but also from the insurance
companies.

A feature of the retail bank sector in the UK is its branch network, which now numbers over 13,000. Many branches are in fact sub-branches or satellites to a larger centre branch. These sub-branches do not have a branch manager as such, but are run on a day to day basis by a supervisor. Many of the corporate accounts which were run from the nearest branch have now transferred to the large centre branches and are looked after by corporate specialists. A lot of the 'back-room' work has been removed from small branches and they are becoming more like financial retailers. Expensive high street property is no longer used for administrative work.

It is the clearing banks which operate the main payment mechanism in the UK. In addition to banks on the CLSB there are also other banks which clear and have seats on the committee, examples include Coutts, Girobank, Yorkshire Bank and Co-operative Bank. The latter acts as a clearing agent for many non-clearers.

Non-clearers will get a clearer to clear for them as their agent. All clearers are members of APACS (Association of Payment Clearing Services). Within APACS are three companies which operate different types of clearing.

Cheques and credit transfers are handled by the Cheque and Credit Clearing Company Ltd. Items handled are said to be handled by Cheque Clearing (formerly known as General Clearing) and Credit Clearing, as appropriate. Some standing orders and direct debits are handled by Credit Clearing. It takes three working days for such items to be 'cleared', that is, for the money to be transferred from bank to bank and be usable without recourse by the recipient of the funds.

CHAPS (Clearing House Automated Payment System) is a same day electronic funds transfer system. There is a minimum figure of £5,000 on each item. It enables large sums to be transferred and be usable very quickly. (A person or company paying a cheque into their branch, by contrast, will not be able to use the funds represented by the cheque for three working days until the item is cleared).

Town Clearing covers same day clearance of cheques with a value greater than £10,000 if the cheques are drawn on and paid into participating clearing branches. Such branches are within a half mile radius of the clearing house and are designated Town

Clearing branches. It is proposed to increase the limit for Town Clearing. It involves messengers 'walking' the cheques from where the cheque is paid in, to the branch where the cheque is drawn. On presentation at the bank counters, provided there are sufficient funds, the money can be debited from the payer's account to that of the recipient of the cheque

BACS Ltd (Bankers Automated Clearing Services) enables external organisations to originate payment instructions which can then be fed into clearing. Instructions can be initiated by physically handing over computer tapes or by transmission of the information via a modem.

EFTPOS (electronic funds transfer at point of sale) fell within APACS and was the body set up to oversee the development of the payment system which enables, for example, retailers to originate funds transfers when purchases are made in their shop.

EFTPOS UK Ltd was closed in 1990.

Cheque Clearing

An outline of how cheques are cleared will enable the main principles of funds transfer to be understood. The process takes three working days.

Day 1

A, the drawer, writes out a cheque for £100 and gives it to B, the payee, in settlement of a debt. A banks with Lloyds and B banks with Natwest.

B pays the cheque into his bank and has his account credited with the £100 as an 'uncleared' item. The money cannot be used yet as it has not been collected from Lloyds, the paying bank. Natwest is the collecting bank.

The Natwest branch handling the cheque will sort it, along with all other cheques received that day into bank order. This is done by a machine reading the sort code, the six figure number which appears in the top right hand corner of every cheque. Bank and branch can be identified by reading the magnetic characters. A list can be made at branch level of all cheques not drawn on the branch itself which have been received that day.

The cheques are bundled and sent overnight to Natwest's clearing department at head office.

Day 2

The cheques are received at head office, where again all cheques are sorted into bank order and valued.

The cheques are then taken to the clearing house where they are handed over to representatives of the banks on which the cheques are drawn. Our £100 cheque will be in bundles handed over to Lloyds.

The cheque is taken back to Lloyds and sorted into branch order and listings are made of values so that A's account can be debited on day 3. The cheques themselves are then posted to the branches on which they are drawn.

Day 3

A's cheque is received at his Lloyds branch, and if in order, with sufficient funds, will be debited to his account. If it is not in order or insufficient funds it is returned to B via the collecting Natwest branch as unpaid.

Inter branch cheques clearly do not need to go into clearing. 'Own' cheques can be handled internally. All that is needed is for the payee to have his account credited and the drawer his debited. The bank itself does not experience a change in the level of its deposits. Only the ownership of the deposit has changed.

The above describes what happens to the cheques themselves. The actual money transfers covering the items through clearing is a separate matter.

Each clearing bank has an account at the Bank of England, its operational balance, which is used to effect the corresponding money transfer.

It would be very inefficient if each cheque were individually dealt with. Their values are already totalled in the clearing process so that net differences in the value of the transfers between banks are all that matter.

At the end of a day's clearing an individual bank will experience either a net withdrawal of funds or a net receipt, so that one adjustment to its operational balance will cover all the millions of items which entered clearing.

Imagine four banks only in the clearing system, see Table 4.5.

The net entries are those made by the Bank of England to each bank's operational balance. This one entry covers all cleared items on a daily basis. The alternative would be to pay each other and have lots of payments and receipts unnecessarily.

Table 4.5   *Lloyds, Natwest, Barclays, Midland*

Each bank will owe money to the other three and be owed money by the other three.

	Lloyds	Natwest	Barclays	Midland	Total owed by each bank
Lloyds owes	x	5	7	9	= 21
Natwest owes	3	x	9	8	= 20
Barclays owes	7	3	x	5	= 15
Midland owes	5	9	4	x	= 18
Total owed to each bank	15	17	20	22	

From the table 4.5 it can be seen that
Lloyds is owed 15 and owes 21 = − 6 net
Barclays is owed 20 and owes 15 = + 5 net
Natwest is owed 17 and owes 20 = − 3 net
Midland is owed 22 and owes 18 = + 4 net

4.2   DISCOUNT HOUSES

The role of the discount houses in the sterling money markets is examined in Chapter 9. In summary they take short term deposits from banks, thus enabling the banks to make liquidity adjustments. These funds are then used to purchase money market instruments such as Treasury bills, commercial bills and CDs. They are the principal market makers in such instruments. They occupy a pivotal role in the Bank of England's open market

Table 4.6 *Members of the London Discount Market Association (LDMA)*

Cater Allen Ltd	King & Shaxson Ltd
Alexanders Discount plc	Seccombe Marshall & Campion plc
Clive Discount Company Ltd	The Union Discount Company Ltd
Gerrard & National Ltd	S G Warburg Discount Ltd

Source: *Bank of England Quarterly Bulletin*, list as at end-Feb. 1990

operations in that it is via them that the Bank relieves shortages of liquidity and takes out surpluses. In this way, short term money market rates of interest can be influenced. Their original function, and one still carried out, is to discount bills of exchange and provide finance in this way to the corporate sector. They are very active in the CD market.

4.3 BRITISH MERCHANT BANKS

The term merchant derives from the time when many such banks began as merchant houses which arranged trading throughout the world and the financing of such trade. Things developed so that eventually direct trading ceased and the financing aspect took over. Once they had developed a sound reputation they could, for a fee, add their name to bills of exchange. In this way it was possible for the drawer on the bill, the actual merchant or seller, to discount the bill at a finer, better rate of discount. Thus acceptance facilities developed, i.e. the bank accepting bills for a fee and the role of Accepting Houses.

Financing of trade, both domestic and international, is now also carried out in areas such as medium term ECGD backed finance for exports, factoring, leasing, hire purchase, insurance and shipping.

Merchant Banks take wholesale deposits and use them in the money markets. They are active in the CD market, both as issuers and purchasers in the secondary market. Funds are also deployed to provide medium term corporate finance.

Fee income is earned as advisers on financial matters to industry as well as in the capacity of underwriters to new capital issues for companies. There are 31 merchant banks recognised by the Bank of England and they include household names such as Baring Bros., Hambros, Rothschild, Hill Samuel.

4.4   OVERSEAS BANKS

From Table 4.1 it can be seen that there is a large number of overseas banks in the UK. The majority are American and Japanese. From Table 4.2 it can be seen that their sterling deposits are relatively small, but that their currency deposits are important, far outweighing those of UK owned banks. This of course reflects their importance in the euromarkets (see Chapter 10).

Most overseas banks set up during the 1960s and 1970s, largely as a result of the growth in the euromarkets at that time and were, of course, a factor in its growth. A further reason for establishment in the UK is to serve local ethnic communities and of late the Japanese have entered the UK market to service its corporate clients who have established themselves in the UK or who wish to do so.

4.5   PRUDENTIAL SUPERVISION

Banking activity needs to be supervised to protect depositors, protect bank counterparties in markets and ensure order in markets by certainty and efficiency. In this way the general well-being and stability of the financial system should result.

In order to maintain confidence in the banking system depositors must be sure that they will be able to withdraw their money when required. The certainty of this can only be assured if the money represented by their deposits has been used to create assets which can be fully liquidated without appreciable loss. If assets cannot realise their balance sheet values then there must be sufficient capital employed in the banks to avoid losses to depositors. There must be sufficient capital so that losses will fall upon the providers of bank capital rather than the depositors.

In the UK the Banking Act 1979 was a response to an EC directive on the co-ordination of banking law. This has been superceded by the Banking Act 1987 and provides the statutory authority and framework for implementing the Basle Convergence Agreement in the UK. The implementation of this agreement must also meet the European Community Own Funds directive on banks' capital and the Solvency Ratio directive. These directives become legal requirements for EC banks in 1992 and 1993 respectively.

Bank Supervision involves assessment of the fitness and properness of a bank's management as individuals, an examination of the adequateness of its financial resources, an examination of its business plan and its management control systems. Furthermore, it is necessary to ensure on-going compliance. This is done by focusing on capital adequacy, the exercise of powers of investigation and direction and a regular exchange of information between bank officials and supervisors.

In October 1988 the Banking Supervision Division of the Bank of England issued a 'Notice to Institutions Authorised under the Banking Act 1987' (BSD/1988/3). It contained the explanation of the way in which the 'Basle Convergence Agreement' (the Basle Accord) would be implemented in the UK

The Basle Committee on Banking Regulations and Supervisory Practices meets at the Bank for International Settlements (BIS) in Basle. It comprises representatives from the central banks and supervisory authorities in the GIO countries. From this committee came the Accord or Convergence Agreement.

UK banks must comply with these rules from June 20, 1989, as transitional arrangements before implementation of the EC directives.

The intention is that a common way of assessing capital adequacy be used within the banking system of the GIO countries. In this way the banks in these countries will be equally safe and no one bank or banking system will have an advantage over another due to there being a lower capital requirement. Banks holding less capital than their competitors will be less safe in that there is less of a cushion provided by the capital should losses on assets occur, causing losses for depositors. In addition, due to the fact that there is much inter bank indebtedness, should one bank get into difficulties and not be able to meet its obligations then this will have an effect on banks which are, for example, a counterparty to the bank in difficulty. If the bank in difficulty has issued a number of CDs, these CDs may be held by other banks as liquid assets. At maturity if they cannot be repaid by the issuing bank then this will affect the stability of the bank holding them as an asset, as a counterparty. This in turn might set off a chain reaction with other banks. If counterparties are unsure of their opposite numbers this makes trading in money market instruments and inter bank lending less certain. Continual assessments have to be made as to the creditworthiness of potential counterparties. This slows up trading and therefore affects efficiency in markets.

Allowing a low capital base also gives banks an unfair competitive advantage over banks where a low capital base is not allowed. A low capital base means less of a return has to be earned and paid to the capital providers, the shareholders. In this way higher deposit rates and lower lending rates can be offered which will attract customers away from the banks with higher amounts of capital.

The main thrust of the Basle Accord is to ensure capital adequacy through applying risk weighted ratios. The Bank of England document BSD/1988/3 referred to earlier details its implementation. There follows an outline of its main provisions. Full details can be obtained from an examination of the document itself.

The main emphasis is on equity capital and disclosed reserves which are treated as Tier 1 capital. A second tier, Tier 2, comprises undisclosed reserves and non equity capital in essence.

A minimum of 8 per cent Tier 1 and 2 capital will be required of banks in relation to the value of their assets on a risk weighted basis, of which Tier 1 will form a minimum of 4 per cent.

Each asset in the balance sheet will be taken at its balance sheet value and then risk weighted according to a standard which reflects the risk that the asset will not realise its balance sheet value on sale. Below are given some examples of the risk weight categories for these on-balance sheet items.

A, 0%   cash, loans to OECD central governments and banks, certificate of tax deposit.

B, 10%   loans to discount houses (secured by e.g. Treasury bills), gilt edged market makers.

C, 20%   unsecured loans to discount houses, cash items in the process of collection.
D, 50%   loans to individuals secured by a first mortgage
E, 100% claims on the non-bank private sector (i.e. normal bank lending not covered in D).

It should also be understood that banks also have a number of off-balance sheet risks which have to be taken into account when assessing bank risk. These items are given credit conversion factors. Examples below.

Instruments
D, 50%   guarantees and indemnities, performance, bid bonds
E, 20%   documentary credits issued by the banks collateralised by the underlying shipments
I, 0%   endorsement of bills
N.B.   endorsement of bills which have not been accepted by a bank carry a credit conversion factor of 100%.

The basic idea is that the required amount of capital is related to the asset values on a risk weighted basis. In this way bank risk can be brought to a common factor. Simply relating the amount of capital to balance sheet value would take no account of the risk of loss to asset values in different banks. Without risk weighting it would be possible for banks with similar balance sheet asset values to have the same amounts of capital regardless of type of capital. One bank might have a very safe asset structure supported by equity capital, whilst another might have a much riskier asset structure supported by non equity capital. If non-risk weighted comparisons were made and capital type ignored, it would be possible for each bank to operate apparently equally safely. Each would have the same balance sheet value for the amount of capital in relation to the balance sheet value of its assets. It would not reflect the differences in safety.

The Banking Act 1987 made the Bank of England the legal supervising authority for the first time and set up a Board of Banking Supervisors. It supervises all authorised institutions – those with net assets greater than £1m.

Its powers include the authority to veto acquisitions and mergers on prudential grounds and to require banks to report all loans larger than 10 per cent of capital. Prior notice must be given before loans can be made which expose more than 25 per cent of capital. Auditors can report on banks' activities without breaching their otherwise statutory duties of confidentiality.

The depositors protection scheme has been increased to 75 per cent compensation for the first £20,000.

4.6 CAPITAL ADEQUACY, BANK OPERATIONS AND PROFITABILITY

The implementation of the Basle Accord in relation to capital adequacy means that banks require more capital to support their assets than perhaps would be chosen if the matter were left to the banks themselves.

Given the asset structure of a bank which currently exists, and which does not meet the capital adequacy criteria, then the appropriate ratios can be achieved either by accumulating more capital of the right type, or by reducing the size of the asset base so that with a given amount of (fixed) capital, assets on a risk weighted basis match the capital currently in place.

Under conditions of falling stock market values, rising interest rates and worries concerning bank safety it may be difficult for some banks to raise the extra necessary capital. Squeezed profitability will also make it difficult to increase reserves from retained profits, especially if a proportion of the bank's assets are 'non-performing'. The alternative is for a bank to reduce the size of its asset base, for example, by securitising its LDC debt and refrain from rapidly increasing the size of its loan portfolio. This poses the same problem for profitability.

4.7 BANK LIQUIDITY REQUIREMENTS

Banks need liquidity in order to repay depositors. Although a very high proportion of an individual bank's sight deposits are withdrawn every day, this does not mean that banks need to have sufficient liquidity to meet this total need. Individual banks also have large fresh deposits on a daily basis to replace those withdrawn. What is needed is liquidity sufficient to meet net differences and to meet unexpectedly large demands.

The Bank of England in its paper 'The Measurement of Liquidity' (1980) stated bank liquidity requirements and laid down that banks should meet thir obligations by

holding sufficient liquid assets
by maintaining a deposit base of varying liabilities
by ensuring that maturing assets matched the maturity of liabilities.

The Bank of England did not wish to use liquidity ratios which should be adhered to by all banks as a standard, but instead indicated that liquidity management was the responsibility of each bank's management, with the Bank seeing that individual bank liquidity needs were met. However, the guideline ratio is 12 per cent, i.e. 12 per cent of assets to be in the 'primary' category below.

Attention has now moved to the Bank of England seeking to define and measure liquidity of banks on the basis of categorising Tier 1 and Tier 2 liquid assets.

Tier 1 would be sterling primary liquid assets, cash operational balances, Treasury bills, eligible bank bills and money at call on a secured basis with the discount houses. Tier 2 would be gilts, 1–5 years to maturity, bank and building society certificates of deposit with one year or less to maturity and interbank loans up to 8 days.

In addition to sterling liquidity, the Bank of England also seeks to ensure that individual banks' currency positions are monitored and that currency risk is managed.

4.8   BANKING AND EUROPE 1992

Progress in liberalising the financial services market, including banking, in the EC, has been slow. The reason for this is that member states have different approaches to their own domestic markets. In some there has been deregulation and open markets have resulted. In others controls still exist. Moves towards harmonisation of regulations resulted in some states attempting to preserve their own regulations on the grounds that their own regulations were best for their customers. Alternatively they wished to keep their own domestic market protected. In addition to this, until 1987 member states could veto EC directives, leading to slow progress towards a single market in financial services.

For these reasons harmonisation of regulations as an approach was abandoned. In its place came a 'home country regulation' approach. This means that, in the case of banking, recognition of a bank in its country of origin will mean that it can operate in any EC state. This approach enables each state to regulate banks in its own way, but does not exclude other EC banks from its market on the grounds that they do not comply with domestic regulations. It is mutual recognition by host regulations of the relevant controls in other EC states.

Granting of a banking licence in one EC state will enable the licensed bank to operate in any other EC state. This, however, does not preclude moves towards harmonisation in relation to the Basle Accord. Thus the objectives are still to harmonise capital adequacy requirements, solvency and liquidity, single large loan regulations, standards of managerial experience, published accounts and depositor protection schemes.

Sufficient harmonisation is clearly necessary if there is to be mutual recognition of each EC state rules by other EC states. If this were not the case then there would be a definite incentive for banks to gain their licence in the EC state with the least onerous, weakest regulations. It is also essential that exchange controls be removed between member states otherwise the full force of competition will not be felt.

As the situation stands it will obviously be possible for UK banks, for example, to set up branches in other EC states without the need for separate approval from the domestic regulatory authorities. It will also mean that they will not need to conform to different capital requirements and therefore have capital located inappropriately from the bank's point of view. A UK bank will be able to open branches according to demand as they see it, they will not be restricted by regulations concerning the number of branches they have as is the case in some member states.

UK banks will be able to offer their services from within the UK to residents in other EC states if they see a commercial advantage in so doing. This will obviously be an advantage in servicing the needs of multi-national companies. If UK banks are able to provide services in the UK to clients, they will be able to offer the same services in other EC states even if banks indigenous to that EC state are prevented from so doing by their own domestic banking regulations.

However, there may be some practical exceptions to these possiblities. States can still have their own 'public good' rules in relation to, for example, consumer protection. In the UK, a UK bank needs to be authorised in relation to parts of its business activities under the Financial Services Act. A foreign EC licensed bank it would seem would not need to be authorised under the Act, but would still have its actual conduct affected by the provisions of the Act. It may be possible that some states would exploit these types of situations and anomalies to protect their own markets from competition.

As the UK is already a very open market in relation to banking activity, the number of foreign banks being testimony to this, it seems that the principle of home country control should result in few changes for UK banks in their own market, but may well open up opportunities outside the UK.

REFERENCES

Molyneux, P. (1990) *Banking: An Introductory Text* (Macmillan, London).

Lewis, M. K. and Davis, K. T. (1987) *Domestic and International Banking* (Philip Allan London).

CHAPTER 5

BUILDING SOCIETIES

5.0 INTRODUCTION

The activities of the building societies can be crudely categorised as those pre and post 1986 and those pre and post competition from the retail banks. The relatively simple role of societies pre 1986 is adequately summarised by the Building Societies Act 1962.

> 'The purpose for which a society may be established under this Act is that of raising, by the subscription of members, a stock or fund for making advances to members out of the funds of the society upon security by way of mortgage or freehold or leasehold estate'.
>
> *(Ch 37, Pt 1, Section 1 (I)).*

This Act has been superceded by the Building Societies Act 1986. Under Section 34 of the Act a building society or subsidiary of a building society may provide the services listed in Schedule 8 of the Act (and the review of Schedule 8 in February 1988). The building societies have been given the power to undertake, *inter alia*, money transmission services, foreign exchange services, personal equity plans, unsecured loans, estate agency, administration of pension schemes, investment services, insurance, and unit trust schemes.

Even so, the majority of the building societies' business is still mortgage finance. Table 5.1 shows the aggregate assets and liabilities for all building societies. Mortgages dominate the assets side with 81.3 per cent of total assets, whilst shares and deposits are the major liabilities with 79 per cent. Building societies engage in substantial maturity transformation (see Chapter 2) as their liabilities are relatively short-term (the majority being accessible within a month) whilst assets are mainly long-term 20–25 year mortgages

The building societies are a major financial group in terms of their size. Total assets at the end of second quarter 1989 stood at £189.8 billion. There were 45 million shareholders and depositors ('shareholders' here is a technical term to reflect that those people with an account at a building society are members of the building society – the term should not be confused with the shareholders of a Public Limited Company) and over seven million borrowers. Building societies are the major providers of mortgage finance in the UK, providing over £152.4 billion of total outstanding mortg-

Table 5.1 *Building Societies' Assets and Liabilities (Book Value, End Period 1989)*

Assets	£m	Liabilities	£m
Mortgages	156198	Shares and Deposits (Retail)	142629
		Accrued Interest	4117
Cash and Bank Balances	20098	Wholesale Liabilities	27728
Local Authority Investments	358		
British Government Securities	4318	Other Liabilities and Reserves	15373
Other	8875		
TOTAL	189 847	TOTAL	189 847

Other Assets = Bank Bills, Building Society CD's, Sterling Treasury Bills, Tax Instruments, Transit and Suspense items and Miscellaneous Assets.

Figures after 1989 Quarter 3 are distorted by the conversion of Abbey National to PLC status.

Source: Financial Statistics, September 1990

age loans (59 per cent of the total) in 1989 and £24.0 billion (approximately 71 per cent) of net new mortgage loans for 1989 (Table 5.2). The building societies had 43.5% of personal sector liquid assets in 1989.

In terms of the structure of the industry, there are over one hundred building societies in existence (Table 5.4) which would tend to suggest ideal competitive conditions, but there is a high degree of concentration, with the assets of the five largest building societies accounting for over 60 per cent of the total assets of the building society industry.

Table 5.2 *Loans for House Purchase*

	Net Advances During Period (£m)			Balances Outstanding End Period (£m)		
	Building Societies	Banks	Other	Building Societies	Banks	Other
1973	1999	310	584	14624	1160	3172
1974	1490	90	859	16114	1250	4009
1975	2768	60	902	18882	1310	4810
1976	3618	80	230	22500	1380	4976
1977	4100	121	141	26600	1520	5006
1978	5115	275	47	31715	1805	5023
1979	5271	597	593	36986	2403	5619
1980	5722	593	1018	42708	2996	6643
1981	6331	2448	710	49039	5444	7505
1982	8147	5078	916	57186	10751	8420
1983	10928	3531	66	68114	14845	8422
1984	14572	2043	457	82686	16888	9147
1985	14711	4223	182	97397	21111	9329
1986	19541	4671	2369	116938	25781	11628
1987	14580	10005	4341	131518	35836	15967
1988	23677	10877	5634	155195	45213	21579
1989	24000	7176	2512	152492	79180	24226

Other = Local Authorities, Other Public Sector, Insurance Companies and Pension Funds, Miscellaneous Financial Institutions.

Source : Financial Statistics, Table 9.4

Table 5.3 *Personal Sector Liquid Assets (£m) (Balances Outstanding, End Period)*

	Building Societies	Banks	Other
1973	16347	16317	10634
1974	18316	19290	10584
1975	22477	19376	11169
1976	25778	20733	12048
1977	31710	21267	13887
1978	36609	24489	16049
1979	42442	30842	18150
1980	49617	37407	20346
1981	56699	41570	24833
1982	66993	51622	22061
1983	77243	55124	24999
1984	90492	58972	28325
1985	103806	63701	30766
1986	115653	71759	32916
1987	129279	79721	35274
1988	149404	96439	36643
1989	139789	143931	37398

Other = National Savings, Local Authority Temporary Debt, Deposits with Savings Banks (up to 1981, after that date included in the banking sector) and Miscellaneous Financial Institutions.

Source: Financial Statistics, Table 14.5

As mentioned above, the building societies' activities can be categorised as pre- and post- competition from the retail banks. Competition tended to be stifled in the 1970s by the operation of the building societies' cartel and by direct monetary controls placed on the retail banks. The breakdown of the cartel and the abolition of the direct monetary controls placed on the banks heralded a new era for building societies, and led to the new legislation referred to above. The influence of the cartel and its

Table 5.4   *Building Societies: Progress*

	No. of Societies	No. of Branches	No. of Shareholders /Depositors ('000)	No. of Borrowers ('000)
1960	726	–	4481	2349
1970	481	2016	10883	3655
1980	273	5684	31551	5383
1981	253	6162	34383	5490
1982	227	6480	37701	5645
1983	206	6643	38911	5928
1984	190	6816	40930	6314
1985	167	6926	42145	6657
1986	138	6962	45614	7182
1988	131	6915	48119	7369
1989	126	–	–	–

Source: Annual Reports of the Chief Registrar of Friendly Societies and the BSC

abolition on the activities of the societies is examined in Section 5.1, and the effect of competition from the retail banks is analysed in Section 5.2.

5.1   THE EFFECT OF THE CARTEL ON BUILDING SOCIETY OPERATIONS

The existence of the recommended rate system tended to encourage balance sheet growth as the major objective of building societies. The recommended rate system effectively formed an interest-rate setting cartel within the sector. Whilst most cartels operate in order to keep prices up by reducing the supply of their product or service, it appears that the building society recommended rate system operated a policy of keeping prices down. The cartel tended to keep lending rates below the market clearing level such that there was a deliberate rationing of mortgage loan supply.

This pricing policy was adopted largely in connection with the perceived role of societies as providers of low-cost housing finance.

The status of building societies as mutual institutions has, however, also been a factor in the operation of the recommended rate system. The building society industry viewed itself as a self-help movement for the benefit of its members. Each building society appeared to be a constituent part of the movement, all involved in the same goal. The building society cartel aimed to limit interest rate competition amongst societies partly to protect the smaller, more inefficient societies. The cartel appeared to run counter to the traditional economic model of a price setting cartel. Most cartels function in order to distribute income from consumers to industry, and to drive out smaller firms.

The recommended rate system, however, had the effect of transferring income from depositors to borrowers (Llewellyn 1985) and of protecting inefficient building societies.

The cartel had a marked effect on the mix of price and non-price competition in the market for retail funds. Whilst the cartel was in operation, changes in the price competitiveness of building societies' services could only be initiated through changes in the recommended rates, and hence a deliberate change in interest rate differentials by a large majority of building societies relative to other retail financial institutions. This resulted in a lower level of price competition than might be expected under a free market system.

Furthermore, the cartel meant that in general, whilst price competition was stifled, competition for retail funds was largely effected through the rapid growth of advertising and the dramatic increase in the number of building society branches. (See Table 5.4.)

There was also, however, scope for more efficient societies to circumvent the constraints of the recommended rate system. In particular, some small societies with low management expense ratios were able to offer premia above the recommended rate.

It would thus appear that the building societies' own portfolio strategies and objectives were a major determinant of the manner in which business was conducted. The building societies' objectives tended to outweigh the portfolio preferences of the members of the building societies and their demand for financial intermediation services.

The effect of the cartel can be seen in Figure 5.1 . The Building Societies Association advised the level of interest rates on shares and deposits (e.g. *ID*) and mortgages (e.g. *IM*). The Stow Report

Figure 5.1 *Effect of the Cartel on Mortage Supply*

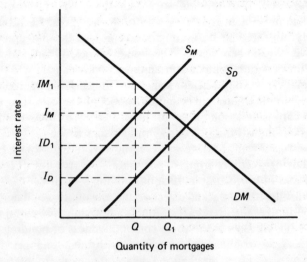

S_M = supply of mortgages
S_D = supply of shares and deposits

(BSA 1979) argued that the effect of operating with low-interest rates that are set at an uncompetitive level meant that there were insufficient funds to meet mortgage demand. For example, if the mortgage interest rate is IM, there will be excess mortgage demand of Q_1-Q at ID rate of interest on shares and deposits, whereas the market clearing level for mortgages is IM_1.

The Prices and Incomes Board (1966) investigation into recommended rates argued that the cartel determined a spread between investment and lending rates that was greater than might be expected under a more competitive system. This tended to deter efficiency by allowing the less efficient societies to survive, whilst at the same time discouraging innovation by providing the more efficient societies with wide margins.

The fixed margin deposit and mortgage rates (set below the market clearing level) led to large surpluses for more efficient societies whilst letting inefficient societies survive. With an inability to compete via interest rates, the existence of large surpluses enabled 'efficient' societies to indulge in non-price competition, as evidenced in the proliferation of building society branches. The Wilson Report (1980, p. 113) expressed the view that the cartel led to inefficiency and a hindrance to competition, and argued that the abolition of the recommended rate system would lead to higher interest rates on shares and deposits (e.g. ID_1) and the ability of societies to meet mortgage demand. It is also noted that one likely impact of greater competition would be to encourage mergers, both smaller societies transferring their engagements to larger ones, and also mergers between larger societies.

After the abolition of the cartel, the building societies showed an increased willingness to accommodate the demand for mortgage loans, whereas previously non-price rationing was in force. This entailed a new interest rate setting strategy, allowing higher mortgage rates rather than the previously adopted policy of pegging mortgage rates below market clearing levels. Mortgage interest rates and deposit rates thus became more fluid and more market related than previously.

5.2 COMPETITION

Monetary controls placed on the retail banks in the 1970's effectively precluded them from entering the personal sector financial market on any significant scale. This meant that the building societies faced relatively little competition from the retail banks.

Largely as a result of the Supplementary Special Deposit (SSD) scheme and the qualitative lending guidelines inhibiting the banks' potential for competition, the building society movement faced a favourable market environment over the majority of the period 1974–1979.

It would be expected, according to traditional economic theory, that the building societies would have taken advantage of the restrictions placed on the banks,

'a combination of restrictive monetary policy and accumulating debt creates the opportunities for non-bank intermediaries to offer more expensive attractions to creditors and hence to compete more actively with banks'

(Gurley and Shaw, 1955, p. 532)

Building Societies represented a special case, however, in terms of their mutuality and the existence of the cartel. The building societies did not actively compete with one another on price terms, and hence probably did not attract as many deposits from the banking system as they may have done if they were competitive.

Some commentators would argue that a major factor affecting the competitive environment was the lack of competitive neutrality (Llewellyn 1986 (a), (b), 1987). In particular, the Committee of London Clearing Banks complained that Building Societies have enjoyed various unfair artificial competitive advantages (CLCB 1977, p. 189).

In relation to the supply of funds to building societies, it has often been argued that the existence of the composite rate tax system gave them a competitive advantage relative to the retail banks (until the extension of that system to the retail banks in April 1985). The composite rate system worked such that, for example, with an ordinary share rate of 9.75 per cent, a basic tax rate of 30 per cent and a composite rate of 25.25 per cent the gross effective yield to tax paying investors is 13.93 per cent, but the gross cost to Societies of their funds is only 13 per cent. Thus the composite rate system allowed building societies to maintain a lower mortgage rate than would be necessary under tax procedures applied to the banking system at the time (BSA 1972). The banks complained that this represented a fiscal advantage in that it acted as an inducement to those paying income tax to deposit with building societies rather than the retail banks.

In the example above, to an investor liable to the basic rate of tax, the gross equivalent yield is 13.93 per cent, whilst for an investor not liable to tax the gross equivalent yield is the same as the net yield, 9.75 per cent. According to the CLCB, building societies benefited to the extent that tax paying investors are more sensitive to differentials in interest rates between institutions than are non—tax payers. Thus the portfolio preferences of the users of the financial system were being affected by the non-neutral taxation considerations between building societies and banks. Boleat (1986), points out however, that the relative competitive advantage is dependent on the elasticities of demand for building society shares and deposits for basic-rate tax payers and those not liable to tax. He disputes the point that those liable to the basic rate of tax are more interest sensitive than those not liable to tax.

Also, it should be noted that whilst the composite rate may mean that societies gain a competitive advantage by attracting money from tax-payers, at the same time they may suffer a disadvantage in attracting money from non-tax payers.

It has also been argued that building societies have received favourable treatment in respect of their corporation tax liability (formerly it was set at a rate of 40 per cent, as opposed to the standard 52 per cent rate applied to the clearing banks) and the exemption from taxation of the capital gains on their gilt-edged securities transactions (provided they have been held for more than twelve months). It should be noted, however, that due to leasing arrangements banks rarely paid the full 52 per cent corporation tax, in fact more commonly banks pay effective tax rates of about 20 per cent.

The main factors affecting the activities of the building societies and banks can be seen in terms of a regulatory matrix (Table 5.5), after Llewellyn (1987) ('regulatory' here used to mean any form of regulation, official or unofficial, that in some way affects the operations of building societies and banks). The functions or business areas which the banks could undertake were largely prohibited by the monetary controls examined earlier, and they were unable to actively compete in the personal sector savings market or the mortgage market. Their pricing policies were also affected to the extent that they were effectively restrained from actively competing for deposits. In addition moral suasion was at times used to affect the lending and pricing policies of the banks.

By contrast, the building societies were not included in the portfolio monetary controls and hence were unrestrained in this manner in terms of their pricing activities. However, the building societies, as emphasised earlier, affected their own pricing by operating the self-imposed interest rate setting cartel, such that they too faced pricing restraints, but as a result of unofficial regulation. On their functional side, the building societies were not constrained by portfolio controls as the banks were, but were more strictly regulated in terms of the areas of business allowed under the Building Societies Act 1962. Re-regulation via a change in the system of monetary control had a particularly immediate effect on the competitive aspect of the mortgage market. Whilst the corset was in operation, the banks were largely inhibited from competing for mortgage business. The direct monetary controls

Table 5.5 Regulatory Matrix for Banks and Building Societies, 1974 – 1980

	Geographical	Functional	Ownership	Pricing	Standards	Business
Portfolio Controls		Y_1	Y_2			
Moral Suasion		Y_3	Y_4			
Legal		X_1Y_5 X_2Y_6				
Self Imposed				X_3		
Self Regulation					X_4Y_7	X_5Y_8
No Regulation	XY					

Key:

X = Building Societies

Y = Banks

Y_1 = Monetary controls affecting the banks' ability to compete in the mortgage market.

Y_2 = Monetary controls affecting the banks' ability to compete on price terms.

Y_3 = Moral suasion by the Bank of England.

Y_4 = Moral suasion by the Bank of England on maximum deposit interest rates.

Y_5 = Legal restrictions on permitted activities of banks.

Y_6 = Legal restrictions on banks' ownership of insurance companies.

Y_7 and

Y_8 = Self-regulation by the Bank of England upon capital and liquidity requirements and standards.

X_1 = Legal restrictions on permitted activities of building societies.

X_2 = Legal restrictions on ownership of building societies, and building societies' ownership of other financial institutions.

X_3 = Self-imposed cartel.

X_4 and

X_5 = Self-regulation by the Building Societies Commission on liquidity, reserves, standards.

acted as an artificial constraint on the banks' ability to expand into this area, by creating a restrictive environment in which they could operate.

Removal of the corset constraint in 1980 correspondingly removed the artificially created environment. The changed conditions meant that retail banks could increase their lending for house-purchase if they so wished. The initial competition between banks and building societies was thus on the assets side of the balance sheet, stimulated by a change in monetary control.

Traditionally, banks have not perceived the building societies as being major competitors because they were not in competition for lending, and because funds attracted by building societies are maintained within the banking system (only the ownership of deposits changes, whilst the total volume of deposits at banks remain unchanged). However, once banks and building societies were competing for mortgage and other businesses, it became logical to compete for deposits.

There was a substantial re-adjustment on the part of the retail banks to rectify a loan portfolio imbalance once the inhibiting controls were removed. In effect, the banks merely adjusted their portfolios to a level that they would have preferred had controls not been implemented. It thus partly represented a once-for-all portfolio adjustment. With the building societies offering mortgage rates below the market clearing level, there had previously existed a mortgage queue, with demand outstripping supply, and hence a certain amount of non-price rationing by building societies. The banks were also able to concentrate on large mortgages (over £30,000) as a result of the building societies' reluctance to lend at the higher end of the market.

Under such circumstances there was scope for profitable lending by the retail banks. Once direct controls were removed, the prime reason for the growth of bank lending for house purchase was that of profitability. Another facet of the banks rationale for entering the mortgage market can be explained in terms of their overall strategy aimed at the ultimate objective of offering a complete package of financial services to the personal sector. Mortgage lending was thus used as a device for introducing other business such as insurance, home improvement loans and unsecured lending, both to extend their customer base and to offer new services to existing customers. The underlying factor, however, was that of profit.

The entry of the retail banks into the mortgage market expedited the breakdown of the building societies' cartel. Several smaller societies had already been offering interest rate premia above the cartel rate. The Abbey National Building Society, then the largest in the UK formally announced its withdrawal from the cartel in 1983. For a short period of time (October 1983 to November 1984), the Building Societies Association issued 'advised' rather than 'recommended' rates of interest, although this was also later abandoned in November 1984. A further significant factor in forcing the breakdown of the cartel, was the increasing reliance placed by the government on funding the public sector borrowing requirement (PSBR) through National Savings. Attractive interest rates were offered on National Savings investment accounts, representing a further increase in competition for building societies.

According to economic theory, in a competitive market system with no cartel restrictions, the entry of new competitors will have significant effects upon both the price and output of the incumbents' product/service. One major effect of the banks competing for retail deposits and mortgage business has been a change in the intensity and mix of price and non-price competition by building societies. Prior to 1980, building societies competed against each other almost exclusively on non-price terms, in particular through the extension of the branch network rather than through price or through new innovative products. The entry of the retail banks into the mortgage market and competing aggressively for retail deposits entailed a shift towards more explicit price competition and an innovation in types of account being offered by both banks and building societies. Indeed, the rapid development of the societies' branch network in the 1970s slowed considerably in the 1980's (Table 5.4).

In the 1970s building society liabilities were dominated by straightforward ordinary shares (over 80% of the total in 1979). In 1980 high interest accounts were introduced, offering premia above ordinary shares, varying withdrawal periods and minimum deposits (sometimes only £500). From 1983 onwards there has been an outflow of deposits from all types of accounts except high interest, and at the end of 1989 they accounted for over 75 per cent of all retail funds at societies. Innovation also occurred in the mortgage market. Loans were advanced for a greater percentage of purchase price than previously, and higher multiples of income were accepted. The building societies policy of charging different rates for loans over £35,000 was also largely competed away.

It has also been suggested that building societies suffer a competitive disadvantage in that regulation constrains the societies to funding the majority (60 per cent) of their mortgage lending in the relatively high cost retail market. Building Societies have only been able to secure wholesale funds since 1981. In view of the structure of interest rates prevailing since then (with mortgage rates and retail deposit rates above money market rates for much of the time) it is hardly surprising that building societies have increased their wholesale funding as a proportion of total funding (Table 5.6).

Table 5.6   *Building Society Retail and Wholesale Funding*

		£m	
	(1)	*(2)*	*(3)*
	Non-Retail	*(Retail)*	*(1) as % of (2)*
1983	1951	76323	2.5
1984	4182	91327	4.6
1985	7269	104816	6.9
1986	13796	116998	11.8
1987	18391	130369	14.1
1988	24255	150778	16.1
1989	27728	142629	19.5

Source: Financial Statistics, September 1990

Moreover, the previous stability of retail funds has tended to fall. The changing competitive positions of competing financial institutions and the increasing financial sophistication of the personal sector means that retail funds can at times be extremely volatile (building societies are also particularly hit by outflows of funds for privatisation issues). Thus the advantage of the stability of retail funds over wholesale has tended to decline.

Furthermore, the marginal cost of retail funds to building societies can be relatively expensive as compared to the marginal cost of wholesale funds. This is because increasing the rate of interest on deposits to raise more funds will increase the rate on funds already deposited with the building society (alternatively a rise in one type of deposit, e.g. term shares, may induce switching from lower rate accounts). Wholesale funds by contrast, will not affect the cost of funds already held at the building society. Wholesale funds can thus be extremely attractive to building societies.

Wholesale funds have the advantage that building societies can actively engage in liability management (as the banks do) which gives societies greater flexibility. Wholesale funds are generally readily available when needed, and can be used to stabilise mortgage lending flows. Indeed, the use of wholesale funds means that building societies can reduce their average liquidity levels. Traditionally, building societies have run down liquid assets at times of low funds inflow to stabilise mortgage lending. If wholesale funds can be used for this purpose, societies can reduce their holdings of low yielding liquid assets. Building societies would be expected to move towards an optimal mix of wholesale and retail funds that minimises costs. Also, portfolio diversification into a greater variety of sources of funds should create greater stability of inflow.

A further factor affecting competition in the retail market is the stipulation that building societies' unsecured lending be limited to £10,000. Some would argue (Llewellyn 1987) that the ability of the retail banks to offer mortgages at the same rate of interest as building societies (despite building societies lower operating ratios) is the ability of the banks to cross-subsidise mortgage lending with their high-priced profitable lending business, such as consumer loans.

The new legislation (Building Societies Act 1986) allows building societies also to engage in such cross-subsidisation with the ability to diversify into unsecured lending. The building societies face a regulatory asymmetry however, in the constraints imposed on the limits to their unsecured lending activities. The limit of £10,000 represents a lack of competitive neutrality *vis-à-vis* the ability of banks to lend unsecured only constrained by prudential limits.

The importance of regulatory change can be seen from the regulatory matrix (Table 5.7) for banks and building societies for post 1980. In contrast to the earlier regulatory matrix, it can be seen that portfolio controls and moral suasion now constrain

Table 5.7 *Regulatory Matrix for Banks and Building Societies Post-1980*

	Geographical	Functional	Ownership	Pricing	Standards	Business
Portfolio Controls						
Moral Suasion						
Legal		X	X			
Self Imposed						
Self Regulation					XY	XY
External Agency		Y			XY	XY
No regulation	XY		Y	XY		

Building Societies = X
Banks = Y

neither banks nor building societies. The retail banks functional areas are no longer limited as earlier by monetary controls, and they have been able to enter the mortgage market. Similarly, they can now compete on price terms with the abolition of the corset and the abrogation of moral suasion on lending to the personal sector.

Although the building societies have been granted substantial new powers in terms of the functional areas of business they are empowered to carry out, they are nevertheless still legally hindered by the Building Societies Act 1986, as outlined earlier. It may well prove to be the case that the removal of the remaining legal constraints on building societies functional activities will be the main catalyst for financial innovation and change in the future. It is also noticeable that there are no official or unofficial regulations affecting the pricing policies of the building societies or the banks, the former having abandoned their self-imposed constraint of the cartel in 1983.

Finally, it is of interest that both building societies and banks are regulated to a far greater degree than before by external agencies, in the form of the Securities and Investments (SIB) and the various Self Regulatory Organisations (SRO's) established under the Financial Services Act, 1986. (See Chapter 12.)

The relative competitive positions of building societies, banks and other financial institutions are as shown in Table 5.8. The gain in market share by the building societies over the retail banks (and the 'other' category) can clearly be seen over the period 1974–1980, when for the majority of the time the banks were constrained by the corset. Building Societies' market share increased from 38 per cent in 1974 to 46.2 per cent in 1980, as opposed to the fall in the banks' share from 40 per cent in 1974 to 31.7 per cent in 1978. On the removal of the corset in the early 1980s the banks recovered somewhat at the expense of the 'other' category to capture 35 per cent of the market in 1983, followed by four years of losing out to the building societies, and then an increase to nearly 45 per cent again at the expense of the 'other' financial institutions. The building societies' share fell to 43.5 per cent by 1989.

A similar pattern emerges from Table 5.9, with the banks providing very few of either net new mortgage advances or outstanding mortgage loans over the period 1973 to 1978, indeed

Table 5.8 *Market Share of Personal Sector Liquid Assets*
(%)

Year	Building Societies	Banks	Other
1973	37.8	37.7	24.5
1974	38.0	40.0	22.0
1975	42.4	36.5	21.1
1976	44.0	35.4	20.6
1977	47.4	31.8	20.8
1978	47.5	31.7	20.8
1979	46.4	33.7	19.9
1980	46.2	34.8	19.0
1981	46.0	33.8	20.2
1982	47.6	36.7	15.7
1983	49.1	35.0	15.9
1984	50.8	33.2	16.0
1985	52.3	32.1	15.6
1986	52.5	32.6	14.9
1987	52.9	32.6	14.5
1988	52.9	34.1	13.0
1989	43.5	44.8	11.6

Other = National Savings, Local Authority Temporary Debt,
Deposits with Savings Banks and Miscellaneous Financial
Institutions.

Source: Financial Statistics, September 1990

losing market share to the building societies over that time. The
building societies thus faced little effective competition from the
retail banks whilst the corset was in operation. The reaction of the
banks to the ending of the corset can be seen in the rapid growth of
market share of net new mortgage loans in 1981 and 1982 at the
expense of the building societies, settling to around 15–16 per cent
of mortgage loans outstanding over 1983–1986, and a recent
increase again in 1989. The building societies' main
market – mortgage loans – thus dramatically changed in the 1980s
in terms of the degree of competition they faced. The banks
poached a large proportion of the market in the early 1980s, and

Table 5.9   *Loans for House Purchase: Market Share (%)*

Year	Balances Outstanding Building Societies	Banks	Other	Net advances in Period Building Societies	Banks	Other
1973	77.1	6.1	16.8	69.1	10.7	20.2
1974	75.4	5.8	18.8	61.1	3.7	35.2
1975	75.5	5.2	19.3	74.2	1.6	24.2
1976	78.0	4.8	17.2	92.1	2.0	5.9
1977	80.2	4.6	15.2	94.0	2.8	3.2
1978	82.3	4.7	13.0	94.0	5.0	1.0
1979	82.2	5.3	12.5	81.6	9.2	9.2
1980	81.4	5.7	12.9	78.0	8.1	13.9
1981	79.0	8.8	12.2	66.7	25.8	7.5
1982	74.1	13.9	12.0	57.6	35.9	6.5
1983	74.3	16.2	9.5	75.2	24.3	0.5
1984	76.0	15.5	8.5	86.4	12.0	1.6
1985	76.2	16.5	7.3	76.9	22.1	1.0
1986	75.7	16.7	7.6	73.5	17.6	8.9
1987	71.7	19.5	8.8	50.3	34.5	15.2
1988	69.9	20.3	9.8	58.9	27.1	14.0
1989	59.6	30.9	9.5	71.2	21.3	7.4

Source: Financial Statistics, Table 9.4

more recently in 1987 and 1988 the 'other' financial institutions have taken up to 15% of net new loans.

5.3   PROFITS/SURPLUS

As mentioned earlier, the mutuality of building societies has tended to mean that they have traditionally aimed for balance sheet growth rather than profits. Indeed, in the past 'profit' was not even mentioned in annual reports. Building societies have in the 1980s become far more profit orientated, mainly through necessity. The abolition of the cartel induced competition amongst the building societies themselves, and the ending of the direct portfolio controls on the retail banks meant that the building

societies faced effective external competition for mortgage lending.

With the more competitive market the building societies were
increasingly pushed towards using profitability as a performance
criteria. Furthermore, full diversification into the new areas of
business allowed under the Building Societies Act 1986 will
require an increase in the capital bases of most building societies,
which can only be raised through increased profitability or through
raising subordinated debt capital (although the latter is limited to
50 per cent of reserves) because they do not have shareholders and
cannot raise funds through rights issues as the banks do.

A further stimulus towards the emphasis on profitability is the
reported desire of some societies to convert to PLC status, as the
Abbey National has already done. Once quoted on the Stock
Exchange, profitability, yield and return on capital will be used by
investors and analysts as yardsticks of performance and will have
to be adopted by the newly converted building society (which
would then technically be a bank, supervised by the Bank of
England). With this route in mind, many building societies will
have to concentrate on profitability in the run-up to conversion in
order to achieve an enthusiastic reception from potential investors.

Given that the larger building societies are now active participants in the wholesale money markets, and are competing with
other financial institutions for those funds, it is likely that lenders
will tend to apply the same criteria to societies when assessing how
much to charge for those funds and profitability is likely to be of
major importance.

Profitability of building societies has tended to be boosted by
the finite stock adjustment of personal sector mortgages after the
abolition of the cartel. The ending of the cartel changed the
mortgage market from one of variable excess demand to one of
excess supply, with a rapid growth in mortgages granted. The
change in the building societies' interest rate strategy after the
ending of the cartel has also increased profitability. Mortgage
interest rates are now far more fluid and market related than
previously, and the spread between deposit and mortgage rates
has been increased, raising profitability. Mortgage lending has
thus tended to be relatively profitable for the building societies',

although it would be expected that the increased competition from banks and other lenders would in the long-term lead to a reduction in margins and a fall in profitability.

As building societies diversify, particularly into unsecured lending, they will be able to cross-subsidise mortgage lending in much the same way as the banks do. In other words, given the growth in societies' unsecured lending, coupled with their lower unit costs than the banks, they may be able to increasingly cross-subsidise their mortgage lending and under-cut the banks.

The Building Societies Commission Annual Report for 1988–89 pointed out that medium sized societies tended to be the most profitable in 1989, whilst the three largest societies had a fall in profitability compared with 1988. The results of the medium sized societies are interesting because they seem to conflict with the assertion of some commentators that this group will face the severest problems into the 1990s, as they are too small to compete with the large building societies, but too large to adopt niche strategies.

Building societies face a zero cost of reserve capital. This is because, as mutual institutions, they do not have to service their capital. Societies thus have free reserves, the level of which can affect profitability. A society with a large volume of free reserves will tend to be more profitable as it will have a relatively high proportion of capital on which interest does not have to be paid compared with its amount of assets which are non-income earning. This results in free reserve income, which provides an endowment effect when interest rates are rising. As interest rates rise, societies will have an endowment effect as interest bearing liabilities will be less than interest bearing assets by the size of the free reserves. This may be a powerful advantage to building societies during periods of rising interest rates.

There are two further aspects to the societies' endowment effect. Interest is only credited to investors' accounts every six or twelve months, and of course additional interest is only earned on the original interest from the date of crediting. Building Societies will thus tend to have a pool of interest free funds that has not yet been credited to investors' accounts. This is particularly important during periods of high interest rates.

Secondly, building societies will tend to make greater provision for composite rate tax during periods of high interest rates. Until these funds are paid to the government (normally quarterly), these interest free funds can be profitably invested.

5.4 CAPITAL AND LIQUIDITY

Capital is required by building societies for two main reasons. Firstly, to maintain confidence in the general public that the society will be able to repay shares and deposits, and secondly to absorb any losses that might occur. Capital thus acts as a cushion against losses which may occur from mortgage defaults, investment losses, and credit losses. The existence of an adequate capital base enables a building society to pay off liabilities when revenues are too low, and to write off assets as losses where necessary without liabilities exceeding assets (i.e. the society becoming insolvent).

With respect to maintaining public confidence, a public measure of capital adequacy is used:

$$\frac{\text{Free Capital}}{\text{Total Liabilities}}$$

Where Free Capital = Total reserves plus bad debt provisions plus subordinated debt minus fixed assets.

In terms of absorbing losses, an operational measure of capital adequacy is used which is not publicly available, and consists of Minimum Acceptable Capital (MAC), below which a building society will be at risk, and Desired Capital (DC), which is used for long-term planning and budgeting activities. The Building Societies Commission maintains that the DC must be at least ½ per cent above the MAC, or the offending building society must change its strategy.

The main feature of the capital requirement is that percentage capital weights are attached to different categories of assets held by building societies according to their riskiness and then the separate capital amounts are summed to give the total capital requirement. Mortgages, for example, require a capital backing of to 6 per cent depending on their riskiness, liquid assets require a backing of approximately 15 to 11 per cent depending on their maturity, and loans 15–20 per cent depending on their risk. (See Table 5.10).

Table 5.10 *Minimum Acceptable Capital Ratios*

Mortgages	1 – 6%
Liquid Assets	1 – 11%
Loans	15 – 20%
Fixed Assets	50%
Development and Residential Property	30 or 50%
Housing for Rent	20 or 40% (long term) (other)
Equity Interest in Shared Ownership Schemes	10 or 30% (long term) (other)
Foreign Exchange Services	10%
Extra Requirement for Small Societies	1% 0.5% (less than (£25m to £25m assets) £50m assets)

International harmonisation of capital adequacy requirements under the auspices of the Bank for International Settlements (BIS) means that the building societies (and the retail banks) will come under the BIS proposals for capital, which are outlined in Chapter 4.

Liquidity refers to the ability to obtain cash at short notice and without capital loss. (See Chapter 2). Building societies need liquidity to meet day to day withdrawals of funds, and to be able to choose between the retail and wholesale markets depending on their relative attractiveness (i.e. not to become too dependent on either), and to cover known differences in cash flows from mortgage repayments, interest receipts, and outflows of mortgage lending and expenses. There are no particular liquidity ratios that must be complied with by building societies, but the Building Societies Act 1986 requires that a sufficient proportion of assets must be kept as liquid to meet liabilities as they come about, and the proportion should take into account the composition and nature of the assets and liabilities of the building society in question. Moreover, liquid assets should be readily marketable, have limited credit risk and should not represent an interest rate mismatch with liabilities. In practice ratios have tended to average around 17–18 per cent.

5.5   1992

For building societies, the effect on the domestic mortgage market is likely to be greater than the impact on their European aspirations (BSA 1989). Very few building societies have started operations in Europe, and it is likely that overseas activities will remain a small proportion of total business for the forseeable future.

At present approximately 2–3 per cent of the market share of the UK mortgage market is accounted for by overseas institutions. It is likely that more overseas operators will enter the UK mortgage market, but it is unlikely that they will have a large effect on the market share of the building societies who are dominant.

Building Societies can at present set up subsidiaries overseas, but cannot lend directly overseas. The overseas subsidiaries cannot lend on land in the United Kingdom or collect deposits in the UK. The relevant directive is the Second Banking Directive which specifically includes mortgage credit under the 'single license' (see Chapter 13) and which has outdated the Draft Directive on Mortgage credit of 1984. A major constraint is that a building society must have assets of at least £500 million to operate. Also building societies should be able to offer mortgages in Europe directly through a branch, rather than through a subsidiary which would be in the awkward position of being able to operate in Europe but not the UK. Finally, it should be emphasised that the European mortgage market is particularly diverse, and will not provide a great boost to the growth and geographical diversification of the building society industry.

REFERENCES

Boleat, M. (1986) *The Building Society Industry* Allen & Unwin, London.

Building Societies Association (1972) 'Do Building Societies have Tax Advantages?' *Building Society Affairs* January, p. 2.

Building Societies Association (1989) *The Building Societies and 1992.*

Building Societies Commission (1988–89) *Annual Report.*

Committee of London Clearing Bankers (1977) Evidence by the CLCB to the Committee to Review the Functioning of Financial Institutions (Wilson Committee) *CLCB* London.

Drake, L. *The Building Society Industry in Transition* (1989) (Macmillan, London).

Gurley, J. G. and Shaw, E. S. (1955) 'Financial Aspects of Economic Development' *American Economic Review* Vol. 45, No. 4, September, pp. 515–38.

Llewellyn, D. T. (1985) *The Evolution of the British Financial System* Gilbart Lectures on Banking (Institute of Bankers).

——(1986a) 'Regulation and Myth' *Banking World* May, pp. 37–39.

——(1986b) 'The Regulation and Supervision of Financial Institutions. Gilbart Lectures (*Institute of Bankers*, London).

——(1987) 'Competition and the Regulatory Framework' *National Westminster Bank Quarterly Review* August, pp. 4–13.

National Board for Prices and Incomes (1966) *'Rate of Interest on Building Society Mortgages'* Report No. 22 Cmnd 3136 HMSO.

Stow, R. (1979) *Mortgage Finance into the 1980's* Building Societies Association.

CHAPTER 6

INSURANCE

6.0 INTRODUCTION

Insurance companies and Lloyds syndicates are important institutional investors in fulfilling their function as a risk transfer mechanism through their intermediation between policyholders and the financial markets. They are custodians of large funds built up from premiums received which are available for investment and from which claims and other expenses must eventually be paid.

Although the primary function of insurance is risk transfer, long term business includes much activity directed at channelling savings into investment with only a minimal risk transfer role.

This chapter looks at risk transfer and the demand for insurance in the wider context of Risk Management. It also looks at pricing, profitability, competitiveness and the investment behaviour of the two main groups of insurance activity.

The activities of insurers are divided into two main groups: long term and general.

6.1 GENERAL INSURANCE

This insurance group has in general a much shorter span than long term insurance between premium and claim. The risk of the event occurring, which is the purpose of the insurance, is in some cases not related to a predictable factor like the age of the owner of the policy. Claims can and do fluctuate because of external factors, e.g. theft risk insurance is affected by rising crime rates but there is not the same degree of predictability which encompasses life, pensions and permanent health risks which make possible long term contracts. General insurance comprises classes such as fire, accident, motor, marine and aviation.

6.2   LONG TERM INSURANCE

Long term insurance includes life, pensions, and permanent health insurance. This represents policies of insurance which are taken out to protect an individual for his or her lifetime or shorter periods. Much life insurance relates to protection and savings over periods of 10 to 30 years. Pensions consist of income paid in retirement for the remainder of a person's life from funds built up during working life. Permanent health insurance relates to protection against disability from sickness or accident during a persons working life.

The function of life insurance is twofold: protection and savings. To fulfil these functions a variety of types of contracts exist which provide the following benefits:

Term Insurance: payment of a specified sum only on death within a fixed term. (Protection only – no investment component).

Whole Life: payment of a specified sum on death whenever it occurs.

Endowment: payment of a specified sum on survival of an agreed term of years or on prior death within the term.

The liability which the insurer has to meet on death is fixed in money (nominal) terms. The premiums which are payable are usually fixed at the outset to take account of expected mortality, investment returns and expenses of administration. Many endowment policies are 'with profits': the sum assured is increased by reversionary bonuses added at regular intervals, however these are not contractual obligations.

Not all life business is transacted on this basis. A growing class of business referred to as 'unit linked' insurance is based on a different concept. It is a development of the endowment or savings end of the life insurance market. The policyholder becomes the direct investor himself receiving an allotment in terms of units which stand in his name in a unit trust or fund chosen by himself from a range offered by the company. The policyholder choses his own funds and can follow their performance and switch between funds if required. The insurance policy becomes in effect an investment vehicle which offers life insurance as well. The insurer does not have to meet any agreed sum at maturity, all of the growth or loss is handed to the policyholder in the form of an appreciation or depreciation of unit values. If the policyholder dies within the term, a payment of the sum assured or value of the units (whichever is higher) is made.

6.3 STATUTORY CLASSIFICATION OF INSURANCE

The Insurance Companies Act 1982 lays down the following classification of insurance to meet the requirements of the EC directives. It does not correspond significantly to the typical

Table 6.1 *Statutory Classification of Insurance*

Long term business
   Marriage and birth
   Linked long term
   Permanent health
   Tontines
   Capital redemption
   Pension Fund Management

Non life business

Accident	Motor liability
Sickness	Aircraft liability
Land Vehicles	Ships liability
Railway Rolling Stock	General liability
Aircraft	Credit
Ship	
Goods in Transit	Suretyship
Fire and Natural Forces	Miscellaneous financial loss
Damage to Property	Legal Expenses

internal organisational structure of insurers where frequently an insurance policy contains several classifications of cover within one policy. The classifications do dictate the structure of the annual returns which must be submitted to the Department of Trade and Industry under the legislative requirements.

The basic division of long term and general business is reflected in the life and non life categories. The subdivisions are shown in Table 6.1.

6.4   INSURANCE SUPPLIERS

1.   Insurance Companies

These comprise limited liability companies owned by share-holders, and mutuals owned by the policyholders. The proprietary companies can raise capital from the equity markets and have tended to grow faster than the mutuals (see below).

Companies can be classified by function as well as ownership into specialist and composite. The latter have grown from offices transacting one class of insurance by acquisition and merger into offices offering the major part of insurance business. Specialist offices offering a limited range of insurance services tend to be more numerous in the long term sector.

Mutual companies distribute their profits to their policyholders. They are also known as Friendly Societies in the sector known as industrial life insurance. Many mutuals have been incorporated into proprietary companies because of the advantage of raising capital from outside sources, but some of the biggest UK life insurers are mutuals (e.g. Scottish Widows).

2.   Lloyd's Insurance Market

This is run by a Council under the Lloyd's Act 1982. It regulates some 29 000 Lloyd's Underwriting Members organised into 400 syndicates which supply insurance mainly to the marine, aviation, property, liability, and motor markets. Insurance is transacted on a basis of unlimited personal liability. The financial resources of Lloyd's members to maintain solvency consists of their capital commitment which is held in a trust fund for the benefit of their insured clients and their remaining personal wealth. One of the functions of the Council is to vet the entry of members to see that they are capable of meeting their underwriting liabilities.

6.5 THE NEED FOR INSURANCE

Insurance can be defined as 'the losses of the few paid for by the contributions of the many'. The ratio between losses and contributions can be described as the mathematical probability of loss (i.e. the risk) based on past experience. In deciding whether to underwrite the risk of, for example fire in a particular factory, the insurer must decide the relevance of past claims experience to the future and, calculate a premium to cover the cost of future claims, expenses, and yield a profit.

Insurance in Risk Management

Insurance is a method of financial risk control whereby a possible loss is controlled in exchange for a much smaller fixed expense – the premium. In accepting contributions or premiums from a lot of customers facing similar types of risk, the insurer creates a fund from which losses can be paid. The risk of the event in question occurring must be quantifiable and ideally an estimable one so that an appropriate premium can be calculated. If the risk of loss is under-estimated the fund will run out. If it is over-estimated the premium will not be competitive against other insurers. The prudent route is to build up a fund which is greater than the anticipated losses in any given period and to charge a premium which is competitive.

Before considering the nature of the risks faced by insurance companies, it is necessary to examine why a need for insurance exists, in those areas referred to as general business.

An individual or a group investing in a business is exposed to a variety of risks. Certain risks which businesses or individuals face carry with them a probability of reward. These can be termed speculative risks, and encompass business activity and investment decision making. The likelihood and amount of profit (risk/ reward) influence people's decisions to undertake business or investment activity. Other types of risk carry no possibility of reward, only of loss. In this category are events such as marine disasters, earthquakes, fires, theft, civil legal liabilities, personal injury and death. These are termed pure risks.

Risk management is a set of techniques which have been developed to identify, evaluate and control all types of risk. The aim is to protect the assets and earning potential of a business by these measures.

If, for example, an individual or a group is considering investing in a new pharmaceutical factory to manufacture a particular drug they could be exposed to some or all of the following risks (whether they realised it or not): —

Direct: Fire, explosion, flood, fraud, structural defect, war.

Consequential: Loss of profits following: fire, flood, strikes, default in supply of materials or power.

Social: Changing medical attitudes towards the prescription and use of this drug.

Legal: The possibility of injurious side effects from use of this drug and costly damages awards in the courts.

Political: Loss of overseas markets by foreign governments imposing tariffs, outbreak of war.

Financial: Competitors undercutting prices, inflation eroding profit margins.

Risk management is concerned with techniques and management strategies to control risk. Any speculative risk presupposes that the factory is able to produce drugs in the normal way for which it was designed. Pure risks, such as fire and flood undermine the assumptions upon which speculative risks are based. They can cause direct damage to the factory and consequential (economic) loss to profits whilst production is interrupted and market share is lost to competitors.

Control of fire risks can for example be minimised by physical precautions such as alarms, extinguishers etc. However there is an irreducible risk which can never be completely eliminated. This risk must be controlled by financial means.

There are two alternatives: risk retention and risk transfer. The first involves setting aside sufficient capital from current profits into a fund to replace the factory and lost profits during rebuilding. There are two consequences to this line of action. Firstly, should fire occur soon after construction of the factory the fund would be too small to meet the losses. The second is that assets which could be used by the business are kept tied up in relatively liquid form for the eventuality of the fire or flood. The second alternative is to transfer the risk of loss to an insurer in exchange for payment of an agreed annual sum, a premium. The potential losses which could be covered by insurance would include the material damage to the factory and profits lost during rebuilding.

Thus insurance is one of the tools available to the risk manager to protect the assets and earning potential of the business from pure risks. It relates to a specific area of the overall control of risk. Other risk management control techniques will be applied to those speculative risks to which insurance is inapplicable. For example investment risks are the province of portfolio planning and lie outside the scope of insurance.

Market pressures and desire for market share could force insurers to cut their premiums below a level at which they can pay claims. The market will eventually correct itself after the marginal companies have become insolvent and premium rates have risen again.

This will clearly weed out the marginal companies but it can also be financially ruinous to the claimants who do not receive the money to which they are entitled.

For this reason there is a strong web of legislation which has been enacted under the Insurance Companies Act 1982 which sets down strict principles to check that insurance companies are being managed by 'fit and proper persons' along sound insurance lines. Criteria are laid down for setting solvency margins, i.e. the amounts by which assets must exceed liabilities. The current situation governing the supervision of insurance will be detailed below.

6.6 FACTORS INFLUENCING THE PRICE OF INSURANCE

There are three factors at work influencing the price of insurance. They are the risk assessment or underwriting factor, the rate of investment return, and the competitive environment or pressures. The legal requirement to maintain a minimum solvency margin will in practice set limits on the lower levels of premium which an insurer can charge.

Risk assessment or underwriting considerations require that a premium charged for a given risk covers the cost of expected claims, administration expenses and a profit element within the agreed period of the insurance contract. In general insurance the period is usually twelve months from the commencement or renewal of the insurance. Long term business, as its name suggests, concerns periods of much greater length related in most situations to the expectancy of human life. Thus general funds are built up to meet liabilities that are essentially short term, whereas long term accumulates assets and liabilities over a much longer period. It also means that long term underwriters cannot vary premiums as frequently to meet changing conditions affecting cost as in general business.

In addition the shareholder's funds and reserves must be sufficiently large to meet the appropriate solvency margins required for both general and long term business by the Insurance Companies Acts 1982. The investment return on the assets held by insurance companies is a vital factor in both long term and general insurance pricing.

General insurance has made underwriting losses on most classes of business for long periods. This means claims and expenses exceeding premium income. Since 1967 for example underwriting losses have been recorded on most classes of business in both the US and the UK apart from brief periods in the early and late 1970s. Only by investment returns exceeding these losses has overall profitability and therefore supply been maintained.

Historically the unprofitability of general business has been affected by two factors. Firstly, the oil price shock of 1972–1982 caused a great slump in demand as industry sought to cut costs. Secondly, the cost of claims has risen faster than premiums.

Long term insurance has traditionally built in conservative estimates of investment returns into its premium structure. This is possible for two reasons. Claims are generally more predictable and so 'matching' of assets to meet future liabilities is made easier. However, the current concern over the impact of AIDS is modifying the general assumption about future claims. This will be dealt with below. Secondly funds are built up to meet liabilities which will arise many years in the future.

Long term insurance has operated in this competitive enviroment but there has been no parallel collapse of demand which affected general business. From 1977–1987 life insurance doubled its share of the personal savings market. Average growth was 9.6 per cent in real terms compared to general which was 4.2 per cent. In addition claims have remained far more stable and predictable than for general business even allowing for the possible impact of AIDS on life insurance claims and reserves for possible future increases in mortality.

6.7 PROFITABILITY

General Insurance

There are two factors which determine the level of profitability of general insurance. Firstly, the profit or loss on underwriting which in simple terms is the surplus or deficit of premium income for a particular year over claims and expenses (i.e. allowances for administration/salaries/commission etc.). The main factor will be claims which usually absorbs about 70 per cent of premium income.

The second factor is the investment income which is derived from the funds under management.

Nearly all insurers currently make a loss on their general business underwriting results. Profitability is maintained because of the successful investment management of insurance companies. Out of the top ten companies those quoted in Table 6.3 made losses.

The high level of returns from investments in the last decade have kept insurers solvent but clearly deteriorating investment returns could force general insurers to take action either by withdrawing from the market or by raising rates of premium. There are several forces at work which are likely to push claims costs higher than they are today.

Recent poor weather has produced large underwriting losses. As an example the 1987 hurricane damage cost more than £1 billion in claims. Motor insurance which in 1988 operated at an underwriting loss of 5.3 per cent of premium income continues to be subject to rising claims costs from a steadily rising pattern of claims frequency and rising spare parts costs and garage charge out costs.

Table 6.2   *Overall Trading Profit of World-wide General Insurance ABI Member Companies*

	£m 1985	£m 1986	£m 1987	£m 1988	£m 1989
Net Premiums Written:	15,796	18,899	19,709	21,902	25,168
Underwriting profit/loss for 1 year account basis					
Motor	− 736	− 638	− 477	− 374	− 780
Fire and Accident	− 1054	− 518	− 479	− 116	− 657
Transfer to Profit and Loss Account for other Business					
Marine/Aviation /Transport	− 56	− 4	+ 52	+ 29	− 175
Other	− 366	− 253	− 228	− 106	− 376
Total	− 2212	− 1413	− 1132	− 567	− 1988
Investment Income	2213	2526	2631	2910	1988
Overall Trading Profit	1	1113	1499	2343	1555
Profit as a percentage of Premiums	0.0	5.9	7.6	10.7	6.2

Source: ABI Insurance Statistics 1985–89

Table 6.3   *Non-Life Underwriting Losses*

	£'000
Sun Alliance	128,900
Royal Insurance	155,100
Eagle Star	143,600
General Accident	98,300
Commercial Union	152,800
Norwich Union	30,900
Guardian Royal Exchange	63,900
Prudential	72,800
Cooperative	24,000
Cornhill	15,057

Source: The Times 1000 1989–90

Long Term Business

This has maintained profitability more consistently than general business. Premium income has tended to grow faster. Over the 10 years 1978–1987 long term business grew by an average of 10 per cent p.a. in real terms compared to 4.2 per cent for general business (*Lloyd's Bank Economic Bulletin*, October 1989).

Long term insurance is underwriting the risk of death. Premiums are collected and invested with the guarantee that they will be paid out at death of the policy holder or at some specific date in the future. Thus there are two variables which can be calculated with a reasonable degree of accuracy: the likely date of death and the investment returns which are likely to be earned by that date. Mortality tables and discounted cash flow tables make the calculation of premiums a relatively easy task. Note however, that the impact of AIDS has to some extent destroyed the predictability of the date of death and companies have been forced to increase their premiums for term insurance (see reinsurance) and set aside greater reserves for the future than they would otherwise have done. Much life insurance is part of the savings market and insurers have not been exposed to any great increase in costs as a result.

Since the Actuaries who calculate these premiums use very conservative assumptions about the rate of investment return, between 3 and 4 per cent per year, there is a high degree of certainty of securing the amounts of money guaranteed by the policy. Since the company will always secure the sum guaranteed there is a very high degree of certainty of profit. If the policyholder has taken out a 'with profits' policy then the insurer will pass on a major part of the profits in the form of reversionary and final bonuses. The balance, usually about 10 per cent, is allocated to policyholders.

This system therefore ensures that the insurer is very likely to make a profit. The profit itself is shared between the with profits policyholders (90 per cent) and shareholders (10 per cent). If the company is owned by the policyholders, i.e. a mutual office, then they enjoy 100 per cent of the profits.

Because the bonuses are not guaranteed at the outset the insurer is not risking having a loss recorded if investment returns prove to be worse than expected. However, with profits policyholders benefit directly from investment performance exceeding the conservative assumptions which are used in the premium rates.

In reality market pressures force the companies to maintain good bonus performance so as to secure an increasing flow of new business. The companies' profitability is directly affected by its investment performance.

Investment Income

General Business: Some £2918 million was received by UK insurance companies on invested funds of their general business during 1988. This represented just over 13 per cent of their total net premium income. Lloyds syndicates received in total £810 million during 1987 representing just 9.1 per cent of premium income.

Long term: The investment income of £12 106 million of insurance companies represented nearly 48 per cent of premium income. This reflects the much longer period over which assets have to be built up to pay claims. Consequently it is possible to invest for a better return than on shorter term scale general business. (see profitability of long term business).

Lloyd's The accounts for all classes of business underwritten at Lloyd's are prepared using the 'three year' accounting convention. Under this method revenue accounts are held open for three years from the commencement of each underwriting year. By that time a

Table 6.4 *Companies Investment Income*

The investment income represents a significant item of revenue for insurance companies especially for life business. The figures below show the investment income received, net of interest payable. They are therefore on a slightly different basis from those figures given in the income and outgoing tables quoted by the ABI in their booklet 'Insurance Statistics 1985–1989'.

Net income	1985 £m	1986 £m	1987 £m	1988 £m	1989 £m
Life	8854	10018	11022	12051	14886
General	2213	2526	2631	2911	3543
Total	11067	12544	13653	14962	18429

sufficiently accurate determination of outstanding liabilities (i.e. claims) can generally be made to permit the account to be 'closed' and the underwriting profit to be determined. The Global Report and accounts at 31 December 1989 accordingly show 1987–1989 as open years and 1986 will be 'closed'. There are problems with closing some syndicate accounts (see below 6.12. Supervision of Insurance).

Lloyd's showed a profit of £509 million for 1987 before tax (see Table 6.7) to the 30 000 names represented at Lloyd's for the year 1987. However the results for the remaining open years 1988 and 1989 are likely to be less profitable as a result of a general softening of rates and in 1989 the impact of some major claims.

Table 6.5 *Lloyd's Capacity and Profits*

	Market Capacity (£bn)	Gross Receipts (£bn)	Net Premiums (£bn)	Pre-tax Profit (£m)
1980	3.4	3.6	–	264
1981	3.5	4.5	–	152
1982	4.1	6.5	2.9	57
1983	4.3	5.7	2.5	35
1984	5.0	6.5	2.9	278
1985	6.6	6.4	3.0	196
1986	8.5	7.3	3.7	649
1987	10.3	–	–	–
1988	11.0	–	–	–
1989	10.9	–	–	–
1990	10.8	–	–	–

Source: Lloyd's of London
    – equals not available
    Gross receipts includes investment and other income, before reinsurance.

Lloyd's of London has severe problems with the number of years of account left open, but reported an improvement in 1989 over the previous year. These are years in which some underwriting syndicates cannot close their accounts after the normal three years because it is not possible to ascertain net profits or losses.

Net profits or losses are not known because of the existence of 'long-tail' risks, which may be claims for business written as long ago as 1940. The major long-tail risks to date have been the insurance and reinsurance of pollution and asbestos risks in the United States which have led to large claims in the 1980s and 1990s. Chatset, the organisation which publishes the Lloyd's League Tables, has argued that Lloyd's will face extinction if it cannot solve this problem, as it is a deterrent to new members.

Given the nature of business at Lloyd's, profits are difficult to ascertain until the end of the three-year accounting period. The last year for which accounts were closed and profits known was 1986, which was an excellent year (see Table 6.5), but profits have fallen since then. The greatest problems are long-tail risks, and the decline in premium income since 1986.

The decline of Lloyd's is apparent in the statistic that the main specialism of Lloyd's, marine insurance, has declined to the stage where three-quarters of world business is written elsewhere.

Plans have been set up to allow names to diversify their risk more widely through Members' Agents Pooling Arrangements (MAPAs), a sort of Lloyd's unit or investment trust. It is hoped that this might reverse the decline in the number of names, many of whom are leaving because underwriting losses can no longer be written off against personal income, because of scandals (Posgate) and because of perceived higher levels of risk (Outhwaite).

Lloyd's costs are rising, from around 7 – 8 per cent of premium income in the 1980's to around 10–12 per cent now (Economist June 16th 1990) through increased costs of regulation, higher salaries and more expensive premises.

Lloyd's has an extremely antiquated fragmented structure. There are 403 syndicates, over 33 532 names in 1988, 260 registered brokers and 224 members' agencies. There needs to be some form of consolidation if Lloyd's is to maintain its share of the world market. Restrictive practices need to be abolished, such as the requirement that all Lloyd's business must be channelled via registered brokers, when in fact many syndicates could sell their business directly. This would at least ensure greater competition and hence efficiency.

One improvement taking place is investment (£125m a year) on improving computer facilities within Lloyd's to speed up handling of claims and to simplify reinsurance settlement. Computerisation should reduce the paper mountain in the same way that is (eventually) coming about at the Stock Exchange.

Lloyd's finally appears to be becoming more aware of the European Market and 1992. Six offices have been set up in Europe to encourage business, and recognition seems to have emerged that Lloyd's is over-exposed to the American market, which is heavily cyclical in nature. There are still rule changes that are needed at Lloyd's to effectively compete for European business however. A particular (self-imposed) barrier to Europe is that registered brokers need to have offices in the proximity of Lime Street. The relaxation of this, and a real opening up of the Lloyd's market to foreign brokers would encourage greater competition and awareness of the European market.

Lloyd's global accounts are divided up into four markets: marine, non marine, aviation and motor. The relative size of each can be seen from the following figures.

Table 6.6 *Lloyd's Profitability by Class*

Year of account 1987	Marine	Non Marine	Aviation	Motor
% of total premium income	35	43	10	12
	£m	£m	£m	£m
Net premiums £m	1466.9	1820.4	428.3	479.3
Underwriting result	146.9	8.7	176.0	80.1
Gross investment return	228.7	428.4	91.4	47.1
Profit for closed year of account	291.9	281.9	246.2	60.8

Source: Lloyd's Global Accounts

Marine: Although the year of account showed a reasonable profit this was lower than for 1986 and the prospects for the 'open years' do not look very promising. This is due to poor trading conditions or 'soft' rates which have forced premiums down to uneconomic levels. In addition major claims such as Piper Alpha, Exxon Valdez, Phillips Pasadena Petroleum explosion and Hurricane Hugo will reduce the level of funds and consequently the amount available for investment.

The losses born by insurers have been cushioned by the high levels of reinsurance available at very cheap rates. When the claims work through the system there will be a return to 'harder' premium rates and profitability.

Non-Marine: The 1987 account was affected by the October 'hurricane' over south east England which resulted in large property claims and the 'run-off' from earlier years of account left open particularly in respect of liability claims for asbestosis and pollution.

Aviation: The profits shown for 1987 are unlikely to be repeated for the 'open' years. Competition has forced rates down and both 1988 and 1989 saw some large losses. Twenty eight Western built airliners crashed in 1988 killing 1004 passengers and claims could exceed $1.3 billion.

Motor: This section showed the best underwriting result reflecting more realistic premium pricing and a reduction in road casualties.

One rule change that will have a beneficial effect is the breaking down of the distinction between the four markets, which will allow Lloyd's to offer policies that cover several types of risk, that many large companies across Europe desire.

6.8   MARKET SHARE

The current state of the UK insurance industry is highly competitive. The largest insurer in 1988, the Prudential, controlled 9.3 per cent of the total world wide premium income of UK companies. The ten largest companies however control approximately 55 per cent of the world wide income. (See Table 6.9).

The proportion of this income controlled by the five largest companies has been declining (see Table 6.9). This is due to the faster growth of long term business relative to general. These larger companies have been relatively more important in the latter sector and have therefore suffered a relative decline.

Table 6.7 *Lloyd's Global Accounts as at 31.12.89*

Global Accounts as at 31.12.1989. *Year of Account 1987*	£m
Premium Income. Net of R/I ceded but inclusive of R/I premiums received from Previous Accounts	8851
Claims Net of R/I recoveries but inclusive of R/I premiums paid to close accounts	8439
Underwriting Result	412
Investment Returns	810
Profit before expenses	1222
Syndicate Expenses	341
Closed Year of Account Profit	881
Names Personal Expenses	372
	509

Table 6.8 *5 Largest UK Companies' World Wide Premium Income*

Year 1988 company	£ Million	% to all companies	
Prudential	4697	9.3	
Royal Insurance	3966	7.8	
Sun Alliance	3112	6.1	34.7%
Commercial Union	2991	5.9	
General Accident	2847	5.6	

Source: The British Insurance Industry 1989/90. A Statistical Review by R. L. Carter and S. R. Diacon

Table 6.9 *Proportion of all Company Premiums controlled by*
the Largest Companies

	1974	1980	1983	1987	1988
5 Largest	44.9%	40.7%	38.5%	34.4%	34.7%
Next 5 Largest	19.6%	20.5%	18.3%	19.8%	20.3%
	64.5%	61.2%	56.8%	53.9%	55.0%

Source: *The British Insurance Industry 1989/90. A Statistical
Review* by R. L. Carter and S. R. Diacon

In 1988 the top ten life companies (long term business)
accounted for approximately 44 per cent of the total premium
income of £22 008 million. This section of the insurance industry
was serviced by 209 specialist companies and 65 composite offices.

The top ten non-life offices (general business) companies
accounted for approximately 65 per cent of total premium income
of £12 652 million. This section of the industry was serviced by 564
specialist non-life companies and 65 composite insurers.

Foreign penetration of the UK market was about 5 per cent by
premium income. This figure increases to about 15 per cent where
foreign owned minority shareholdings are taken into account.

The UK life insurance industry is not particularly large by world
standards because pension funds have played a much larger part
than in other countries. It is only ninth in terms of sums insured
per person with an average figure of £9354 (1986) or the equivalent
of less than one year's average earnings. This compares with
£49 100 for Japan and £22 816 in the USA. However, overseas
sales for the UK life insurance industry have grown by 11 per cent
per annum in real terms over the period 1978–1987 compared with
9.3 per cent in the UK. Overseas income now represents 18 per
cent of total long term income.

This compares with 42 per cent of companies overseas general
business income from companies. The UK represents only 4 per
cent of the world market but British companies have 10 per cent of
it. The contribution to the UK balance of payments credits of all
insurance is £3.8 billion of which the majority is derived from
general insurance. The biggest single market for UK exporters of
insurance is the USA (35 per cent) compared with the EC of 20 per

cent. This is due to the protected nature of the European market. In many EC countries local regulations on the movement of life funds prevent the movement of investment overseas and act as a form of exchange control.

The negotiations until now on the 1992 Single European Market have been slow in creating a market for insurance. The non life directive in June 1988 created more freedom for cross-border insurance of large risks such as marine, aviation, and transport than for mass risks and does not cover motor risks. A draft life directive is under discussion which will give freedom to individual rather than group life insurance to sell life policies in a separate passive mode. The proposal is that the Directive provides for the possibility of Policyholders to use their initiative in seeking life insurance in other member states subject to those states' rules.

The slow evolution towards a single market has encouraged European insurers to establish affiliates or make take-overs in other countries abiding by the local laws and regulations.

6.9   ASSET PORTFOLIOS

Insurers are custodians of funds built up from premiums to pay claims. They also build up reserves against years when unexpectedly large claims occur. In a typical general insurance company about two thirds of the assets represent provisions to meet estimated liabilities to policyholders, i.e. claims. The remaining one third represents shareholders funds (or free reserves) to meet the legal and practical requirements for a 'solvency margin'.

These funds are invested and earn a return which is added to the fund. Outflows from the fund are used to pay the claims, expenses, and profit of the insurer.

Portfolios are a mixture of Government securities, equities, debentures, property holdings and the like. The nature of the investment portfolio is decided in relation to the type of business which the company is underwriting and the need to match the investment portfolio with the potential cash requirement needed to meet claims.

General insurance has about one-fifth of the invested assets of the long-term, life insurance and insured pension schemes. Its net income is proportionately smaller. A higher proportion of the

Table 6.10   *Investments Life and General Insurance 1988–89 ABI Member Companies*

The table below shows the way in which funds were invested at the ends of 1988 and 1989. Differences in investment patterns exist between life and general insurance to reflect the very different nature of the liabilities incurred.

| Funds/Assets | Life Insurance | | | | General Insurance | | | |
| | 1988 | | 1989 | | 1988 | | 1989 | |
	£m	%	£m	%	£m	%	£m	%
British Government authority securities	33 606	15.6	32 711	11.9	6182	14.6	5709	11.1
Foreign and Commonwealth Government, Provincial and municipal stocks	6 110	2.9	6817	2.5	7277	17.2	7044	13.7
Debentures, loan stocks preference and guaranteed stocks and shares	15 325	7.1	22 884	8.3	5549	13.1	8733	16.9
Ordinary stocks and shares	102 230	47.5	14 3391	52.0	11 803	27.9	16 207	31.9
Mortgages	10 841	5.0	13 493	4.9	1656	3.9	1989	3.9
Real property and ground rents	35 881	16.7	42 240	15.3	3507	8.3	4335	8.4
Other investments	11 126	5.2	13 939	5.1	6370	15.0	7518	14.6
Total invested assets	215 119	100	275 475	100	42 344	100	51 535	100
Net current assets	192		395		4236		5904	
Total	215 311		275 870		46 850		57 439	

Source: ABI Insurance Statistics 1985–89

general insurance funds are invested in loans or guaranteed stocks and preference shares. These are more secure and marketable but generally provide a lower return than equities. This is because general insurance is about annual contracts so there is no continuing commitment to renew premiums. Claims are more volatile and less predictable than long term business. Premium rates can be subject to intense market pressure which leads to insurers actually making losses on their underwriting operations. Thus a bigger proportion of the fund must be kept liquid compared to long term.

A comparison for the overall figures between long-term and general business shows that there is a higher proportion of long-term funds held by UK insurers in ordinary stocks and shares; 52 per cent in 1989 compared with 31.4 per cent for general insurance. General insurance held a greater proportion in loan stocks and debentures. The latter are more secure assets in the short term and therefore more realiseable.

The investment portfolio of a company writing general insurance business is likely to be geared to a shorter term cash requirement than that of a life company which can generally look to a longer term relationship between cash requirements for matured and surrendered policies. However, this general rule can be reversed by a general insurer which is increasing its level of business. Premiums are paid in advance of a period of cover being granted. In this situation it is possible to pay claims from previous years from the premiums for current years premium receipts. Whilst this situation exists it is possible to invest some of the technical reserves for the long-term. Only in the event of a long-term decline in the amount of business being written is there a necessity to realise all or part of the investments representing the reserves (=provisions).

Long-term funds invest a bigger proportion of their funds in equities. They are expanding more rapidly in terms of premium income compared to general business. Claims are more even and predictable than general so liquidity requirements can be met from new premiums.

Pension funds tend to hold a bigger proportion of equities and index linked gilts than straightforward life because their liabilities are in real rather than nominal terms. Life insurers on the other hand tend to hold their investments in fixed interest investments such as gilt edged because a large part of their liabilities is in nominal terms. That is, their liabilities are fixed at the commencement of the contract and do not escalate with inflation. Many modern insurance contracts do provide inflation proof death benefits but to the present time they still form a minority of the total sums insured which are in force.

Where future liabilities are in real terms the selected investment medium must show a growth which is faster than the rate of inflation. Historically equities have shown returns above the rate of inflation but this is accompanied by greater risk than fixed interest investment.

This traditional approach of life companies to invest heavily in the fixed interest market had been eroded by two factors, political and competitive. Firstly, the Gilt market has shrunk as the size of the National Debt has shrunk. Secondly, competitive pressure to show better returns for policyholders has been created by unit linked insurance contracts offering more specialised investments particularly in equities. Traditional life insurance companies are now increasing their holdings of corporate bonds, property and equities.

6.10   REINSURANCE AND COINSURANCE

Reinsurance and coinsurance are two mechanisms which have evolved to increase the strength and capacity of individual insurers.

By its nature the potential liabilities of an insurance company are always greater than its assets. The critical factor is the proportion of potential liabilties which become actual. Insurers spend a great deal of effort in trying to determine this proportion and base their premium rates accordingly. The calculation can only be an estimate because of the inexactitude of the exposure to risk. There can therefore only be an estimate of the amount of capital necessary to support the exposure.

Reinsurance and coinsurance do not reduce the total losses. Instead they ensure that the losses are shared between a large number of shoulders rather than one pair. In this way the risk of insolvency is reduced because losses do not fall on one company or Lloyd's syndicate.

Reinsurance differs from coinsurance in that in the former, the direct office, dealing with the customer takes the business risk of the reinsurer's insolvency. Coinsurance between several insurers means that the customer accepts the consequence of an individual insolvency amongst the coinsurers. In short there is a contractual relationship between a direct office customer and any coinsurers but not with the reinsurer.

Two examples of the operation of reinsurance can be seen in the October 1987 gales and the Piper Alpha disaster. The former incident gave rise to total losses costing the insurance industry over £1117 million from a large number of small claims. The latter gave rise to the biggest single insurance loss to date estimated at $1.4 billion. The Piper Alpha loss covers not only property damage to the rig but liability claims for death and injury. The final figure in this case will not be finalised for many years until all the litigation surrounding the liability claims has been settled.

In the October 1987 gales some £376 million will be recovered from the Reinsurance market and £414 million in respect of the Piper Alpha disaster. Reinsurers themselves retrocede (reinsure) a large proportion of the risk they carry back to direct insurers who have not themselves taken any direct part of the risk. All these separate transactions reduce the individual exposure to risk of the direct insurers which accepted the original risk on Piper Alpha by sharing the loss with Reinsurers and Retrocessionaires.

Reinsurance markets tend to be more international than domestic insurance markets. This is because domestic insurers are more likely to be affected by domestic incidents such as those described above. Thus claims will be partially met indirectly by payments received from overseas reinsurers.

The London Reinsurance company market in 1988 received about 25 per cent of its premium income from the UK. The other major areas were:

USA	23 per cent
Europe	14 per cent

On the general business side world wide underwriting losses after retrocession recoveries were sustained averaging approximately 12 per cent on worldwide premiums. Only part of the property insurance portfolio representing 16 per cent by premium income and aviation insurance (3.7 per cent) made profit on underwriting. The viability of the Reinsurance market would only be sustained by the investment returns which are earned on the premiums. This is the consequence of the over-capacity which the industry was experiencing at the period 1988. In the short term when investment returns begin to decline the industry will have to increase its rates so as to maintain its solvency margins. Reinsurance Offices Association Statistics 1982–89).

Long-term reinsurance (reassurance) is concerned with the reinsurance of the mortality risk of life and pensions business. The investment risk to the direct office of providing guarantees is effectively reduced by their low level where they exist and the widespread sale of unit linked contracts which do not provide guarantees.

Unit linked and with profits business contracts with substantial investment content pass the risk of the investments to the policy-holder. Thus the major area of risk which the insurer has to carry is related to mortality.

A large part of the mortality risk is reinsured. Thus the reinsurance market is concerned with factors leading to fluctuations which increase the mortality experienced above that which was allowed for in the reinsurance premium rates. The long-term trend of mortality in life insurance has been steadily improving and until the advent of the AIDS problem this was thought to continue. It is estimated that this disease will have an adverse impact on the future trends of mortality. Various projections have been calculated by the Institute of Actuaries working party on AIDS. A large increase in mortality is foreseen. Its extent will depend on factors such as government action and the development of successful drug treatments. This information has been taken very seriously by the Reinsurance industry because of its exposure to the mortality risk and consequent impact on its profitabilty.

The response of the Reinsurance market to this problem is dictated by the contractual nature of long term business. Terms and premium rates are fixed for existing business. Thus if rates are to harden they can only apply to new business which is currently being sold. Any response will therefore only affect a minority of the insured risks for a considerable period into the future. This contrasts with general business where new premium rates and policy conditions can be imposed at renewal.

The three areas in which a Reinsurer can influence a direct office are underwriting, risk premium rates and product design. In all three areas the AIDS problem has led to changes. Direct life offices have adopted progressively more stringent selection procedures, e.g. lifestyle questionnaires and HIV blood tests from some applicants blood. Term insurance rates have been generally increased to the levels recommended by the Institute of Actuaries AIDS working party. Exclusion clauses have been introduced into many permanent health insurance contracts. The Reinsurance market and the direct life market have developed close working relationships. They have been instrumental in raising the standards of underwriting in direct offices by training assistance and technical cooperation. In addition they have provided expertise in the development of new forms of cover by drawing on their expertise drawn from a wide range of claims experience.

Table 6.11 *Sample of Life Reinsurers Premium Incomes*

In 1987 the revenue premium income of nine prominent life reinsurance companies based in the UK was as follows:-

British and European	£7 827 883
Gerling Global	£2 094 000
Mercantile and General	£101 404 952
Munich Re	£9 972 644
NRG London Re	£17 180 000
Skandia Re (UK)	£5 606 000
Swiss Re (UK)	£38 468 000
Victory Re	£35 958 000
World Wide Re	£16 661 000
	£235 172 479

Source: Money Marketing Life Reinsurance Report, 29.9.1988

6.11 SUPERVISION OF INSURANCE

Insurance has traditionally been a closely supervised industry because of the consequence for policyholders of company failure. Legislation affecting life insurance, requiring minimum deposits for companies transacting this class of business was first required under the Life Assurance Companies Act 1870. The supervision of general business began with the passing of the Assurance Companies Act 1909 and legislation has continued ever since with a great increase in volume during the 1960's and 1970's. This was caused by a series of company failures and the impact of the EC on legislation.

The First Council Non Life Establishment Directive 73/239/ EEC was instrumental in bringing about the 1974 Insurance Companies Act and subsequent statutory instruments under the Act. This legislation brought some harmonisation of the UK and Europe in the field of solvency margins, definitions of classes of business and the authorisation of insurance companies in the general business area. In 1979 the EC issued Life Establishment Directive 79/267/EC which was followed by the Insurance Companies Act 1981.

All current legislation has been codified by the Insurance Companies Act 1982 and Statutory Instrument number 1654 (Insurance Companies Regulations). The EC directives and the legislation makes the carrying of life and non-life business subject to an authorisation requirement which must be met by those seeking to transact insurance. In particular it provides that insurers in one member state obtain authorisation for branches to be established in other member states. It also sets up a harmonised regime for the financial supervision of insurers. In addition to the assets necessary to meet their underwriting liabilities undertakings must possess a supplementary reserve known as the solvency margin which is to be represented by free assets. Detailed rules are laid down for the calculation of this margin for life and non-life business.

Life solvency margins are based on the actuarial liability (present liabilities plus the present discounted value of future liabilities). Non-life margins are based on the premiums and claims. The legislation contains directives concerning undertakings which fail to possess the required margin, concerning the transfer between undertakings of some or all of their portfolio of policies, the withdrawal of authorisation and branches of non-community companies.

For this reason there is a strong web of legislation which has been enacted under the Insurance Companies Act 1982 which sets down strict principles to check that insurance companies and Lloyds are being managed by fit and proper persons along sound insurance lines.

Capital and Reserves

This represents the shareholders interest in the business. It is important to the viability of insurance companies that the solvency margin which is required by government regulation is defined as the company's capital and free reserves. Why is this?

The insurance company's requirement for capital derives from the nature of insurance. In providing insurance the company needs to ensure that over a period of time, usually a year, the premium income will provide sufficient money for the payment of claims, the administration costs of the company and some profit. However, there can never be a guarantee that this state of equilibrium will be maintained over any one period of account. The actual incidence of claims will be subject to external factors beyond the company's control and the premium which can be charged will be subject to market pressure.

Premium rates in general business tend to follow cyclical trends already described. During periods of high premium rates and profitability additional insurers move in and compete forcing down rates and often the standards at which a particular risk is regarded as insurable.

Thus profitability is by no means guaranteed. Capital is required so that claims can be fully covered during periods of unprofitable underwriting. Without this capital cover the policyholder would not be paid claims in years when losses occur.

This shareholder capital is intended to provide financial backing as a last resort. In practice insurance companies create free reserves out of profits in years when claims remain relatively low and/or premium rates remain high. These reserves are usually great enough to withstand losses arising in the 'bad' years.

The capital subscribed is only needed as a last resort and is therefore available for investment. This contributes to the profitability of the company and the shareholders' dividends. Long term business has a different cost structure compared with general business. The initial cost of setting up can exceed its premium for a period of up to two years because the majority of the commission is paid during this period. After claims, selling costs form the biggest part of an Insurer's costs. In addition there are other setting up costs such as medical fees for large life insurance proposals which have to be recouped. This phenomenon is referred to as the 'new business strain' by Actuaries.

Thus a company requires a higher capital commitment during its early years when it is being established. Profitability will be established when the proportion of new policies to old policies is reduced. When a policy has been 'on the company's books' for over two years it will become profitable to the insurer. It needs a spread of new and established policies to be viable. Therefore in the early years capital is required to overcome the strain on profitability created by this problem.

Lloyd's is also supervised under the Insurance Companies Act 1982 and various Statutory Instruments. Security is maintained not only by external legislation but by internal regulation issued by the Council of Lloyd's which sets limits on the volume of business which members can accept in any one year by reference to their level of Funds held at Lloyd's in the form of personal and special reserve funds and deposits. These limits are monitored by underwriting agents at syndicate level.

In addition each member of Lloyd's is required to pass an annual solvency test as at 31 December by providing sufficient acceptable assets to meet their future underwriting liabilities which are calculated in a manner presented by the Council of Lloyd's and approved by the Secretary of State. Members who fail to comply by the due date are suspended from underwriting and amounts sufficient to cover the shortfall are earmarked from the Central Fund.

Lloyd's as a whole completes a solvency margin statement as part of its statutory return to the Department of Trade and Industry. At 31 December 1989 Lloyd's achieved eleven times the required solvency margin.

Lloyd's financial resources come from two sources: its members and a Central Fund. The individual members are liable for their underwriting commitments and the greater part of these resources represent that of the members (£18 345 million as at 31 December 1989).

The Central Fund and the assets of the Corporation of Lloyd's exist as an ultimate safeguard if an individual member is unable to meet their liabilities. The members' resources are divided into Technical Reserves and Members' means. The former consists of a syndicate underwriting balances in respect of the two open years of account. The members' means consist of Lloyd's deposits and, personal and special reserve funds and their personal wealth. Only certain assets qualify for inclusion as 'means' so as to ensure that a high proportion is in the form of readily realiseable assets.

The Outhwaite syndicate of over 1600 members has lost over £200m, and the final sum will probably be over £300m. There is under capacity at Lloyd's at present, with syndicates writing less than two-thirds of their capability according to the capitalisation of 'names'. Capacity has remained at around £11 bn since 1988 (see Table 6.5), but there are fears that Lloyd's will not be able to cope with a growth in business, given the decline in the number of names.

6.12 EC AND INSURANCE

The main objectives of 1992 in relation to insurance are:-

   (i)   harmonisation of supervision
   (ii) mutual recognition by host regulators of the relevant controls in other EC countries.
   (iii) regulation of insurance companies by parent (home) regulators.

As stated earlier full harmonisation is too difficult a task, and liberalisation of the insurance market takes a similar line to that of the banking market.

The theoretical ideal is a position whereby insurance companies have both freedom of establishment and freedom of services. The former means the right to set up an insurance business in any EC country, with terms being no more onerous than that of local insurers (these may in themselves be onerous, but that is another matter). Freedom of establishment has now existed for a number of years. The latter refers to the ability to sell insurance policies EC–wide, and has been far more problematic in implementation.

The main framework for the provision of non-life business was set out in the second non-life Directive of 1988. This distinguished between two types of non life insurance, characterised by their degree of risk. The first category is *large risks*, which relates to insurance for large firms (500 employees or more, turnover of 24m ECUs or more, and a balance sheet of 12.4m ECUs or more – two of the three criteria to be satisfied). All marine, aviation and transport business is deemed to be large risk. The directive allows for transactions in large risk business across borders, with home country regulation. Mass risk relates to all other non-life business, and requires authorisation from the *host* country, which generally is very time consuming. Motor insurance is classified as a mass risk, but is to be regulated separately.

In addition, under the 'cumul' rules an institution cannot provide insurance business overseas by both an establishment and a services basis, only one or the other.

Liberalisation of life assurance has so far not taken place. At present insurers are only allowed to sell life assurance overseas if it has been gained on an 'own initiative' basis, i.e. if overseas customers have contacted the insurer on their own initiative, cross-boarder advertising being largely prohibited. The scope for such business is obviously limited.

Also, many EC countries have strict demarcation lines with respect to permissible areas of insurance business. Many countries have laws separating life from non-life business, such that UK composite insurers that offer both types of insurance are at present restricted from competing.

The taxation of premiums differs among EC countries, ranging from zero to around 30 per cent, and until this is harmonised, those policies from low tax countries will be cheaper than in higher tax countries, other things being equal.

There is thus a disparity between the opportunities for UK companies in the mass risk and large risk non-life markets, and between non-life and life business. The large risk market is already extremely competitive on an international scale, whilst the stipulation of host country regulation for mass risks has hindered cross border business. Similarly, non-life business in general is becoming more liberalised, in contrast to the life market which still remains national in character.

6.13   CONCLUSION

Despite its problems insurance remains a vital exporter of financial services for the UK and its continued strength is important to the UK economy's balance of payments. In 1989 insurance companies, Lloyds and brokers contributed £2 927 million (47 per cent) of the total net invisible earnings of UK financial institutions of £6 184 million. This compares with the next biggest, Securities Dealing, which contributed just under 20 per cent and banking where there was a negative net outflow of £678 million. (Source: Central Statistical Office).

REFERENCES

Dodds, J. C. (1987) *The Investment Behaviour of British Life Insurance Companies* (London: Croom-Helm).

Daenger, B. J. (1984) 'Solvency. The problem of evaluating insurers' Vol. 72 of *The Journal of the Insurance Institute of London*.

Frost, A. J. and Hager, D. P. 'A General Introduction to Institutional Investment' *The Institute of Actuaries London*.

Tutt, L. W. G. and S. I. M (1989) 'Financial Aspects of Life Business' Chartered Insurance Institute, London.

——(1989) 'Financial Aspects of Pensions Business.' Chartered Insurance Institute, London.

Williamson, Dan (1988) 'Management II: Insurance Companies.' The Chartered Insurance Institute, London.

Lloyds Bank Economic Bulletin October 1989 Number 130.

'Insurance Statistics 1985–1989' 'Association of British Insurers, Aldermary House, 10–15 Queen Street, London EC4N 1TT.

'Reinsurance Statistics 1982–1988' Reinsurers Offices Association, Aldermary House, 10–15 Queen Street, London, 1 Lime Street, London EC4N 1ST.

'Global Report and Accounts 1989' Lloyds of London, 1 Lime Street, London EC3M 7HA.
'Statutory Statement of Business made by the Council of Lloyds' as at 31 December 1988.

CHAPTER 7

NON-BANK FINANCIAL INTERMEDIARIES

7.0 INTRODUCTION

This chapter explores the functions of the diverse grouping of financial institutions known as non-bank financial intermediaries and comparisons are made between unit trusts and investment trusts, and the impact of pension funds on the operation of the financial system are considered. The effectiveness of venture capital funds in promoting seed-corn businesses is analysed, and the changing role of venture capital funds is detailed. The operations of the National Savings movement are set out and the special status of National Savings is emphasised. The activities of finance houses in providing credit facilities are also examined.

7.1 UNIT TRUSTS

Unit trusts are an investment vehicle for persons and companies to obtain a share in a diversified portfolio of assets. Funds contributed to a unit trust are invested in a variety of assets ranging from liquid to relatively illiquid – bank deposits, equities and loan stock (both UK and overseas), local authority debt and government securities. Investors contribute funds in order to obtain a share of the stream of dividends and any capital gains that accrue on the portfolio of assets. Of course the 'Units' are bought by investors, and these units are priced according to how many are in existence and what the total value of the trusts' net asset holdings are (e.g. £50m net assets and 5m units means each unit is priced at £10).

The offer price of units (the price at which they are sold to investors) and the bid price (the price at which they are bought by investors) are worked out day-to-day, and are determined by the daily market value of the net assets of the trust. Various fees and charges make up the difference between the offer and bid prices, such as profit, brokerage charges, trustees' fees and contract stamp, although the maximum permissible spread is regulated by the Department of Trade and Industry. The largest spread allowed between offer and bid prices is 15 per cent of net asset value. If the net asset value of the trust were £50m and there were 5 million units in existence, then the net asset value of one unit would be £10 and the largest permissible offer price would be £10.75 with a possible bid price of £9.25, giving a 15 per cent spread. In general, spreads tend to average around 6 to 7 per cent.

It should be recognised that there is no secondary market for units, they can only be bought and sold from the unit trust itself. Unit trusts must buy back any units investors wish to sell, at the prevailing price, and so investors can obtain liquidity at any time, although of course if instant liquidity is required the transaction may have to be carried out at unfavourable prices, and so units should be thought of as long term investments with a deposit account held at a bank or building society for liquid funds.

Unit trusts are run by two separate companies, a trustee company, and a management company. The former acts as the overseer of the unit holders' income and assets on their behalf. The trustee company, which is often a subsidiary of a major financial institution such as a large insurance company or bank, checks that investments of unit holders' funds are in line with the general investment strategy of the fund as stated in the trust deed. The management company, which again is often a subsidiary of an insurance company or bank, is in charge of actually making and carrying out investment decisions, and selling and buying back units. Unit Trusts are open-ended, which means that their size can grow or diminish according to the demand for units.

As stated above, investment decisions are carried out in accordance with the broad policy set out in the trust deed, but the limits of the investment policy are in turn delineated by the following conditions (LAUTRO):

1. Investment in commodities and property are not permitted. (Although see the section below on Property Unit Trusts).

2. A minimum of 75 per cent of the value of the portfolio must be invested in securities which are quoted on a recognised stock exchange. A maximum of 25 per cent of shares can be invested in shares on the Unlisted Securities Market. A maximum of 5 per cent can be invested in unquoted shares.
3. No more than 10 per cent of the share capital of any single company can be held.
4. No more than 5 per cent of the value of a unit trusts portfolio can be invested in any single company, *at the time the investment is made*. If after the investment is made the value of the shares rises, intervention is not necessary by the trustees as long as the value of the shares does not increase to rise above 7 ½per cent of the value of the portfolio. It is generally regarded that liquidity is a very important factor in the management of unit trusts, given the ability of unit holders to require payment for the resale of their sales on any day, and the above conditions relating to investment policy largely reflect the need to plan for adequate liquidity.

Net new investment in Unit Trusts in 1989 was £3866 million, and funds under management stood at £58 159 million.

Money invested in unit trusts has grown throughout the 1980's, particularly in 1986, with funds under management growing by 63 per cent. The number of unit holder accounts has also grown, particularly in the bull market years of 1985 to 1987. The number of accounts faltered slightly after the crash, and appear to have settled at around 4.8 million. The number of trusts has grown from 493 in 1980 to 1379 in 1989, with many commentators predicting a certain degree of rationalisation in the 1990's, although there is no evidence of this as yet.

During the 1980s income growth in unit trusts has been high (£1000 invested in a unit trust in 1989 would have yielded £142, compared with £81 in a building society). Several factors encouraged the growth of unit trusts in the 1980s: the abolition of restrictions on unit trust charges and the abolition of exchange controls, both in 1979. The third was the abolition of capital gains tax on unit trust portfolios in 1980.

Life insurers have historically placed a proportion of their funds in unit trusts because capital gains on units were tax exempt until sold. Tax exemption is to be closed by the Inland Revenue in 1991, however, and life companies have recently withdrawn substantial

Table 7.1   *Unit Trust Industry Statistics*

	Funds under Management (Year end) £m	Net Investment as % of gross Sales %	Unit Holder Accounts m	Number of Trusts
1960s[1]	1412	70.8	2.39	205
1970s[2]	3936	14.1	1.82	459
1980	4968	20.2	1.72	493
1981	5902	55.2	1.79	529
1982	7768	50.9	1.80	553
1983	11689	60.9	2.04	630
1984	15099	49.3	2.20	687
1985	20308	56.5	2.55	806
1986	32131	60.0	3.41	964
1987	36330	43.5	5.05	1137
1988	41574	23.3	4.89	1255
1989	58159	36.4	4.88	1379

[1] at end of 1969   [2] at end of 1979
Source: Unit Trust Yearbook 1990

sums from unit trusts (£63.8m net outflow in June 1990). Most of the funds withdrawn are actually from unit trusts owned by the life insurers through subsidiaries, and a switch away from unit trusts will be a substantial structural change, as life companies held 44 per cent of unit trust funds at the end of 1989. Life companies are to be assessed each year on the gains on their units, and taxes spread over seven years. Life companies have until the end of 1991 to switch their unit trusts into the underlying shares without tax penalties. Such substantial flows of funds as these show the effect that the tax system or changes in the tax system can have on the patterns of finance in the UK.

Nearly 95 per cent of UK unit trusts' assets are held in company securities (both UK and overseas). Ordinary shares dominate the UK company securities section and the overall portfolio, accounting for around 56 per cent of total net assets. British Government securities are insignificant by comparison, with only 1 per cent of the assets (see Table 7.2). Short-term assets account for around 5 per cent of total assets, and have been becoming more important in recent years. (Table 7.3). Overseas securities grew markedly after the removal of exchange controls in 1979 largely at the expense of UK company securities, but as with overseas investments by investment trust (see next section) have fallen away slightly in recent years.

Table 7.2 *UK Unit Trusts; Assets and Liabilities*

End of Year Market Values 1988

	£m	
Short-Term Assets:		
UK:		
Cash and UK Bank Deposits	2032	
Local Authority Temporary Debt	41	
Other short-term Assets	249	
Overseas short-term Assets	173	
Short-term Liabilities	(438)	
Total Net short-term Assets		2057
Foreign Currency Loans		(489)
British Government Securities		501
UK Company Securities:		
Ordinary Shares	24040	
Preference	858	
Loan Capital	868	
Total		25766
Other UK Investments		205
Overseas Company Securities		14738
Other Overseas Investments		187
Total Net Assets		42965

Source: Financial Statistics, August 1990

Short term assets are held for investment opportunities, and the government's privatisation programme, coupled with high interest rates on liquid assets may explain the increased popularity of cash and other short term assets in recent years.

UK Property Unit Trusts are 'unauthorised' in that they do not have to be authorised by the DTI because of the fact that they do not deal with the general public (major investors being pension funds and charities). As their name suggests, they invest largely in

Table 7.3   *UK Unit Trusts; Asset Distribution Holdings at end year, Market Values %*

	Net Cash and Short-Term Assets	British Government Securities	UK Company Securities	Overseas Company Securities	Other Net Assets	Total Net Assets
1980	3.7	1.5	71.2	22.8	0.8	100
1982	4.5	4.2	60.2	29.8	1.3	100
1984	6.1	3.8	55.0	33.9	1.2	100
1986	4.4	1.7	54.8	38.4	0.7	100
1988	4.7	1.2	59.3	33.9	0.9	100

Source: Financial Statistics, various issues

property (see Table 7.4) and are exempt from income and capital gains tax.

Unit trusts are regulated by the Life Assurance and Unit Trust Regulatory Organisation (LAUTRO) and the Investment Management Regulatory Organisation (IMPO), and they have a Unit Trust Association (UTA) which carries out supervision on an informal basis, and is more of a lobbying body on behalf of the unit trust industry.

Table 7.4   *UK Property Unit Trusts; Aggregate Assets Amounts Outstanding, Market Value 1988*

	£m	%
Cash, bank balances and other current Assets	84	8.9
Property:		
UK	1	0.1
Overseas	681	72.4
Other Assets	174	18.5
Total Assets	940	100

Source: Financial Statistics, August 1990

There are a certain number of tax barriers to selling UK unit trusts in the EC: (Yearbook 1990).

1.   UK tax has to be deducted from income payments such that the investor has to reclaim the tax.

2. Income from a UK unit trust invested in foreign shares is lower than a locally based one because of UK corporation tax.
3. UK unit trusts are the only ones in Europe taxed on 'Trading Profits'.

Unit Trusts have been allowed since 1985 to operate across EC borders.

The UCITS (undertaking for collective investment in transferable securities) Directive of 1985 sets out minimum requirements for unit trusts, in terms of information policies of owners, investment policies of trusts, and marketing aspects. With regard to marketing, unit trusts which comply with the directive can be marketed in any EC country, and will have to abide by host country advertising restrictions.

Products that contain both life and unit trust elements will still be regulated by separate member countries.

7.2 INVESTMENT TRUSTS

Investment trusts are similar to unit trusts in that they allow persons and companies to obtain a share in a diversified portfolio of assets and have a specialist fund manager to control the portfolio, but are fundamentally different from unit trusts in other ways.

Investment trusts are mis-named in that they are not trusts as properly defined, but are in fact actually limited companies quoted on the stock exhange. Moreover, the scope for advertising is limited, as they are prohibited by the Companies Act to advertise their own shares for sale (as are all quoted companies). Advertising is limited to a new issue by an investment trust, and to investment trust saving schemes.

The Securities and Investments Board's Retail review Committee recommended in 1990 that investment trust savings schemes should be allowed to be advertised with the same degree of freedom as unit trusts. There is still the limitation however that this relates only to investment trust savings schemes, such that investment trusts cannot advertise their shares directly. This is a great step forward as advertising should reduce the level of ignorance of the investing public that apparently exists according to a survey by the Stock Exchange and the Association of Investment Trust Companies. It was found that even existing shareholders had had a very limited knowledge of the savings schemes that investment trusts offer.

Investment trusts can issue debentures and warrants as well as equity, and can retain capital gains from investments and retain other income if they so wish, whereas unit trusts cannot. Investment trusts are closed end funds, while as stated earlier, unit trusts are open ended. The broad policies of investment trust companies are set out by a board of directors, and as with any limited company they are limited by the articles of association and shareholder approval. Day-to-day running of the trust is carried out by specialist fund managers, often by merchant banks.

As with the shares of any quoted company, prices can vary quite substantially according to their supply and demand, which in turn can be determined by a variety of market factors. Investors buy a general claim on the investment trust, rather than buy the assets as in a unit trust.

Management fees of investment trusts are considerably lower than those of unit trusts because of the wide disparities in money spent on advertising, although with the changes in rules on advertising for investment trusts, their fees are likely to rise.

In terms of regulations as to permitted forms of investment, investment trusts are only limited by the listing requirements of the Stock Exchange:

1. No more than 10 per cent of total investment to be tied up in any one company.
2. Holdings of unlisted shares must not account for more than 15 per cent of total investment.

In practice the majority of investment trust assets are held in quoted company securities, although they are also free to invest in property and trade in currency options and futures, none of which unit trusts are permitted to do.

The major element of investment trusts' asset portfolios is ordinary shares, with UK and overseas ordinary equities accounting for nearly 90 per cent of total assets net of short-term liabilities. Holdings of government securities and property are relatively insignificant (Table 7.5). Relatively few government

Table 7.5 *Investment Trusts: Aggregate Assets. Amount Outstanding End Year, Market Value 1989*

	£m	
UK Short-Term Liabilities:		
Bank Borrowing	(191)	
Other	(102)	
U.K. Short-Term Assets:		
Cash and Bank Deposits	823	
Certificates of Deposit	53	
Local Authorities Temporary Debt	82	
Other	116	
Net UK Short-Term Assets		781
Overseas Short-Term Liabilities	(90)	
Overseas Short-Term Assets	278	
Net Overseas Short-Term Assets		188
Total Net Short-Term Assets		969
UK Investments:		
British Government Securities		199
Listed Company Securities:		
Ordinary	10472	
Preference and Loan Capital	669	
Total		11141
Unlisted Company Securities		
Ordinary	723	
Preference and Loan Capital	126	
Total		849
Public Corporation Securities		40
Unit Trust Units		63
Other Financial Assets		45
Property		60
Other Real Assets		1
Overseas Investments:		
Government and Municipal Securities		44
Company Securities:		
Ordinary	10587	
Preference & Loan Capital	437	
Other	63	
Total		11131
Total Assets Net of Short-Term Liabilities		24343

Source: Financial Statistics, August 1990

securities are held, and although overseas securities grew in the 1980's, European equities are in fact a relatively small proportion of the total.

The removal of exchange controls allowed diversification of portfolios to continue on an international scale, and it should be recognised that the increasing globalisation of markets through deregulation and liberalisation also contributed to the growth in holdings of overseas securities. This shift towards overseas equities can clearly be seen in Table 7.6. The proportion of assets accounted for by overseas equities grew rapidly from 36.6 per cent of the total in 1980 to 49.3 per cent in 1984. There appears to have been a certain degree of retrenchment after the initial enthusiasm, with overseas securities standing at around 45 per cent of the total at the end of 1988. This growth in the proportion of overseas equities in the portfolios and subsequent decline has been mirrored by a fall in the importance of UK company shares over 1980–1984, but a resurgence since then at the expense of overseas securities.

Shorter-term assets are kept at relatively low levels and tend to be used for investment transactions and repayment of loans.

Reserves and provisions in Table 7.7 refer to investment income and realised capital gains that have been retained for reimbursement.

Table 7.6   *Investment Trusts' Asset Distribution, End Year, Market Values %*

	Total Net Short-Term Assets	British Government Securities	UK Company Securities	Overseas Company Securities	Other Assets
1980	2.7	3.1	55.4	36.6	2.6
1982	2.4	1.9	46.0	44.7	5.0
1984	2.6	2.0	41.6	49.3	4.5
1986	2.1	1.5	44.2	47.7	6.2
1988	3.3	1.8	48.6	43.6	2.7
1989	3.9	0.8	48.9	45.0	1.3

Source: Financial Statistics, August, 1990

Table 7.7 *U.K. Investment Trusts: Medium and Long-Term Liabilities and Capital. Amounts Outstanding, End Year, Market Value 1989*

	£m
Issued Shares:	
Ordinary and Deferred	3064
Preference	177
Loan Capital	1534
Other UK Debt:	
Sterling Bank Borrowing	299
Foreign Currency Bank Borrowing	124
Other	
Other Overseas Debt:	
Foreign Currency Borrowing	161
Other	15
Reserves and Provisions	19027
Total	19019

Source: Financial Statistics, August 1990

Shareholders = Value of Issued Shares + Reserves + Provisions
Equity

Notice from Table 7.7 however that investment trusts have a low level of gearing (borrowing in relation to equity).

Liabilities and short-term assets are at book value, foreign currency items are translated into sterling at middle-market exchange rates, real assets and investments are at market value.

Shares in investment trusts are often priced below their net-asset (NAV). The discount on the share can be worked out using the formula:-

$$\text{Discount} = \frac{\text{NAV Minus Market Value of share}}{\text{NAV}} \times 100$$

Investment trust shares can also trade at a premium where the market value of the share is greater than its NAV:

$$\text{Premium} = \frac{\text{Market Value of Share Minus NAV}}{\text{NAV}} \times 100$$

It is generally the case that a discount exists for a variety of reasons. Breaking up the investment trust would involve costs, and selling large blocks of the shares on the market would probably depress their price, such that the shares are 'discounted' when in a portfolio of an investment trust. Obviously investment trusts' management expenses need to be paid and corporation tax paid, again reducing the value of the shares relative to the underlying assets if they were held by the investor. Also investment trust shares may be less marketable or liquid than others, as they are not actively traded by institutional investors.

One of the major problems of investment trust shares trading at a discount is that the company becomes a relatively attractive proposition for predators, particularly other financial institutions wishing to buy a ready-made diversified portfolio of assets (at a discount).

Pension funds, in particular, are interested in buying investment trusts that have a wide discount to net asset value in order to build up their portfolios. At the time of writing, British Coal Pension Fund is making a contested bid for Globe, Britain's largest investment trust, with over £1.09 billion of assets, and more than 40 000 shareholders. The intention of a predator (as with British Coal Pension Fund) is to buy the shares of the investment trust at a premium to market prices (to induce investors to sell) but still at a discount to NAV.

From the investors point of view, discounts can be good as they effectively increase the ability of the investment trust to create income relative to a given investment of funds. For example, if there is a 25 per cent discount on shares valued at 200p, NAV of each share would be 250p. £10 000 invested in shares would have an underlying NAV of £12 500 (ignoring transactions costs) with which the investment trust can generate income.

Investment trusts are regulated by the rules of the Companies Acts, which lay down requirements with respect to number of shareholders, form of financial accounts, constitutional structure, etc. and by the listing requirements of the Stock Exchange (see above). The Association of Investment Trust Companies (AITC) has no formal regulatory powers, but is rather a voice for the investment trust industry.

7.3 PENSION FUNDS

Pension funds can be conveniently divided into state schemes and private schemes. State or public sector schemes are generally referred to as 'pay-as-you-go', whereas private funds are generally externally funded. Pay-as-you-go means that the present pension benefits are provided through the taxation system. Those in work are paying for the pensions of those past retirement age at the current time, rather than for their own pensions in the future. This situation where current pensions are paid for out of current income does not present a problem for governments, as they should always have the power to raise funds through taxation. Private sector companies do not have this luxury however, and operate on a funding scheme where money placed into the fund is used to finance future pension payments.

A number of reasons exist as to why companies run funded schemes. Perhaps the most important reason is that if the company should go bankrupt, the pension fund (which is normally administered by an appointed financial institution) would not be affected, which can be contrasted with a pay-as-you-go system where obviously there would be no employees left to finance current or future pension benefits. The second reason (and also a powerful one) is that funded schemes benefit from favourable taxation.

Examples of pay-as-you-go include the National Health Service, the Armed Forces, the Civil Service and teachers, although it is somewhat of an anomoly that the pension schemes of Nationalised Industries, e.g. British Coal, British Rail, are in fact externally funded, when there is no clear rationale as to why they should be.

In terms of financial intermediation it is only externally funded schemes that carry out an intermediary function, as the funds collected for future pension payments are invested in financial assets (and a small proportion in real assets – property and works of art) in order to earn a return on investments to be able to pay out future pensions, whereas in pay-as-you-go funds are merely transferred from present employees to present pensioners, with no financial intermediation taking place.

Most pension schemes are 'final salary' schemes, with the pension being a proportion of the employee's final salary at retirement multiplied by the number of years of pensionable service. Specific schemes differ in their elements: for some final salary may be the best of the last three or five years or the average, or may be based on earnings as opposed to salary.

A popular form of scheme is the 'managed fund', generally administered by insurance companies whereby the funds of several pension funds are combined to form one large portfolio, and the portfolio is often divided into units that are owned by the pension funds, the value of the unit being equal to the market value of the assets held in the whole portfolio divided by the number of units issued. Pension funds can further diversify their portfolios by investing in a spread of these units across different managed funds (insurance companies have in fact set up specialised managed funds that are largely made up of specific investments, to allow such diversification across managed funds by pension funds).

The size of the pension fund is a major determinant of the extent to which managed funds are used. Medium-sized funds may have a small proportion invested in managed funds, with the majority of assets in its direct control, large pension funds are likely to have totally direct control, whilst smaller funds may simply invest in a range of managed policies.

If a pension becomes large enough to move away from managed funds, specialist fund managers are normally used to invest the assets, and extremely large pension funds such as British Coal tend to employ a team of specialist investment advisors.

Changes in pension provision came about with the passing of the Social Security Act 1986 and the Finance (No. 2) Act 1987. The changes came about because of the costs of the State Earnings Related Pension Scheme (SERPS), the need for pensions that could be moved along with a change in jobs, and the wish to provide the public with more freedom of choice in their pension plans.

The main changes included the ability to contract out of SERPS, voluntary membership of occupational schemes, and the availabil-

ity of personal pensions through a wide range of intermediaries – insurance companies, friendly societies, banks, building
societies and unit trust groups.

Personal Pensions are 'money purchase' plans whereby the
retirement benefits depend mainly on the amount of funds paid in
and the return on investment, whereas the company schemes can
be either money purchase or 'final salary', where the benefits are
based on the employee's salary and length of service.

Pension funds are massive institutions and rival insurance
companies in terms of size. As with insurance companies, pension
funds are tremendously important to the efficient working of the
secondary market of the Stock Exchange. The majority of the
pension funds' assets are company securities, both UK and
overseas, and especially ordinary shares. At the end of 1988 UK
and overseas ordinary shares accounted for around 67 per cent of
total net assets (Table 7.8). British Government securities are also
important, at around 13 per cent of total net assets, with particular
emphasis on index-linked and long-dated stocks. Land, property
and ground rents are also significant, at approximately 8 ½ per
cent of the portfolio. There was substantial growth in the early
1980's in overseas shares after the abolition of exchange controls,
and holdings of both UK and overseas equities have grown rapidly
(Table 7.9).

Holdings of overseas securities of course allows for greater
diversification of the asset portfolio, and often offers higher yields,
especially in the Far East in recent years.

Fund managers are increasingly developing portfolios that track
world indices. If this trend continues, then pension funds, for
example, will steadily off-load domestic (UK) equities in favour of
European and other stocks. Indeed, over the period March 1989 to
March 1990 pension funds increased their holdings of European
equities from 6 per cent to more than 8 per cent. This should not
be cause for alarm, however. It is likely that overseas institutions
will simultaneously be increasing the proportion of UK equities in
their portfolios. Short-term liquid assets are held for active trading
purposes and for buying long-term investments.

Pension funds have used property unit trusts as a cheap method
of diversifying into the property market, without the problems
associated with actually dealing in the properties themselves.

'Other' assets include unit trust units, local authorities mutual
investment trust, property unit trusts, loans and mortgages, UK

Table 7.8   *UK Pension Funds: Assets Portfolio Holdings at end of Year Market Values 1988*

	£m
Short Term Assets:	
UK:	
Cash and Balances with Banks	8760
Certificates of Deposit	986
Other Financial Institutions	390
Treasury Bills	–
Local Authority Bills and Temporary Money	696
Other	795
Overseas Short-Term Assets:	575
Short-Term Liabilities	(435)
Long-Term Borrowing	(261)
British Government Securities:	
Index Linked	6005
Up to 5 years	563
Over 5 and up to 15 years	12610
Over 15 years and undated	7905
UK Company Securities:	
Ordinary Shares	115455
Other	3477
Overseas Securities:	
Ordinary Shares	28024
Other	699
Government Securities	1019
UK Local Authority Securities	130
Unit Trust Units	1930
Local Authority Mutual Investment Trust	6
Property Unit Trust	1405
Loans & Mortgages:	
To Parent Organisation	66
Other	250
Overseas	25
UK Land, Property and Ground Rents	18164
Other Investments	4545
Debtors Net of Creditors	734
Total Net Assets	214518

Source: Financial Statistics, **August 1990**

Table 7.9 *Selected Asset Holdings of Pension Funds, %*

	Short Term Assets	British Govern- ment Securities	UK Company Securities	Overseas Company Securities	UK Land Property and Ground Rents	Other
1980	4.7	21.8	46.8	8.4	15.5	2.8
1982	3.6	21.7	44.2	12.2	12.5	5.8
1984	4.1	18.3	48.6	14.0	9.2	5.8
1986	3.7	15.4	52.0	17.0	7.3	4.6
1988	5.7	12.7	55.6	13.9	8.5	3.6

Source: Financial Statistics, various issues

local authorities securities, plus other investments, minus short-term liabilities and long-term borrowing.

As can be seen from Table 7.10 private sector pension funds are by far the largest by asset size, with nearly 68 per cent of the assets of all pension funds.

Given that the end product is a pension some time in the future, then the majority of assets are viewed as long term. As can be seen from the table, around half of pension funds' assets are UK company securities. According to modern portfolio theory (MPT) pension funds ought to hold a 'core' portfolio of securities in large blue chip companies that are rarely traded, (i.e. held for the long term) around which 'satellite' shares in smaller less well known (less well analysed, and therefore possibly inefficiently priced – see Chapter 11) companies are actively traded in order to make short-term capital investments. It does appear that many large pension funds do carry out such a policy, with many of them attempting to replicate the FTSE 100 Index with their core portfolios so that the returns will match the market. There are no specific regulations relating to the structure of pension funds' asset portfolios.

UK pension funds are exempt from both capital gains tax and income tax on their investments, and hence there is no preference (according to the taxation regime) for preferring income over capital gains or vice versa, nor any constraint on the volume of trading (apart from transactions costs).

Table 7.10   *UK Pension Funds. Analysis by Type of Fund, Total Assets, Holdings at end of Year, Market Values 1988*

	£ million	%
Local Authorities	29289	13.7
Other Public Sector	40667	18.9
Private Sector	144562	67.4
	214518	100.0

Source: Financial Statistics, August 1990

Property might seem to be an unusual investment for pension funds given its volatile nature, but its inclusion can be defended on the grounds of past long-term returns that have been a good hedge against inflation. Many smaller pension funds invest in property unit trusts, some of which specialise in overseas property, and hence gain portfolio diversification in their own portfolios by including property, but also benefit from being diversified in the property market.

The regulation of pension funds tends to be far lighter than for insurance companies as they are bound by trust legislation, and because the companies that offer pensions have an incentive to make sure that schemes are adequately administered as they are responsible for the benefits they have agreed upon for their employees (even though they rarely run the fund themselves).

Pension funds must gain approval from the Superannuation Funds Office (SFO) – part of the Inland Revenue – to gain the tax advantages relevant to pension funds (although this does not relate to protection for pension scheme members).

The National Association of Pension Funds (NAPF) acts as the lobbying body on behalf of the pension industry, but has no specific regulatory powers, nor does the Occupation Pensions Board (OPB) which comments on pension matters that are referred to it by the Secretary of State (and also has responsibility for issuing contracting out certificates). Indeed, it is something of an anomaly that there is no self regulatory organisation for the pension fund industry. Specific areas of controversy where an SRO for pension funds would be useful are in disputes over investment strategies of funds, in fund surpluses, and in pension fund 'holidays'.

Pension fund surpluses arise as a result of assets growing faster than liabilities. This may occur through the return on assets being higher than the growth in earnings or salaries. The question arises as to what should be done with the surpluses that arise. One method of reducing surpluses has been for companies to take contributions holidays (although generally these are not extended to employee contribution holidays) whereby they do not pay any contributions for a period of time. These can be useful for the company as the money that would have gone into the pension fund can be used to boost profitability (particularly useful during a takeover bid), or for the financing of projects.

Another method has been to increase the benefits paid by the pension fund, although this has been rarely used, nor has a refund to the company from the pension fund, as it requires approval from the SFO.

In relation to contribution holidays, Goacher *et al.* (1987) point out that stock market prices can at times be dependent on the increase in profits derived from the contribution holiday, which could at times increase volatility, and lead to inefficient pricing of shares.

Pension fund surpluses can be dangerous in that they may encourage corporate takeovers in order to strip the pension fund, although many companies nowadays have very carefully worded trust deeds for their pension funds to limit the chance of takeover.

There has been a certain degree of controversy in recent years over the practice of self-investment by pension funds. Pension funds ought to be immune from the performance of the company to which they relate, so that employees' pensions are safeguarded even if the company is experiencing difficulties. With self-investment however, a downturn in the company's fortunes can cause problems for the pension fund. In 1987 for example, the value of Victor Products' (an engineering group) pension portfolio was reduced by £400 000 due to poor results of the company, and the fact that a quarter of the funds' portfolio were self-invested in Victor Products.

The Investment Committee of the National Association of Pension Funds recommends that shares held in the parent company should be based on the proportion of the share in the All Share

Index, (in order to allow Index 'tracking') or 2 per cent, whichever is lower. Further problems with self-investment can occur when a pension fund invests heavily in its parent company's shares in order to fend off a takeover bid, particularly if those shares are bought at a premium during the bid, and have to be off-loaded at a loss afterwards.

In relation to Europe and 1992, it is expected that there will be substantial growth in many markets (particularly Spain), although at the present time EC rules and regulations on pensions are still being liberalised. Freedom of services will be one of the most important directives, and British firms are likely to be extremely active in the European pensions market. (See also Chapter 13.)

A recurring complaint from industry has been that pension funds are too short-term orientated, to the detriment of the companies in whose shares they deal. (See Chapter 13.)

7.4   VENTURE CAPITAL

Venture capitalists provide equity and other types of long term funds to unlisted companies which have no or little past performance record. Backing small growth companies is extremely risky in terms of possible failure of the companies, but this risk tends to be counterbalanced by high rewards in the form of long-term capital gains. One of the major risks stems from an 'information asymmetry' (Dixon 1989) where the knowledge of investors as to the prospects of companies is extremely low. Rarely do the investors have a documented past record to analyse, nor are they able to glean information from historic share price data. Similarly, those starting up the business have a lack of knowledge of the methods and management systems used by venture capital funds. The risks involved are thus extremely high, and it is generally recognised that close management control of these companies by the venture capital funds in necessary, as compared with the more remote approach of investors on the Stock Exchange. Venture capitalists attempt to fill the information gap by close examination and control of companies, which should reduce the risk of loss. Assistance is provided through financial expertise, technical abilities, and management expertise.

The growth of venture capital funds in the UK has been substantial in the 1980s and is the result of a number of factors. In the bull markets of the eighties long term investment funds were attractive to investors, and there was also a steady demand from new businesses starting up and from management buyouts that became popular. The unlisted securities market, the Third market and the over-the-counter market provided business with something to aim for and provided investors with a method of disposing of their interests (an 'exit route' in the terminology). Finally, the venture capital industry in America was a useful model to adopt.

The venture capital industry has grown rapidly in the 1980's and into the 1990's, from around twelve in the mid 1970's to approximately 124 at the present time. Total investments in 1989 (latest figures available at time of writing) amounted to £1.7 billion, and UK venture capitalists dominate the European market, with around 55 per cent of total venture capital investments (ECU 23 billion, £16.3 billion).

There are a number of different forms of venture capital funds:

1. *Captive funds* – generally subsidiaries of the large UK insurance companies, banks and pension funds, which provide them with capital for investment.
2. *Independent funds* – raise capital from a diverse range of sources, such as private investors and institutions.
3. *State owned funds* – those which manage the Business Expansion Scheme (Set up in 1983 to encourage investment by private investors in unquoted companies, through tax relief at their marginal rate up to £40,000 in a year) and the Scottish and Welsh Development Agencies, set up to fund growth in their particular areas.
4. *Semi-independent* – some funds have emerged recently that are linked with a financial institution, from whom funds are received, and also attract funds from elsewhere.
5. *Corporate venturing* – some large companies (e.g. BP, Shell) take an equity stake in smaller companies (often in a similar line of business) to encourage innovation and growth, although the size of these funds is relatively small.

Most captive funds are open ended, that is, they have no predetermined size or duration, and will be dependent on the general strategy of the financial institution to which they are linked. Independent funds tend to be closed ended, and have a pre-set strategy and investment size and duration.

In terms of size, independent funds are the largest, with over 75 per cent of total venture capital funds invested. Special mention should be given to 3i which is the largest single venture capital provider in the UK. It is jointly owned by the Bank of England and a group of clearing banks. It originates from the Industrial and Commercial Finance Corporation (ICFC) and Finance for Commerce and Industry (FCI) set up in 1945 on the findings of the MacMillan Committee that a gap existed in the provision of long term capital funds to small businesses.

Table 7.11   *Venture Capital Investment in the UK (Numbers)*

	1987		1988		1989	
	No.	*%*	*No.*	*%*	*No.*	*%*
Start up	191	16	202	15	177	13
Other Early Stage	133	11	182	13	344	25
Expansion	641	53	639	47	473	35
Buy out/buy in	217	18	282	21	333	25
Secondary Purchase	26	2	51	4	24	2
Total	1206	100	1356	100	1351	100

Source: Financial Times, 9 July 1990

Criticisms have recently been raised as to the increasingly short-term investment attitude of venture capital funds in the UK. The Bank of England (1990) argues that the venture capital industry has done little to reduce the funding gap and indeed that it may be getting larger. The figures in the table above seem to confirm this point of view. There has been a large growth in the number of buy-out/buy-in deals carried out, at the expense of start-up business. Buy-out/buy-in business now accounts for a quarter of investments made by venture capital funds, whereas the number of startups account for only approximately 13 per cent (Table 7.11). Venture capitalists thus seem to be moving away from riskier start-ups and towards more established companies in buy-out situations. Particularly acute problems appear to be found in the area of raising seed-corn capital (pre start-up capital, less than £250,000, the riskiest type of venture capital) and that venture funds are looking for shorter term returns (BEQB 1990).

The amount of funds channelled towards buy-out/buy-ins has risen to 61 per cent of the total in 1989, whereas that for start ups has fallen to only 6 per cent (start-ups and other early stage only account for 15 per cent of total funds invested).

Table 7.12 *Venture Capital in the UK (amount)*

	1987 £m	%	1988 £m	%	1989 £m	%
Start up	75	8	70	5	86	6
Other Early Stage	45	5	60	5	129	9
Expansion	278	30	402	31	319	23
Buy-out/buy-in	513	55	733	56	867	61
Secondary Purchase	23	2	33	3	19	1
Total	934	100	1298	100	1420	100

Source: Financial Times, 9 July 1990

UK pension funds are the largest provider of capital to venture funds (over 30 per cent of the total).

Some would argue that the compound rates of return required by venture capitalists – on average 20 per cent to 25 per cent p.a., but sometimes up to 50 per cent for start ups – are too high, but this is difficult to argue against given the nature of the investments involved and the high degree of risk. Institutional fund managers, including those responsible for venture funds, are increasingly pressurised to perform against their competition, and this has resulted in more regular reports on funds, greater investment in buy-outs with fast exits and therefore short-term profits, and performance targets for businesses that may lead to short-term objectives. New entrants to the venture capital industry are now low in number, probably reflecting the size and strength of incumbents in attracting the available funds, and it is likely that concentration will occur, creating larger institutions, possibly to the detriment of independent venture capitalists who tend to specialise in particular markets.

One argument is that venture funds apply inadequate investment criteria in assessing potential start ups. A survey (Dixon

1989) has shown that arbitary, internal rate of return figures are used (up to 60 per cent) for start-ups, and that the Capital Asset Pricing Model is ignored. This may be one reason why venture capitalists argue that profitable start-up opportunities are rare – perhaps they do exist, but that the theoretically correct investment criteria are not being applied and so they cannot be found – although no concrete evidence exists for this link.

European Venture Capital is likely to exhibit fast growth over the next decade, and UK venture capitalists have the expertise to be very powerful competitors (see Chapter 13).

7.5   FINANCE HOUSES

There are 47 finance houses in the UK. Finance houses are a diverse grouping of financial intermediaries that carry out a variety of instalment credit facilities for the personal sector: hire purchase, credit sale, conditional sale, secured and unsecured personal loans, revolving loans and repayment loans.

For the industrial and commercial sector services include leasing, factoring, industrial hire purchase, commercial loans and stocking loans, and block discounting.

1.   *Hire purchase* – personal customers hire goods for an agreed length of time and buy them at the end of the period for a low price. The goods are owned after the last instalment.

2.   *Credit sale* – the customer buys the product (and legally owns it from day one) but pays by instalments.

3.   *Conditional sale* – the price of the product is paid by instalments, but the product remains in the ownership of the seller for a pre-set period of time, often until the last instalment has been paid.

    With these three methods of finance the finance house provides the funds and a percentage rate of interest. The seller of the goods may wish to simply pass on the interest charges to the customer, or may wish to push up the price of the product and market it as zero interest finance.

4.   *Secured and unsecured personal loans* – loans are provided for fixed periods of time, often at fixed rates of interest and

equal instalment payments. For larger loans security may be required. Obviously there is intense competition from banks and building societies.

5. *Revolving loans* – personal customers under this type of arrangement can borrow a multiple of monthly payment, e.g. £30 per month may be paid to the finance house which allows up to 15 times that amount to be borrowed (£450).

6. *Repayment loans* – customers pay fixed monthly repayments based on what the Finance House expects the market interest rate to be over the period of the loan, and at regular interval or the end of the loan, the difference between actual and estimated interest rates is calculated, and the difference is paid or received by the customer.

For commercial customers services include:

1. *Leasing* – these are mainly used for large plant and equipment. A lessor (in this case a finance house) hires out capital equipment to a lessee, and the ownership of the equipment rests with the lessor. Two main types of lease exist, financial and operating. With the former rental is set up at such a rate that the full cost of the equipment is recovered plus a return, whilst with the latter the contract is shorter and the same equipment may be leased to a number of lessees. The lessor receives capital allowances against tax.

2. *Factoring* – factoring services can involve the full operation of companies' invoicing and debt collection, credit protection through cover on sales made, and payments of up to 80 per cent of debts in advance of collection. With many businesses waiting up to two-three months for payment, and research showing that many companies fail through poor cash flow, factoring is a very important service to industry.

3. *Industrial Hire Purchase* – the same as hire-purchase for personal customers but for items of capital equipment.

4. *Commercial Loans* – either secured or unsecured, and used for a variety of purposes.

5. *Stocking loans* – used specifically to allow companies to hold necessary volumes of stock, as in car dealerships.

6. *Block discounting* – a finance house may buy a 'block' of debtors from a company at a discount, and follow them up

for the company. Cash flows are improved and possible defaulters removed.

On both the personal and commercial side of their business finance houses experience intense competition, both from within the industry and from without in the form of building societies and banks.

For non-bank finance houses the assets portfolio is dominated by the supply of credit to the personal sector (see Table 7.13), although credit to industrial and commercial companies is also important. The majority of funds tend to come from the banking sector, although commercial bills are also important.

Finance houses use the wholesale money markets to borrow around 25 per cent of their funds, and raise another 30 per cent from commercial banks. The rest of their liabilities are raised through deposits from the general public, share capital and deferred taxation. One of the major problems faced by finance houses is that of interest rate risk, given the volume of fixed rate lending business. If interest rates change adversely, finance houses could find themselves funding fixed rate loans with more expensive floating rate loans. Finance houses are regulated by the Consumer Credit Act 1974 and the Director General of Fair Trading.

Credit business to both the personal and corporate sector (but especially the former) are likely to grow in the future, providing substantial opportunities for Finance Houses (see Chapter 13).

7.6   NATIONAL SAVINGS

The main role of the National Savings movement is to collect the savings of small or relatively unsophisticated savers in order to finance borrowing by the public sector. The variety of National Savings instruments is extremely diverse, and the degree to which various governments have utilised the National Savings sector as a method of raising finance has tended to vary over the years.

The National Savings Bank has a large branch network in that its services are provided through post offices and sub-post offices, although of course the nature of these outlets differs considerably from those of the building societies or retail banks.

Table 7.13 *Non-Bank Credit Companies: Aggregate Balance
Sheet. Holdings at end of year, book values 1989*

	£m	%
Assets:		
Cash and Balances with Banks	212	2.4
Certificates of Deposit	3	0.03
Other Current Assets	660	7.4
Loans and Advances:		
Block Discounts	1	0.01
Finance Leases	1011	11.3
UK Industrial and Commercial	1547	17.3
Personal Sector	5226	58.4
Other Assets	73	0.8
Physical Assets	213	2.4
Total Assets	8949	100.0
Liabilities		
Commercial Bills	802	9.0
Short-term Borrowing from Banks	4437	49.6
Long-term Borrowing from Banks	1513	16.9
Borrowing from Other Financial Institutions	218	2.4
Other UK Suppliers	215	2.4
Overseas	21	0.2
Other Current Liabilities	757	8.5
Capital Issues	138	1.5
Reserves	848	9.5
Total Liabilities	8949	100.0

Source: Financial Statistics, August 1990

As can be seen from the amounts outstanding in various
instruments there are a number of different types of saving
available, the most popular of which are National Savings Certificates, Ordinary Accounts and Investment Accounts (it is not the
intention to describe in detail all of the instruments available, as
descriptions are readily available from post offices).

Many National Savings instruments pay tax free interest as this
is more sensible than the government paying a higher gross rate of

interest and then having the administrative cost of collecting the tax on those interest payments. Unfortunately this also means that non-tax-payers lose out to an extent as they would prefer a higher gross interest rate that is subject to a person's rate of income tax. National Savings are not part of the composite rate tax system (unlike building societies and banks) in which the composite rate is deducted at source and cannot be reclaimed by non-tax-payers. As interest is paid tax free on National Savings there is a competitive advantage in attracting the savings of those who do not pay tax.

One of the major differences of the Department of National Savings relative to other financial intermediaries is that it does not hold an asset portfolio to back up liabilities held, and therefore is not constrained by the need to adhere to liquidity, solvency or capital adequacy regulations (given that funds are backed by the Treasury and are therefore essentially default-free).

National Savings were particularly competitive in the 1980's when emphasis was placed on raising government funds from this source, largely because it relieved the need somewhat to borrow from the banking system which created credit and therefore inflationary conditions, and because of the fear that government borrowing in the long-term capital markets would tend to 'crowd-out' industrial and commercial companies from that market, and impede their ability to raise funds for capital investment and long-term growth.

Index linked National Savings Certificates were popular up until the early 1980's, but with a fall in inflation they have tended to be eclipsed by the popularity of fixed interest certificates which accounted for about 16 per cent of total assets in 1990. Investment accounts have offered competitive rates in the late 1980's and now account for over 22 per cent of the total assets portfolio.

7.7   VARIOUS SCHEMES

In 1971 the Bolton Committee reported on the financing of small companies in the UK and concluded that an 'equity gap' existed in terms of difficulty of raising funds up to £250 000. It was also recognised that an 'information gap' existed in relation to the knowledge of entrepreneurs as to the sources of finance available to small firms. The Wilson committee largely concurred with these

Table 7.14 *National Savings: Amounts Outstanding in Various Instruments at end period 1990 Q1*

	£m	%
National Savings Certificates:		
Index Linked:		
Principal	2922	8.1
Index Linked or Bonus	1425	3.9
Fixed Interest:		
Principal	5886	16.3
Accrued Interest	2694	7.4
National Savings Stamps/Gift Tokens	2	–
British Savings Bonds	–	–
Premium Savings Bonds	2334	6.5
Income Bonds	8211	22.7
SAYE/Yearly Plan:		
Index Linked:		
Principal	116	0.3
Accrued Interest	–	–
Accrued Index Increase or Bonus	114	0.3
Fixed Interest:		
Capital	643	1.9
Accrued Interest or Bonus	94	0.3
National Savings Bank		
Ordinary Accounts	1561	4.3
Investment Account	8029	22.2
Deposit Bonds	779	2.2
Capital Bonds	489	1.4
Other Securities on National Savings Register	866	2.4
Total	36195	100.0

Source: Financial Statistics, May 1990

views, and pointed out the specific problems of small firms in raising long term finance, whether loan or equity. In 1986, the Committee on Finance for Industry, an arm of the National Economic Development Office emphasised that although lending facilities were becoming more available from the banking system, a major problem still existed with a need for a greater proportion of equity funding for small businesses.

The Loan Guarantee Scheme (LGS) and the Business Expansion Scheme (BES) are government initiatives that have been set up in order to facilitate the channelling of funds from financial institutions to small businesses (thus these schemes are 'enabling mechanisms' rather than forms of financial intermediation). The LGS is a system whereby the government guarantees loans provided by banks to small businesses in situations where the risk may be high and finance might not otherwise be provided.

Set up in 1981 and operated by the Department of Trade and Industry, the LGS has been heavily criticised as a tool for helping channel funds to small business because of the high cost of the funds involved. On top of the lending margin over base rate which the banks charged, a risk premium was added to cover the guarantee, making funds extremely expensive. In June 1984, small businesses were also required to provide security for the first time under the scheme, which obviously deterred many potential entrepreneurs and damaged the usefulness of the scheme. Moreover, Robson Rhodes the Accountants found that many firms that were proceeding along conventional lines in terms of raising finance, often suddenly moved to being financed totally under the LGS.

The aim of the Business Expansion Scheme (BES) is to increase the availability of equity capital to companies. The main incentive to investors is income tax relief on an amount up to £40 000 p.a. invested in ordinary shares of unquoted (i.e. not quoted on the main exchange, the USM, the Third market or the over-the-counter market – see Chapter 11 for definitions) companies, and capital gains on selling the shares are exempt from Capital Gains Tax (CGT). Shares cannot be sold for five years, however, or the various benefits will be lost to the investor. Firms thus benefit from a solid investor base, and of course there is not the problem of high levels of gearing as with the LGS. Set up in 1983 under the Finance Act, the BES has been a major facilitator of the channelling of funds to businesses (Peat Marwick 1986), many of which would apparently not have been able to raise capital without the help of the BES, although it was also reported that very little of the funds were provided for seedcorn businesses.

One problem for small businesses is that capital needs to be reinvested over a number of years yet there are no special allowances provided by the government for doing so. Perhaps one method would be to allow small firms to set aside a percentage of profits into a tax free investment vehicle on the understanding that it is to be used for reinvestment within 5 – 10 years.

There is some argument for a form of National Investment Bank, although there is considerable doubt as to the real necessity (Budd 1986). The objective would be to provide funds for startups and for small and medium-sized businesses in general. The rationale is that traditional financial institutions have in some way failed to find funds for these sectors, as outlined above. The main difference between a NIB and say, venture capital funds would be that:

1. Loans would be at subsidised rates of interest (provided through the taxation system).
2. Funds would be available long term.
3. 'Different' investment criteria would be used from those traditionally employed.

Subsidised rates of interest are needed it is argued for times when interest rates are high due to monetary policy as in the 1990's, which might discourage start-ups and result in bankruptcies of small firms if loans are not available, and because rates charged by financial institutions are too high. The first case is probably justifiable, but the second is unlikely, given that financial institutions have to take adequate account of the risks involved. Competition is relatively strong in UK corporate banking and would suggest reasonable costs of borrowing *vis-à-vis* the risks taken on.

As has been seen with venture capital funds, there may be some evidence of difficulty of raising long term funds for under £200 000, and a National Investment Bank may indeed fill this gap.

The greatest problems emerge from the third main difference between an NIB and financial institutions. 'Different' lending criteria would relate to businesses that have significant regional growth prospects or growth prospects in general – large growth in employment, those with good export or import substitution potential, and those involved in new technologies. Such a list is not exhaustive, and the major problem for a NIB would be to identify companies that fall in the above categories, which is by no means an easy task. Problems also arise over companies that receive funds but subsequently do not perform as expected. Will further funds be withdrawn and the company allowed to fail with loss of jobs, or will it be supported as a 'lame-duck' reintroducing many of the industrial problems of the UK of the 1970s?

REFERENCES

Bank of England (1990) 'Venture Capital and the United Kingdom'. *Bank of England Quarterly Bulletin*, February.

Budd, A. (1986) 'Do We Need a National Investment Bank?' *National Westminster Bank Quarterly Review*, August.

Dixon, R. (1989). 'Venture Capitalists and Investment Appraisal'. *National Westminster Bank Quarterly Review*, November.

Goacher, D.J. and Curwen, P.J. (1987) *British Non-Bank Financial Intermediaries* (Allen and Unwin, London).

Peat Marwick (1986) 'The Business Expansion Scheme' (Inland Revenue).

CHAPTER 8

THE BANK OF ENGLAND

8.0 INTRODUCTION

The Bank of England occupies a central position in the UK financial system in terms of its main activities and areas of responsibility. This chapter describes the various roles that the Bank takes on, and puts them in the context of the overall powers that it enjoys, particularly in relation to the supervisory activities carried out and the possibility of the emergence of a European Central Bank. Given the pervasive influence of the Bank of England over the UK financial system, it is no surprise that later chapters also contain a great deal of further information on its business.

8.1 FUNCTIONS AND STRUCTURE

The Bank of England is the central bank of the United Kingdom, and carries out a variety of traditional central bank functions. The Bank is a nationalised corporation, and has an organisational structure as set out in Fig. 8.1.

The Bank of England's balance sheet has traditionally been divided into two separate sections – the issue department and the banking department. The issue department is concerned with the issue of notes by the Bank, and is classified as part of the public sector in the national account. The banking department deals with all the other banking business, is classified as part of the banking sector, and falls within the UK monetary sector.

The issue of banknotes is the sole function of the issue department, the notes being fiduciary backed by government securities

Figure 8.1 *Organisation of the Bank of England*

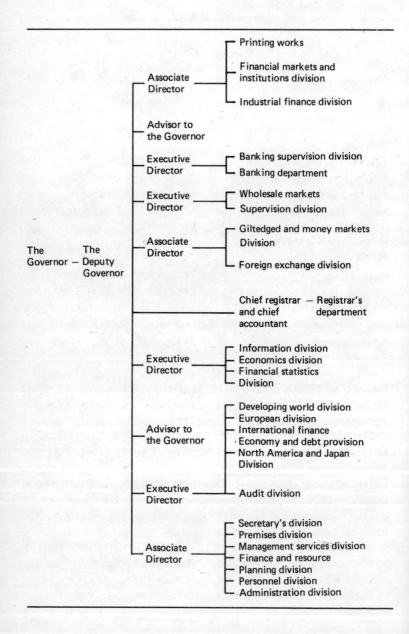

Table 8.1 *Assets and Liabilities of the Bank of England: Year End 1990*

Issue Department			
Liabilities	*£m*	*Assets*	*£m*
Notes in Circulation	15020	Government Debt	11
Notes in Banking Dept.	9	Govnmnt. Securities	10009
		Other Securities	5,009
	15029		15029
Banking Department			
Liabilities		*Assets*	
Public Deposits	454	Notes and Coin	9
Bankers' Deposits	1665	Cheques in collection	429
Other Deposits	1288	Treasury & other bills	1540
Taxation & Creditors	89	Investments	876
Payable to Treasury	72	Advances	650
Reserves	765	Accounts Receivable	383
		Subsidiary Companies	71
		Premises & Equipment	375
	4333		4333

Source: Bank of England Report & Accounts 1990

rather than backed by gold. The liabilities of the issue department are thus simply notes in circulation in the economy, plus the operational balances held at the Bank.

Government securities and debt refer to British Government and government guaranteed securities, Treasury bills and any special Treasury liability, and advances to the National Loans Fund. Other securities are local authority deposits and bonds, commercial bills, company securities and miscellaneous securities.

The main areas of activity of the Bank of England can be grouped under the following categories:

(1) Banking role. (2) Lender of Last Resort. (3) National Debt Management. (4) Monetary Policy Role. (5) Note Issue. (6) Foreign Currency Exchange Market Intervention. (7) Supervision.

(1) Banking Role

The Bank of England acts as banker to a variety of customers, many of whom would be atypical clients of a commercial bank:—

(*a*) Banker to banks and other financial institutions – every commercial bank has an account with the Bank of England in which 'operational deposits' are kept in order to settle interbank debts from the cheque clearing system, and for payment of funds due to the government (and, conversely, funds paid by the government to the banks). Operational deposits make up approximately a fifth of bankers' balances held at the bank, the remainder being made up of non-interest bearing cash deposits that banks are required to keep at the Bank of England to provide it with an income. In recent years the Bank of England has become more profitable as a result of high interest rates and good yields on the investments that these non-interest bearing deposits are placed in. [N.B. these non-operational non-interest bearing deposits are in no way connected to monetary policy or control of the money supply].

(*b*) Banker to the Government – the Bank of England maintains the 'public deposits' of the government from which payments are made into and out of. Public deposits include the National Loans Fund through which all transactions involving the National Debt (see below) pass through, the Exchequer (tax revenues), the Paymaster General (including the Exchange Equalisation Account – see below), and the National Debt Commissioners. The Bank of England merely acts as a bank in terms of these accounts, with the government making the decisions as to the level of public deposits. The Public deposits are usually relatively small, as surplus cash is utilised for repayment of government debts.

(*c*) Overseas Central Banks and International Institutions – the Bank holds accounts for a variety of international financial organisations, including the World Bank, the Bank for International Settlements (BIS) and the International Monetary Fund (IMF), and organises international transactions that originate from intervention in exchange markets.

(*d*) Private customers – the number of these is small, and are mainly made up of staff members of the Bank and some UK organisations. There is no pretence of competition with commercial banks for private sector business, and there is some suggestion that the accounts are maintained in order for the Bank to keep in touch with banking practice, although the degree to which such experience accrues is likely to be limited given the small number of accounts relative to a commercial bank.

(2) Lender of Last Resort

The Bank of England acts as lender of last resort to the domestic banking system, in that it will provide funds to the banking sector when it is short of cash. Shortages may occur through large outflows of funds from the banks to the government (into the governments accounts held at the Bank of England) or due to a large need for cash by customers, and may occur on a daily basis. Lender of last resort facilities are provided through direct loans to the banking sector, or by purchasing Treasury bills or commercial bills (mainly the latter in recent years) from the banking system. The Discount houses usually act as a conduit in such transactions (see Chapter 9 on more detail relating to these operations). If it so wishes, the Bank can provide assistance only at penal rates of interest, if for example it wishes interest rates to change as part of its overall monetary policy of controlling the money supply.

(3) National Debt Management

Complementary to its role as banker to the government is the responsibility for administering the public sector debt. This includes financing any public sector borrowing requirement (PSBR) that exists as a result of a shortfall in government revenues compared with expenditures, or at times managing the public sector debt repayment (PSDR) when government income is greater than government expenditure. In addition, the Bank is responsible for funding the constant flow of maturing government debt instruments, and carrying out open market operations in respect of private sector holdings of government debt in response to desired policy objectives. The Bank also attempts to smooth the flows of funds between the government and the private sector that are the product of its activities in the government debt market.

To avoid large outflows of funds on the redemption of a large government debt issue, the maturing stock is bought by the Issue

Department (see below) of the Bank over a period of time to avoid shocks to the financial system. When a large debt issue is undertaken, the Bank will underwrite a large proportion of the issue and slowly sell them to the market over a period of time to avoid excess supply of government debt.

(4)   Monetary Policy Role

The fundamentally most crucial function of the Bank of England is the responsibility of carrying out monetary policy operations. Specific policy objectives are set by the government, and put into action by the bank, although the Bank has an important role as adviser to the government on monetary policy matters. It is in a strong position to provide sound advice, given its close links with institutions in the financial system and in its capacity as the collector of financial statistics from the banks.

The dominance of monetarist strategies in the 1980s and start of the 1990s has meant that monetary policy has played an extremely important role in overall economic policy, with control of the money supply and inflation being of prime importance. Monetary control instruments can generally be divided into market controls and portfolio (or non-market controls). Of the former, the main techniques are market intervention through open market operations (see Chapter 9), intervention in the foreign exchange markets, and lender of last resort facilities. Portfolio controls consist of special deposits, supplementary special deposits, reserve requirements, directives, and moral suasion. Portfolio controls were used intermittently through the 1970s, but have fallen out of favour in the 1980s and early 1990s with the recognition that they distort the workings of the financial system, and that methods of circumventing the controls exist (see Hall 1983).

The experience of the monetary authorities in carrying out a policy of control of the money supply has not, however, been a happy one (Leigh-Pemberton 1986). The Bank of England did not appear to have fully considered the problems of financial change at the introduction of the Medium Term Financial Strategy (MTFS). The Bank maintained in 1980 that although targets were set, it was possible that structural change and financial innovation may affect the relative growth rates of the aggregates, but that the problem was not insuperable (Green Paper on Monetary Control 1980).

In view of future events, however, it appears that the problem of financial change was underestimated. In contrast to the initial confidence of the authorities as to the insignificance of changes in the financial system for the operation of monetary control, the monetary authorities progressively emphasised the importance of financial institutions during the MTFS and subsequent analyses of the MTFS. Official publications have tended to cite the effects of change in the financial institutional framework as the major factor for the problems experienced with monetary control, yet the Bank of England's conclusion that monetary policy is affected by financial change is not a new viewpoint. Indeed, the notion that the behaviour of financial institutions needs to be taken into account when examining the efficacy of monetary controls has a long, although perhaps not popular, pedigree. The 'institutionalist' school (comprising, *inter alia*, Gurley and Shaw 1960, Tobin 1963, Radcliffe 1959) first warned of the possible dangers of 'traditional' monetary theory, which has promulgated the view that the financial system is essentially a static equilibrium system, a mere unchanging backdrop against which policy operates.

Opposed to this, the institutionalist school takes the actions of financial institutions as being of central importance in the conduct of policy. It is recognised that observed statistical relationships may change over time due to changes in financial markets. Even if a policy of controlling the money supply may be optimal at present, if previously held relationships break down under rapid financial change, then the rationale for controlling the money supply may disappear. With financial innovation, traditional instruments may become obsolete in influencing the money supply.

The Radcliffe Report (1959) emphasised in stronger terms the problems associated with financial change and maintained that it is impossible to define money, because there is no clear criterion with which to determine those assets that are part of the money supply. Obviously, if it is impossible to define the money supply, it is impossible to control. This view has since been reflected in official commentary during and after the MTFS. The impact of increased competition between building societies and banks has been blamed as a major determinant of the observed change in relationships among the various monetary aggregates, and between them and nominal incomes. The activities of building societies and banks have been given prime consideration when assessing the appropriate definition of money and the problem of implementation of monetary control (Bank of England, Dec. 1984).

One of the main reasons cited has been the importance of liberalisation of credit markets and the introduction of new types of financial assets (Bank of England, March 1982).The authorities have given special emphasis to the financial instruments offered by banks and building societies (Bank of England March 1983).

Although little detailed research has been carried out in the UK on the effects of financial innovation and structural change upon the appropriate conduct of monetary control, it appears that there is a consensus opinion that the effects of financial change necessitate that monetary policy be conducted in a *discretionary* manner.

Not only may policy have to be carried out in a discretionary approach, but the authorities may be constrained to,

> 'muddling through in a discretionary, but unrigorous manner.'
>
> (Goodhart 1986, p. 101)

Where does this leave the operation of monetary policy? It appears that there have been major changes in the rationale and operation of the MTFS as a result of the effects of financial innovation, which would indeed seem to suggest a degree of discretion is necessary in policy actions. Currie (1987) has noted that there are some who maintain that policy is turning full circle back into a fully discretionary mode.

Currie (1987) provides reasons for the continuation of some form of medium term strategy. He maintains that it would provide greater certainty for economic agents as to the governments likely policy reasons; the government could establish/maintain a reputation for consistency and commitment. It would provide built-in automatic short-term policy responses, and would provide consistency between short-term and medium-term policy actions.

(5) Note Issue

The Bank is responsible for printing and issuing banknotes and coins in the UK. New notes and coins are withdrawn by banks

of England. Notes withdrawn by the banks will show a fall in the
value of the 'notes in Banking Department' (a liability of the Issue
Department) and an increase in the value of 'notes in circulation'
(another liability of the Issue Department).

(6) Foreign Currency Exchange Market

Intervention – the management of the Treasury's Exchange
Equalisation Account (EEA) is carried out by the Bank of
England. The EEA contains the deposits of the UK's gold and
convertible foreign currency reserves that are used to intervene in
the exchange markets to stabilise the exchange rate of sterling, or
to raise it or lower it relative to other currencies.

(7) Supervision

The Bank of England is responsible for the supervision of all banks
under the Banking Act 1987. The institutions were categorised
under the Act as 'recognised banks' (which offer a wide range of
banking services and have net assets of not less than £5 million),
and 'licensed deposit takers' (those institutions that do not meet
the requirements for recognised bank status). A major change was
made however after the need for the Bank of England to rescue
Johnson Matthey Bankers (JMB), a recognised bank, such that
the categorisation of licenced deposit takers and recognised banks
was abolished and a single category of bank established for
regulation. The main problem stemmed from the fact that there
was an asymmetry of regulation in that recognised banks were less
strictly regulated than licensed deposit takers. It is interesting to
note that this situation was in contrast to an earlier serious
problem in the banking system, the secondary banking crisis of
1973–1974, in which less well known banks were subject to less
regulation than the more stable institutions.

The Bank of England evolved as the regulator of banks largely
through its operations in the financial markets. The institutions
preferred to be regulated by 'one of their own'. Llewellyn (1986)
points out that until 1974 banking supervision was carried out by

the Bank's Discount Office, which was responsible for money market operations. The Bank of England has a great deal of power over the financial markets because of its role as lender of last resort.

The Banking Supervision Division was established in 1974 mainly as a result of the secondary banking crisis in 1973–1974.

8.2   POWERS/CHANGING ROLE

The influx of foreign banks into the domestic financial market has undoubtedly reduced the ability of the Bank to carry out monetary control through moral suasion or supervision through the traditional informal networks. The ability of the Bank to operate through such systems is largely through the historical building up of relationships and the ingrained tradition of the banks to accept such a system because of their desire to be watched over by 'one of their own'. Overseas financial institutions often come from a far different system in which rules and regulations are far more explicit, and tend not to be fully conversant with a less transparent form of control as operated by the Bank. The growth of overseas financial institutions in terms of their numbers has been a major factor in the formalisation of supervision with more emphasis on the 'rulebook' and a relative decline in the less formal traditional system.

The Bank of England has lost some independence in recent years because of the formalisation of what were previously informal supervisory activities. Notably the Banking Acts of 1979 and 1987, the FSA 1986, the Basle Concordat and capital adequacy arrangements have all meant that the Bank has lost a certain amount of discretion in implementing supervision (see Chapter 12).

8.3   INDEPENDENCE OF THE BANK OF ENGLAND – THE EUROPEAN CENTRAL BANK AND PRIVATISATION OF THE BANK OF ENGLAND

A common currency and a European Central Bank are necessary for a fully integrated European market. A European Central Bank would operate a lender of last resort facility for individual nations' central banks, and would aim at stability of the European economy through interlocking economic policies within the EEC. The West German finance minister has formally requested that 'Euro-fed' – the future European Central Bank (if it comes about) be based in Frankfurt, which would obviously undermine the position of the Bank of England.

The Bundesbank wants national Central Banks to be made independent, and of course for the European Central Bank to operate independently with respect to price stability.

The European Central Bank would have members consisting of the governors of the national banks, and other members chosen by the European Council, according to the Delors report. The problem that exists is that factions of governors who are members of the European Central Bank and who disagree with its policies may join together to frustrate them at the national level. The ability of the European Central Bank to carry out policy will depend upon the independence of the individual central banks.

Under the 'hard ECU' proposal put forward by the then Chancellor of the Exchequer, John Major, a new institution would be set up to manage the hard ECU, the European Monetary Fund (EMF). The EMF would not carry out national monetary policy decisions, so this would not interfere with the Bank of England's role in this area, although the EMF would act as an indirect constraint on domestic monetary policy and would be in control of ECU interest rates, which would eventually be expected to influence national interest rates.

Initially then, the Bank of England would still be responsible for carrying out UK monetary policy, but would be slowly overtaken to some extent by the EMF's control of ECU interest rates and control of the supply of ECUs.

There has been some debate over the necessity of maintaining a central bank, when it is possible to have a free banking regime in which banks would be free to print their own notes to satisfy the demand for cash. Opponents of free banking argue that a lender of last resort (i.e. a central bank) is needed, and that inflation would be rampant under free banking because of the banks' ability to print notes at will. This would not be the case, however, if each bank that was allowed to print notes was forced to repay the face value on demand (in gold, for example) such that convertability would restrain the banks from issuing too many notes. Certainly, if convertability did not exist, few would accept the notes of banks if there existed the chance that they might be worthless in future years. It is also argued that a lender of last resort would not be needed because of the ability of banks to issue their own notes backed up by their deposit base (Dowd 1990).

Mullineux (1985) argues that many functions carried out by the Bank of England could be done so by private sector institutions. He maintains that foreign exchange intervention and management of the Exchange Equalisation Account could be carried out by private institutions, as could the banking role, and monetary policies designed by the Treasury could be implemented by a major commercial bank for a fee. The only functions that necessarily have to be carried out by the Bank of England are lender of last resort facilities – even supervision could be carried out by a self regulatory organisation (SRO – see Chapter 12) for the banking system.

Mullineux does not make it clear, however, what the advantages would be of dismantling the Bank of England and the major functions being carried out by the private sector, indeed it is difficult to see of any real benefits, although the disadvantages could be major. Housing all of the traditional Central Bank functions under one roof has the advantage of considerable economies of scale in collecting and analysing data and the interdependencies of departments.

It is often pointed out that governments manipulate the economy to engineer booms in periods immediately preceeding elections, to the detriment of the economy, often by manipulating the money supply. It is therefore argued that the operation of monetary policy should be taken out of the hands of the government which is politically motivated and into the hands of the Central Bank, which is neutral but has a reputation to uphold (such a situation exists in Germany, with the Bundesbank deciding on monetary policy).

It could be argued however that according to the theory of bureaucracy the Central Bank would operate monetary policy to suit its own needs, and also that monetary policy ought to be operated by a body that is accountable to the electorate (a central bank is not, although the Bundesbank does not appear to suffer from the above problems).

REFERENCES

Bank of England (1982) 'Transactions Balances – a New Monetary Aggregate'(BEQB June).

Bank of England (1983) 'The Nature and Implications of Financial Innovation'(BEQB September).

Bank of England (1984) 'Changing Boundaries in Financial Services'(BEQB March).

Bank of England (1987) 'The Instruments of Monetary Policy' (BEQB August).

Currie, D. (1987) 'Options for UK Macroeconomic Policy' *Oxford Review of Economic Policy (3) 3*.

Dowd, K. (1990) 'The Case for Free Banking' *Economic Affairs* Aug/Sept.

Green Paper on 'Monetary Control' (1980) Cmnd 7858, March (HMSO London).

Goodhart, C.A.E. (1986) 'Financial Innovation and Monetary Control' *Oxford Review of Economic Policy (2), 4*.

Gurley, J.G. and Shaw, E.S. (1960) *Money in a Theory of Finance* (The Brookings Institution, Washington DC).

Hall, M.J.B. (1983) *Monetary Policy since 1971: Conduct and Performance* MacMillan, London.

Leigh-Pemberton, R. (1986) 'Shifting Frontiers in Financial Markets: Their Causes and Consequences', in Fair, D. (Ed) *Shifting Frontiers in Financial Markets* (Martinus Nijhoff, Netherlands).

Llewellyn, D.T. (1986) 'The Regulation and Supervision of Financial Institutions', Gilbart Lectures (Institute of Bankers, London).

Mullineux, A. (1985) 'Do we Need the Bank of England?' *Lloyds Bank Review*, July.

Radcliffe Committee (1959) *Report on the Working of the Monetary System*, Cmnd 827, HMSO London.

Tobin, J. (1963) 'Commercial Banks as Creators of Money' in Carson, D. *Banking and Monetary Studies* (R.D. Irwin Inc. Homewood).

CHAPTER 9

STERLING MONEY MARKETS

9.0 INTRODUCTION

A market can be said to be a place where buyers and sellers meet to make an exchange of goods (or services). Those with more goods than they have need for their own consumption will sell to those who have insufficient goods for their needs.

A money market works in a similar kind of way. It is a financial market where essentially short term capital is raised – those with excess money lend to those who have insufficient for their needs. It is where surplus and deficit units are brought together; many of such units are financial intermediaries. The process involved is a direct one, lender and borrower deal with each other directly, although arrangements are often made through brokers acting as agents.

The sterling money market in London is the device used by banks and others to adjust their liquidity. Every day bank deposits are withdrawn and fresh deposits made so that at the end of each day liquidity for each bank will be different from that at the beginning. Some banks will be more liquid, typically those which have received net deposits, and some will be less liquid, those which have experienced net withdrawals.

Either condition is unsatisfactory from the banks' point of view. To be over liquid means that profit opportunities are being passed up. To be under liquid means that an individual bank may not be able to fully clear its cheques, standing orders, direct debits and other bank giro items the following day, when individual depositors wish to make withdrawals. Clearly confidence in a bank would quickly suffer if cheques were returned unpaid due to a bank having insufficient funds in its operational account at the Bank of England, if a clearing bank.

Therefore there are benefits to both liquid and illiquid banks in using the money market to adjust liquidity positions near to its ideal. Those with excess liquidity wish to become less liquid and lend money at a return they would otherwise not receive, to those with insufficient liquidity; those with insufficient liquidity are prepared to pay for funds. Virtually all funds come to the bank at a cost, so these money market funds are no different in this respect.

In fact in many ways they may be preferable to funds raised in the 'ordinary' way at branch retail level. Funds raised on the money markets are wholesale, large amounts, so that the expense of raising them is quite small in that it does not require an expensive branch network to attract deposits in small amounts.

The market being described is the London interbank market. Rates of interest in this market are of importance and significance as will be seen later. They are known as LIBOR or LIBID (London Inter Bank Offer Rate and London Inter Bank Deposit). Other parts of the money market are concerned with the buying and selling of money market instruments. These instruments are sold to increase liquidity and bought by those who wish to reduce liquidity, in what is known as a secondary market. The largest market here is that for Certificates of Deposit (CDs).

It should be understood that the market does not have an actual geographical location, but that the market is the activity which takes place between financial institutions, using the various instruments and facilities to make liquidity adjustments, to maximise returns on money they are holding.

It should also be appreciated that activity between market participants is used by the Bank of England, directly and indirectly to implement monetary policy via interest rate changes.

9.1   THE DISCOUNT AND PARALLEL MARKETS

The money market is traditionally split into two categories, the discount market and the market which runs 'parallel' to it, the parallel market. To some extent the distinction is arbitrary, but still perhaps useful nevertheless. It is easy to distinguish between the two markets – the discount market has as one of its participants the Bank of England, participating in its capacity of 'lender of last

152

Table 9.1 *Discount Market and Parallel Market*

DISCOUNT MARKET

Participants
Discount Houses
Bank of England
commercial banks (Bank of England relationship with these very limited)
bill broking firms (v. small, no relationship with Bank of England)
Accepting Houses

Instruments
Treasury bills
eligible bills issued by UK local authorities
eligible bank bills
sterling commercial paper

during period of acute cash shortages –
gilt-edged stock and promissory notes in relation to ECGD guarantees.
Certificates of Tax Deposit

PARALLEL MARKET

Participants
commercial banks
discount houses
finance houses
local authorities
companies

Instruments
interbank deposits
Certificates of deposit (CDs)
local authority deposits
finance house deposits
inter-company deposits
commercial bills

resort', an important function dealt with later in this chapter. The parallel market has no participation by the Bank of England; a further distinction is that the discount market activity is on a secured basis – in the parallel market it is unsecured. Apart from this the participants in both markets are often the same but not exclusively.

The discount market is arguably unique to London and currently consists of eight discount houses (refer to Table 4.6 for members). A small number of bill broking firms are involved – they act as agents (brokers) in bringing together those wishing to sell instruments and those wishing to buy. The object is to match required amounts and maturities at the right rate. Also participating are the money dealing departments of commercial and eligible banks and Accepting Houses; the latter accept bills of exchange for a fee. This enables the bill to be traded at a 'fine' rate of discount. Before looking at each market in detail it would be helpful if a basic principle could be understood.

9.2 PRICE/YIELD RELATIONSHIP OF FINANCIAL INSTRUMENTS

There is a simple relationship between the price of a financial instrument and its yield, i.e. the financial return from holding it.

Initially a Treasury bill will be used as an example. For the purpose of understanding the basic relationship between price and yield, the following needs to be explained, without going into a lot of detail here concerning the issue of Treasury bills.

Treasury bills are issued by the Bank of England on behalf of the government. By selling Treasury bills the government is borrowing money from the original purchaser of the bill and the government repays the loan on an agreed day; in the case of Treasury bills this is usually 91 days after issue. On day 91 the Treasury bill is said to mature – the original purchaser is lending money to the government. Like any lender the buyer will wish to make a return as a reward for loss of use of the money and for the risk of non repayment when the loan expires. In practice the risk of default of non repayment is nil so far as lending to the government is concerned. A return for loss of use of the money is still required and if no return were made then buyers would not lend to the government and would lend elsewhere, for example, by making a bank deposit.

Treasury bills pay no rate of interest. So how can a return be earned from purchasing one? Quite simply a return can be made by paying a lesser amount today for the bill than will be repaid at maturity, 91 days in the future. The difference between the purchase price and its value at maturity (nominal value) will be its yield or return; the bill will therefore be sold at a discount to its nominal value.

This yield can be expressed as a return in percentage per annum terms so that comparisons across a range of financial assets can be made.

The following formula can be used

$$(i) \quad \frac{N - P}{P} \times \frac{365}{n} \times 100 = r\% \text{ p.a.}$$

r = percentage return expressed on a per annum basis
N = nominal value, i.e. the sum paid by the government when the Treasury bill matures. Could also be said to be its maturity value.
P = price paid by the buyer on a given day.
n = days to maturity.
(note: $N - P$ = money return for holding bill, for 91 days in this case)
Using a numerical example, let:
N = £5 000
P = £4 900
n = 91 days

$$\frac{5,000 - 4,900}{4,500} \times \frac{365}{91} \times 100 = 8.9\% \text{ p.a.}$$

Note the following relationships:
1. If the price falls the yield rises, for example, price falls from £4 900 to £4 800

$$\frac{5\,000 - 4\,800}{4\,800} \times \frac{365}{91} \times 100 = 16.71\% \text{ p.a.}$$

2. If the price rises the yield falls, for example, price rises from £4 900 to £4 950

$$\frac{5\,000 - 4\,950}{4\,950} \times \frac{365}{91} \times 100 = 4.05\% \text{ p.a.}$$

Thus there is an inverse relationship between price and yield, as one rises the other falls, or as one falls the other rises.

A reworking of the basic formula allows a price to be calculated for a desired return.

(ii) $\quad P = \dfrac{N}{\dfrac{r \times n + 1}{365}}$ r = percentage return expressed as a decimal

As has been explained, Treasury bills have a life, usually of 91 days (occasionally Treasury bills of different maturities are issued). The original purchaser may hold the Treasury bill to maturity if he so wishes, present the bill for repayment and pocket the difference between the original purchase and its nominal, maturity value. As demonstrated, a percentage per annum return can be calculated for comparative purposes with other types of financial investment.

The purchaser of the bill can, if he so wishes, sell the bill before maturity. In fact the bill can be sold, re-discounted, any number of times before maturity and there can be any number of holders during its life.

When a new Treasury bill is issued, it is issued in the primary market. When the original holder sells to another it is traded in the secondary market and all subsequent sales will be in the secondary market.

There is a ready market in financial instruments like Treasury bills because there are always plenty of willing sellers and buyers at any one time. Buyers are temporarily too liquid and therefore wish to reduce liquidity by buying. Sellers are too illiquid and therefore wish to sell, the proceeds making them more liquid.

Treasury bills are held as liquid assets. Liquid assets are assets which can be readily sold without experiencing *significant* capital losses/gains or losses/gains in interest. The question then arises, at what price should a Treasury bill be sold on a given day?

Each day during its 91 day life, it should increase in value a little. This increase in value is the equivalent of the return or interest that could, for example, be expected on a bank deposit for each day that the relevant sum of money is on deposit. (In practice market expectations can alter the price from the values suggested here. See later for details). In practice, two way prices are quoted, sell and buy. A single (true yield) rate of 8.9 per cent p.a. for illustrative purposes is used.

Using formula ii prices on various days can be calculated and are summarised in Table 9.2.

Table 9.2   *Treasury Bill Prices according to Maturity*

Nominal value of Treasury bill = £5,000

day no.	0	20	50	70	91
days to maturity	91	71	41	21	0
price £	4891.46	4914.91	4950.51	4974.53	5000.00

This information can be plotted, as in Figure 9.1.

It is apparent that the appropriate price can be calculated or read off the graph for each day during the life of the Treasury bill.

The forgoing calculations were made and represented graphically to give a return on an 8.9 per cent p.a. basis. Clearly the prices shown would only have been achievable if 8.9 per cent p.a. were the prevailing rate of return on Treasury bills throughout the 91 days.

Suppose the following were to happen:

8.9 per cent is the current rate of interest on Treasury bills on day 0, the day of issue.

Price £4,891.46 is therefore appropriate on day 0 to give the 8.9 per cent rate of return. (See Table 9.2.)

Figure 9.1 *Treasury Bill Prices According to Maturity*

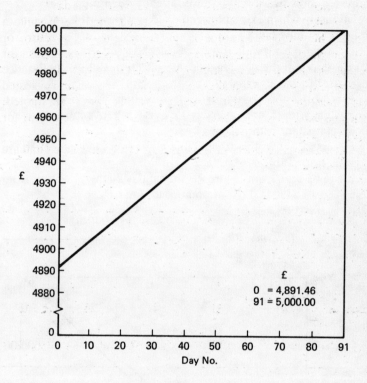

```
       £
       0  = 4,891.46
       91 = 5,000.00
```

But, what happens if, for example, on day 20, rates of interest were to rise for reasons we need not be concerned with here?

From Table 9.2 the price on day 20 to give an 8.9 per cent return would be £4914.91.

Would anyone buy at this price? Clearly not. If interest rates had increased, buying at this price would give a return inferior to that obtainable elsewhere.

Does this make the Treasury bill unsaleable, and therefore have to be held to maturity by the current holder?

Yes, it is unsaleable at this price of £4914.91 but can be made saleable if the price is adjusted so that a return at the new, higher, current rate of return can be earned.

A few moments thought should reveal that the price needs to be adjusted downwards. We have already identified the inverse relationship which exists between price and yield. If the yield rises then price must fall.

By using the formula ii we can calculate and graph new prices consistent with the new, higher rate of return (let us say the new rate rises to 10 per cent).

It is worth noting that for each price there is a rate of return consistent with it, or conversely for every rate of return there is a price consistent with it.

Figure 9.2 shows the original line plotted on Figure 9.1 with the figures from Table 9.3

It can be seen from Figure 9.2 that at day 20 the price falls from £4914.91 to £4904.60 (from point *A* to point *B*).

Figure 9.2   *Treasury Bill Prices following a Change in Yield*

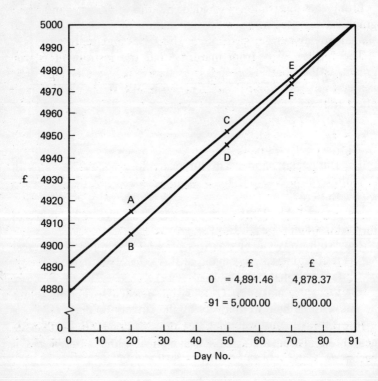

Table 9.3 *Calculation of New Treasury Bill Prices following a Change in Yield* using formula ii

Nominal value of Treasury bill = £5,000

day no.	0	20	50	70	91
days to maturity	91	71	41	21	0
price £	4878.37	4904.60	4944.47	4971.40	5000.00

In a similar fashion, had the interest rate fallen on day 50 then the price would have fallen from price C to price D. On day 70 it would have fallen from price E to F. Conversely, had the interest rate fallen, then prices would have risen. (This effect not illustrated).

From the illustration provided by these figures, and their graphical representation, a further feature of Treasury bills, and similar money market instruments, becomes apparent.

The further away from maturity that the instrument is, the greater is the price effect following an interest rate change. The nearer to maturity that the instrument is, the smaller is the price effect following an interest rate change.

$$AB \quad > \quad CD \quad > \quad EF$$
$$£10.31 \quad > \quad £6.06 \quad > \quad £3.13$$

This is true not only in absolute terms, but also in relative terms too.

AB is a greater proportion of A20 than CD is to C50, which in turn is of greater proportion than EF is to E70.

$$AB = 0.21\% \text{ of A20}$$
$$CD = 0.12\% \text{ of C50}$$
$$EF = 0.06\% \text{ of E70}$$

It is this feature of price/yield relationships that ensures that the nearer an instrument approaches maturity, the more liquid it becomes.

It is necessary to remember that the speed with which an asset can be turned into cash is not a sufficient characteristic of an asset to make it liquid. It must be readily convertible into cash without sustaining significant capital loss (or loss of interest).

Clearly the nearer an instrument is to maturity, the less significant is the risk of capital loss (or gain) should interest rates rise (or fall).

There is one further point worth realising. It may seem that a holder of a bill can avoid making a loss should he retain the bill, rather than sell it, if interest rates should rise. However, a loss is still sustained, even if the bill is held to maturity and not sold. It is earning an inferior return to that currently being earned elsewhere as a result of the rise in interest rates. The holder is locked into the old, lower rate of return and cannot enjoy the superior returns now available. In this way a loss is being experienced, the return on money being forgone. Furthermore, the Treasury bill may have to be sold for liquidity adjustment purposes.

This inverse relationship between price and yield applies to all financial instruments, whether they have no rate of nominal interest attached to them, as with a Treasury bill, or interest as usually with a CD.

9.3　MONEY MARKET INSTRUMENTS

At this stage, the financial instruments traded in the money markets, introduced earlier, can be usefully described in more detail. A reminder, they are:

Treasury bills
CDs
Bills of Exchange
Local Authority Bills
Sterling commercial paper

in addition to which there are a number of market deposits:

Local authority
Finance house
Inter-bank

9.4   TREASURY BILLS – INSTITUTIONAL ARRANGEMENTS

Treasury bills are negotiable, bearer government securities, and represent a charge on the Consolidated Fund. As a proportion of government debt they represent a small amount, however, they do have significance in relation to Bank of England operations in the money market and their number and therefore value outstanding is currently increasing slightly.

Treasury bills can be issued to the public in two ways. Every Friday at 1.00 pm they are issued by allotment to the highest bidder by tender, or by allotment to the highest bidder when the Bank of England wishes to absorb a money market surplus on a particular day. Bids are by invitation to discount houses and to the clearing banks by this latter method.

In addition, Treasury bills can be issued at any time to government departments and the Issue Department of the Bank of England. These are known as tap bills and the rate of discount is set by the Treasury.

Treasury bills are usually issued with a maturity of 91 days, but 61 day bills and sometimes greater maturities are used. Treasury bills have also been issued denominated in ECUs. At the weekly tender each tender must be for not less than £50 000. Bills are allocated to those offering the highest prices until the total amount on offer is used up. It is an obligation of the discount houses to bid for Treasury bills at the weekly tender; the proportion of each issue that individual discount houses tender for is agreed with the Bank of England and corresponds to the size of the capital base of the discount house. The number of bills allotted and the prices (quoted as a percentage discount) can be seen in the money market report of the Financial Times on the following Monday. Very occasionally the Bank of England will refuse all offers at tender. (See later in chapter for reasons.)

Even if a large cash shortage in the money market is anticipated for the following week, as is usually so, Treasury bills will still be announced to be on offer for that week in order to ensure the preservation of a market in the bills. (The purchase of Treasury bills takes money out of the money markets as it flows to the government, therefore sales of Treasury bills during a shortage creates a greater shortage. Significance of which will be seen later in this chapter).

9.5   CDs (CERTIFICATES OF DEPOSIT)

CDs are literally a certificate given by a deposit-taking institution like a bank or building society to acknowledge the existence of a deposit made. The issue of sterling CDs in the UK was made possible under a provision of the 1968 Finance Act. Prior to this US$ CDs were being traded in London. Sterling CDs have a minimum value of £50 000 and are issued to the value of £1 000 000 in increasing multiples of £10 000. Not all banks are authorised to issue CDs by the Bank of England; the primary market exists between the original depositor and bank. A secondary market exists when the original depositor, holder, wishes to sell the CD before it reaches maturity. The main participants in the secondary CD market are the Discount Houses.

Sterling CDs are issued at par (i.e. with the value of the primary deposit being made) on an interest to maturity basis for 28 days to 5 years. However, recently they can be issued for maturities for as little as 7 days to enable them to compete with the sterling commercial paper market. They are fully negotiable instruments.

For CDs with a maturity of one year or less interest is paid at maturity. For those with a maturity greater than one year interest is paid gross annually. The deposit taker does not repay the deposit before maturity; thus the necessity and usefulness of the secondary market.

CDs can be obtained in the primary market, for example by a company with excess funds. Then, when it has need of the funds, it can be sold in the secondary market and in this way the maturity does not have to match the need exactly.

Discount Houses, banks, building societies will be ready purchasers of secondary market CDs, and sellers, in order to adjust their day to day liquidity. In this way there is always a ready market.

As with all such financial instruments bid and offer (buy and sell), i.e. two way prices are quoted. The price at which CDs are traded is a reflection of their maturity value plus 'accrued' interest. 'Accrued' because the interest has not yet been actually paid by the original deposit taker. Due to this a small adjustment, downwards, in the price occurs, to compensate for the dealer being short of funds.

The following example illustrates this point.

Formula iii

Proceeds formula for CDs with maturity of less than one year

$$P = N \times \frac{(365 \times 100) + (r \times T)}{365 \times 100 + (y \times n)}$$

N = principal amount originally placed on deposit
r = nominal rate of interest given on CD
T = original maturity in days
y = current yield on CDs in the secondary market for this class of CD
n = days to maturity when CD sold in secondary market
P = price of CD being traded

To apply formula in first instance assume that yield and nominal rate of interest on the CD are the same

i.e. y = 10%
$\quad r$ = 10%
and N = £100,000
$\quad T$ = 180 days
$\quad n$ = 90 days

$$P = £100,000 \times \frac{(365 \times 100) + (10 \times 180)}{(365 \times 100) + (10 \times 90)} = £102,406.41$$

This gives an actual return for holding the CD for 90 days of £2,406.41.

This is slightly less than would have been obtained on an ordinary fixed deposit for 90 days at 10 per cent. Such a deposit would give interest of:

$$\frac{10 \times 90}{365 \times 100} \times £100\,000 = £2465.75$$

The dealer is paying £2,406.41 90 days before interest is actually paid by the original deposit taker. This cost is calculated on a 'discount to yield' basis at 10 per cent.

i.e. £2,406.41 $\times \dfrac{10}{100} \times \dfrac{90}{365}$ = £59.34

i.e. the short fall £2465.75 − £2406.41 = £59.34

It can be seen that the inverse price/yield relationship applies to CDs, as all other financial instruments. This can be seen by taking the example of falling interest rates giving capital gains on holding the CD.

Using same figures as before, in Formula iii, let

$$y = 8\%$$

this gives a price as follows:

$$P = £100\,000 \times \dfrac{(365 \times 100) + (10 \times 180)}{(365 \times 100) + (8 \times 90)} = £102\,901.66$$

As a result of falling CD yields the price has risen from £102 406.41 to £102 901.66.

A similar calculation for rising yields would show an appropriate fall in price. (For the moment ignore why yields might fall).

Equally, with the use of appropriate figures, it would show that CDs become more liquid, the nearer they get to maturity, i.e. the nearer to maturity they get, the smaller is the loss or gain as a result of changes in prevailing yields. The same affect as was seen with Treasury bills.

9.6 BILLS OF EXCHANGE

Bills of exchange are of various types, but all conform to a common set of criteria. They can be referred to as bills, drafts or acceptances and often come with a label – bank bills, bank drafts, time drafts, bankers acceptances are some examples.

Firstly it would be useful to understand the mechanism by which a 'standard' bill of exchange is created, then to see how other types occur.

There is a buyer and a seller. In a straightforward way the seller provides goods or services to the buyer, presents an invoice and is paid on the due date (more or less). This is how most domestic, commercial transactions are conducted. Some, however, and many transactions concerned with foreign trade, are covered by a bill of exchange whose value equals the value of the sale. Section 3 of the Bills of Exchange Act 1882 provides an exact definition of a bill of exchange.

The sequence of events to create a bill of exchange is illustrated in Figure 9.3.

1.   Goods/services are supplied by the seller to the buyer, thus creating an obligation to pay a sum of money. Usually a certain amount of trade credit will be given so that payment will be some time after delivery of goods or services.
2.   Bill drawn by seller on buyer. The bill of exchange is written out initially by the seller who becomes the drawer. It is usually written on a standard form, but not necessarily. The

Figure 9.3   *Creation of a Bill of Exchange*

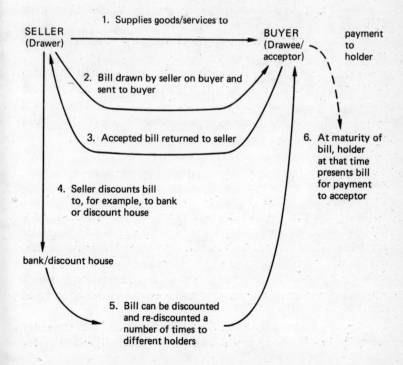

bill in question here, because trade credit is being given, will mature when the payment is due for the goods/services. It is known as a term, tenor or usance bill. When the bill matures the buyer/drawee/acceptor has to pay the sum of money on the bill (see 6.). By 'drawn on' simply means that the named buyer is identified as the party who should pay the sum of money involved.

In this way the buyer becomes the drawee, the person upon whom the bill is drawn. The bill is then sent to the buyer.

3. On receiving the bill the buyer must 'accept' the bill, having agreed to do so as part of their contractual obligations under the sale of goods or services. If the buyer believes such an obligation does not exist, then clearly the bill can be ignored and the matter does not proceed further as far as is concerned here. The bill is accepted by the buyer/drawee writing on the face of the bill the word 'accepted' and must be signed and dated. The buyer is now the drawee/acceptor of the bill, who then returns it to the seller.

4. The seller can, if he so wishes, simply keep the bill to maturity and present it for payment (as in 6.). There is little to be gained from this however. What the seller now has is something of immediate value – the undertaking of the buyer to pay a certain sum of money at a future date. It is possible to borrow money using this undertaking, or promise to pay, as security.

Who will lend money against this security? Discount Houses, banks and some other financial institutions.

Clearly, no one is going to lend, for example, £50 000 today, if the item being relied upon for repayment, the bill, is worth £50 000, and payment is in, say 60 days. Were £50 000 lent today against repayment of £50 000 in 60 days time this would be the equivalent of the lending institution lending at zero interest. Therefore a lesser sum will be lent and the difference between the sum lent and the full amount will equate to the 'interest' being charged. The bill will be discounted, sold for a sum less than its maturity value. The principle is that explained when discussing Treasury bills earlier in the chapter.

Discount Houses derive their name from the discounting of such bills of exchange.

5. The original discounting institution, a bank or discount house, for example, might well find itself short of liquidity before the bill matures. In which case it will be able to re-discount the bill to similar institutions who have excess liquidity. In holding the bill it will increase in value day by day and thus earn a return – return whose value will always be better than that for simply holding liquidity solely in the form of 'cash'. Each time the bill is re-discounted the discounter becomes the holder of the bill.

In practice most trade bills are discounted once and then held to maturity. The market for re-discounted paper is 'thin' in that the risk is greater and the names of the parties to the bill will often be unknown. Thus trading becomes less easy and sure.

It should be noted that some bills carry a 'definitive' rate of interest. This is a rate of interest written in such a way that the final maturity value of the bill can always be calculated. This is necessary so that the bill can be accurately discounted.

6. On a particular day the bill will mature. That is, it will be due to be paid by the accceptor. The current holder of the bill will present it for payment and all being well receive the full value.

Clearly the financial standing of the buyer/draweee acceptor is being relied upon, and a certain risk will attach to non-payment. The greater the risk of non-payment, the greater will be the expected return for discounting. That is, the greater the risk, the greater will be the discount and the greater will be the cost of borrowing experienced by the original discounter, the seller.

However, under the provisions of the Bills of Exchange Act 1882, in the event of non-payment by the acceptor, each holder of the bill can gain redress from previous holders, leaving the original discounter the right to recover the relevant sum of money from the drawer. The logic of this is that the drawer is in the same position he would have been in had he not discounted the bill. He would have remained unpaid, and the loser in the matter. He has used the bill as security to borrow money; if that security turns out to be worthless, then he should be liable for compensation to the lender of funds. It should be noted that in some other legal systems the drawer is not liable in this way and can discount 'without recourse'.

Bills being discounted and re-discounted is part of the Sterling Money Market at work. Such bills must be drawn in sterling and payable in the UK.

The bill described above would be known as a commercial or trade bill. If the drawer (due to recourse) and the drawee were highly credit rated then the bill would be a fine trade bill and would attract a finer, smaller discount, i.e. a lower effective rate of interest, due to the smaller risk of default.

Clearly the financial standing of the drawer and drawee are important in determining the rate of discount. If the drawee were, for example, a bank, then a bill accepted by such a bank would be more marketable, i.e. more liquid. It would also 'cost' less to discount it.

A bill accepted by a bank would therefore be a bank bill. Some banks are known as eligible banks (see later in the chapter) and create eligible bank bills, or simply eligible bills.

The sequence of events in the creation of a bank bill is in Figure 9.4, and is only a modification to that for commercial bills.

This section of the market is generally known as London Bankers' Acceptance Market. In order to provide the acceptance facility banks charge a small acceptance commission of $\frac{1}{16} - 1\frac{3}{4}$ per cent per annum.

It must be remembered they must pay on maturity, whether or not they actually receive the covering funds from the seller, having been paid for the underlying commercial transaction by the buyer. Not to pay at maturity, would be to say the least, extremely damaging to the bank's credit rating and would completely destroy confidence in it.

Bank bills are traded in the money markets in the same way as trade bills, except that the rate of discount is different (smaller) and they are more marketable due to the much lesser risk of default. In this way bank bills may be re-discounted a number of times before maturity. There is an active secondary market in such 'paper'.

Figure 9.4 *Creation of a Bank Bill*

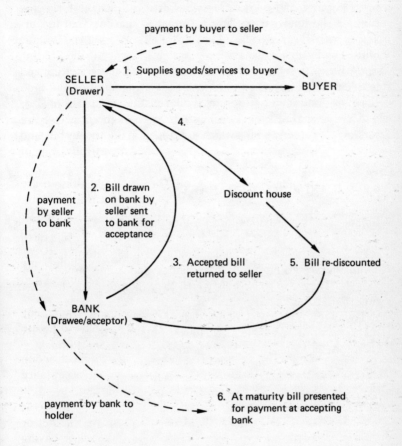

9.7 LOCAL AUTHORITY MARKET

The Local Government Act 1972, Schedule 13, as amended by Schedule 70 of the 1985 Act, allows local authorities to issue bills, technically Local Government Promissory Notes. Occasionally they are called revenue bills or money bills.

They are normally issued by tender with a tenor of 91 days or less, usually 6 months. All issues have to have approval from the Bank of England if they are to be re-discountable at the Bank of

England and attain eligible status. It is this status which makes them popular and marketable. (See later in chapter for significance). The tender procedure is similar to that for Treasury bills and as with Treasury bills, most LA bills are taken up by discount houses and clearing banks.

LA bonds normally have a maturity of 1 year and 6 days, but can be issued for up to 5 years tenor. They are quoted on the Stock Exchange and underwritten by similar institutions to those which underwrite share issues. Local authority stocks provide long-term funding. It is the LA bills which are traded in the money markets.

9.8   FINANCE HOUSE MARKET

Finance Houses provide funds for hire purchase, leasing and trade stock financing. They raise funds for these purposes by borrowing mainly from wholesale banks, taking deposits from insurance companies, pension funds, companies and some private individuals. They also draw bills which they then discount to obtain funds and issue CDs.

Today it is a relatively minor part of the sterling parallel money market due to many Finance Houses obtaining bank status, and therefore able to raise their funds on the sterling inter-bank market.

9.9   STERLING INTER-BANK MARKET

This market has already been used at the beginning of the chapter to introduce the concept and purpose of 'the money market'. It is a very important market in that it is the main link between all other sectors of the money market in London and participants include not just banks, but just about every area of the finance community. Main participants are indeed banks, the clearers plus all others in the banking sector (see Chapter 4), merchant banks and accepting houses and foreign central banks. In addition there are pension funds, insurance companies, large companies, finance houses, discount houses. Business is conducted via money brokers, of which there are currently six.

Essentially those institutions with surplus funds lend to those with insufficient funds to meet their requirements. Most transactions are £½ million plus and funds are lent on an unsecured basis. Most are for three months or less, right down to over-night or at call. Most deals over three months would be made with a CD due to their greater flexibility in that the depositor can gain back the deposit by selling the CD in the secondary market.

It is in this market and the CD market that the clearing banks now obtain the majority of their deposits. The cost of interbank deposits is crucial to setting base rates, as additional deposits are obtained by borrowing in this market it can be seen that LIBOR represents the marginal cost of funds to the clearing banks.

As a guide clearing banks seem to use 1–3 month LIBOR ± ¼ per cent as a basis for setting their base rate. The 'guide' is just that and is not intended as a rigid rule. Base rate can be often seen to be outside this guideline, due mainly to expectations in future movements in interest rates (see later in chapter).

Many large commercial customers of the clearing banks have their deposit and borrowing interest rates linked to movements in a particular maturity of LIBOR.

9.10   CENTRAL MONEY MARKETS OFFICE

Up until the Autumn of 1990 all money market instruments when bought or sold were physically delivered to the buyer, usually by messenger in the City of London. Therefore during every working day many thousands of items had to be delivered causing a great deal of work, plus a security risk. During early 1990 $297m worth of securities were stolen from a City messenger and whilst a general alert went out should any unusual presentations for payment be made at maturity to minimise the risk of loss, it is nevertheless true that this kind of occurrence causes a certain difficulty due to the fact that invariably the instruments in question are bearer instruments.

To deal with such difficulties and unnecessary travel of pieces of paper the Bank of England announced in November 1988 that it would set up a Central Money Markets Office (CMO) to develop a book entry transfer system to enable money market instrument paper to be 'immobilised' and eventually be 'dematerialised'. It provides a central depository, in its initial stages, for the paper once it has been raised. The paper then remains at the Bank and ownership is transferred by change of registration only. The transfer is effected by an electronic book-entry system, which also actuates the associated payment instruction.

There will be two types of participation, direct membership and indirect participation. Direct members have an account with the CMO and are be able to input instructions and receive details of deliveries of instruments on a terminal on their own premises. Tariffs will apply. In addition direct members arrange for money settlements to be made and received.

Indirect members will buy and sell instruments and make and receive money settlement through a direct member who in turn will levy a charge for the service.

All instruments allowed into the CMO system must be payable at maturity by a CMO member. Whilst the system remains paper based, the actual certificates and bills that make up the instruments will be held in a safe custody vault at the CMO.

It is anticipated that the system will eventually further develop, in addition to that of a paper-less system, to include, for example, automatic payment of any interim interest due on CDs or provide an automatic 'parcelling facility'. This would enable parcels of instruments to be made up to a given value, type or maturity for sale and thus improve their marketability.

9.11 THE ROLE OF THE BANK OF ENGLAND IN THE STERLING MONEY MARKETS

This section will attempt to demonstrate how the Bank of England operates in the sterling money markets and thereby influences the level of interest rates in those markets. It will also explain how market rates indirectly affect sterling interest rates generally, and specifically bank base rates.

In the seventh Mais Lecture (reported BEQB, Aug. 1987.) the Governor of the Bank of England said:

'There is a popular perception that the monetary authorities dictate the general level of interest rates, and of course it is true that we are able to exert a very considerable influence on it. But the extent of our influence should not be exaggerated. The financial markets are themselves an immensely powerful influence which we can never afford to ignore. At times, if market sentiment is uncertain and if the authorities are relatively confident in their view of the appropriate policy stance, the Bank's lead may be readily followed. But at other times, if we sought to impose a level of rates against strong market opposition, we are liable to be forced to change our stance...We need always therefore to try to work with the grain of the markets to achieve the required effects.

...Often our aim will be to slow the momentum of an interest rate movement sought by the markets rather than obstruct it altogether.

In seeking to influence the size and timing of interest changes we can operate with a higher profile – through publicised 2.30 p.m. lending to the market, for example, which is the equivalent to the earlier MLR announcement; or we can operate more discreetly through varying the scale of assistance in relation to the market's needs or the terms on which we lend privately to the discount houses. When there is an interest rate change, we can either follow a move in base rates initiated by the clearing banks or we can choose to anticipate a move that they might make on the rates prevailing in the interbank market.'

The operation of the sterling money markets and the role of the Bank of England will be built up from a relatively simple picture.

Firstly, imagine that the UK is a closed economy, with no foreign trade, with no capital flows of money to or from abroad and with no government sector. In this case all money transactions would be between UK residents and UK companies within the UK (i.e. the UK M4 private sector). Most of these transactions would take place via bank accounts. Company A paying company B would mean a transfer of deposits from company A's bank to company B's bank. These transfers would take effect when netted out with all other transactions across the operational balances of each bank with the Bank of England.

At the end of a day's banking some banks are going to be more liquid, as a result of net deposits and other banks are going to be less liquid than they were at the beginning of the day's business, as a result of a net withdrawal of deposits.

This position of under or over liquidity is unsatisfactory in each case. Under liquid banks will have insufficient liquidity to meet demands on deposits the next day. Over liquid banks will have money balances earning no return, so that profit opportunities are being lost. This will affect their ability to pay a return to their shareholders and meet their running expenses, including being able to pay interest on the deposits, where appropriate, that they have taken.

It is to the mutual advantage of both sets of banks, those over liquid and those under liquid, for those over liquid to lend to those under liquid. Money is lent and borrowed in this way on the interbank market. Money can be lent at varying maturities and money settlement will be achieved via changes in operational balances at the Bank of England. (See Chapter 4.)

In addition banks will also hold a set of liquid assets in the form of Treasury bills, various types of bills of exchange, LA bills etc., as has already been described earlier in the chapter. Liquidity adjustment can also occur via appropriate buying and selling of these money market instruments, instruments held for this specific purpose, where they can be readily exchanged without significant loss. Holding them of course means a return is being earned that otherwise would be forgone.

In a closed economy with no government sector where no money either enters or leaves the system it would be possible for total liquidity adjustment between banks to occur in such a way.

More realistically, however, we have to allow that money does enter and leave the system so far described. Money leaves the UK private sector, the system, and flows to the government sector when tax of any kind, for example, is paid. Company A paying its corporation tax from its bank deposit will cause Bank A to lose the deposit to an account at the Bank of England. It does not end up with another bank as would be the case were, for example, an invoice to Company B paid. Thus payments to the government cause loss of liquidity to the banking system as a whole.

On the other hand government expenditure results in an increase in liquidity within the system. If Company A receives payment for supplying defence equipment to the government, then the payment results in an increase in Company A's bank account, without a decrease in any other M4 private sector bank account.

Net inflows or outflows clearly determine the liquidity position of the banking system on a day to day basis.

In a closed economy (Figure 9.5) the circled banks which find themselves over liquid can lend to or buy money market instruments from the under liquid banks (uncircled).

In an economy with a government sector (Figure 9.6) a net outflow of funds to the government (where taxes exceed expenditure on a particular day) results in the banking system being under-liquid.

Figure 9.5 *Liquidity Adjustment, Closed Economy*

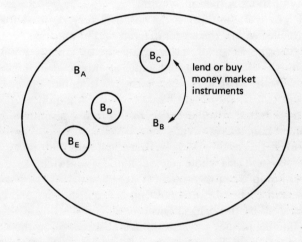

Figure 9.6 *Liquidity Adjustment, Open Economy*

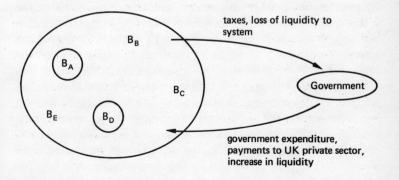

A net inflow of funds from the government (where expenditure exceeds taxes on a particular day) results in the banking system being over liquid.

N.B. On a daily basis different banks become under or over liquid quite fortuitously as a result of the transactions conducted by their customers.

It can also be seen that in reality the UK economy is an open one, with a foreign sector. Thus UK residents, companies and private individuals can make or receive payments to or from abroad. The extent to which these are in sterling or exchanged into sterling, will also have a corresponding effect on the sterling liquidity of the UK banking system.

Under or over liquidity is an unsatisfactory position for individual banks within the system. Even within an open economy, with a government sector, a certain amount of liquidity adjustment can be made between over and under liquid banks in the system. Even when the system as a whole is, for example, under liquid, there will still be individual banks with over liquidity. They can lend to and buy from other banks. In this fashion a partial adjustment can always occur.

However, there will always be individual banks left under liquid when the system as a whole is under liquid. (And vice versa, banks left over liquid when the system is over liquid.)

As remarked before, this position is unsatisfactory and cannot be 'tolerated' by the banks concerned.

Building up further towards a picture of reality, in the UK we have the system of discount houses. These have various rights and obligations under the auspices of the Bank of England. One of their obligations is to always provide two-way prices on the discount money market instruments which have been considered in this chapter. This means they must always be prepared to either buy or sell securities when approached to do so by one of the banks.

The result of this obligation, under conditions of the system as a whole being under liquid, is that the shortage ends up with the discount houses, either with all of them, or with individual houses. Banks having the right liquidity will not enter the money markets. Thus all banks which find themselves illiquid will naturally seek to relieve the shortage by offering to sell securities to the discount houses. In addition many banks will have money market loans at call with discount houses. In conditions of liquidity shortage they will call back these loans, requiring the discount houses to repay the money lent to them. In both ways, the shortage ends up with the discount houses.

There is only one final source of relief with regard to the shortage of liquidity and that is the Bank of England, specifically performing its role of lender of last resort. The Bank deals mainly with discount houses and only on a very limited basis with the commercial banks. As described, the shortage essentially ends up with the discount houses. They, in turn, if short of funds can expect to relieve their shortage, balance their position, either by selling eligible bills to the Bank or by borrowing funds from the Bank, against collateral provided.

By eligible bills is meant any instrument which the Bank is prepared to buy as part of its money market operations to adjust liquidity in the banking system. They include the government's own instruments which it issues, Treasury bills, certificates of tax deposit, as well as eligible Local Authority bills and eligible bank bills. As seen earlier, in a rather circular fashion, eligible bank bills are bills of exchange accepted by an eligible bank. In turn, an eligible bank is one whose acceptances will be rediscounted by the Bank of England, that is will be purchased by the Bank from the discount house holding them.

Such bills have to meet a number of criteria, apart from the credit rating of the bank which accepts the bill. They include an original maturity of no more than 187 days, be payable within the UK and be for an identifiable underlying trade transaction. They must not be accommodation bills, where no underlying transaction exists, where the bill has been accepted so that it can be discounted for capital purposes. On 23 September 1988 the list of eligible banks numbered 158.

During periods of acute cash shortages the Bank may purchase gilt-edged stock under a repurchase (repro) agreement. Here the discount house/bank agrees to buy back the gilt at a future date. This is an exceptional facility and most shortages are relieved by outright purchases by the Bank, against same-day settlement.

Usually, no distinction is made between types of bill, but occasionally the Bank does so. Purchases may also be confined to certain maturity bands as below:

band 1   1 – 14 days
band 2   15 – 33 days
band 3   34 – 63 days
band 4   64 – 91 days

Maturities refer to the remaining maturity, not the original. Thus the Bank does not usually purchase bills with a maturity greater than 3 months. It does not usually purchase eligible bank bills within seven days of their acceptance.

It should be emphasised that the Bank only buys eligible money market instruments. The reason for this is clear. When the instrument matures the Bank will present it for payment to the relevant institution. In the case of Treasury bills it is the government which will be paying – no loss effectively possible there. In the case of bank bills it has to be sure that the acceptor bank will be in a position to pay, thus the requirement of eligibility. Often in money market reports as published in the Financial Times trade bills or commercial bills will be referred to in relation to purchases by the Bank of England. They will always be eligible bank bills and not true trade bills and their nomenclature in this context can only be described as a kind of shorthand and corresponds to the requirement that they must be drawn for transaction not capital purposes.

When there is a shortage of liquidity in the banking system, the Bank of England invites discount houses to offer for sale eligible instruments to the Bank. Open market operations are made via the discount houses, but can also be conducted directly with the major clearing banks. The preference is, however, for the discount houses. They are easier to manipulate, they have less money and depend on the Bank largely for their livelihood. There is a great deal of liaison between Bank and discount houses, all are visited once per week by a bank official from the Money Markets Office to explain reasons behind actions taken in the markets by the Bank. Clearers are also visited in a similar way.

The Bank makes an estimate of what the liquidity position of the banking system will be on a day to day basis for several weeks ahead. Estimates can be quite accurate once two days in advance are concerned. Government departments give information on expected major flows of money. In a similar fashion treasury departments of banks and discount houses also make their own estimates to enable them to plan their strategy for their 'book' of money market instruments.

The market is given the estimate of the liquidity position for the coming day's business at 9.45 a.m. on their information screens. Usually the first operations by the Bank are at 12 noon. This is when, under positions of market shortage of liquidity, discount houses are invited to offer eligible instruments for sale. It is for the discount houses to tell the Bank the rate at which they wish to sell – the Bank may accept or decline the offers. The 'stop' rate is the rate below which the Bank will not buy – it may differ for different maturity bands. The market is not told the stop-rate but of course those houses which offered other bills and were declined will know.

Not all the shortage is taken out early on. This is because if the estimate of the liquidity position is incorrect it will cause large changes in market rates of interest, the undesirability and significance of which will soon be seen.

Exceptionally, if there is a large shortage then the Bank will offer an 'early round' of assistance. Here discount houses can make telephone offers of sale of instruments. Having decided which, if any, offers to accept, the Bank will publish, as at all times of assistance, the amount and types of bills purchased, with the appropriate maturity bands and spread of discount rates given. If the forecast liquidity position has changed significantly by the 'usual' first round of assistance at 12 noon, then a revised forecast is given. No details of the factors creating the change are given.

By practice banks withdraw their callable funds with the discount house by 12 noon, but they may offer their surpluses to them up until the close of business in the afternoon. For this reason any shortages in the system can be expected to be revealed in the discount houses' position by 12 noon.

At 2.00 p.m., if there are any further revisions of significance in the market's position they are published. If there is still a sizeable shortage, then further assistance is given, though not necessarily at the same rates and maturities as earlier.

If a market surplus of liquidity is forecast, then the Bank will only act at 2.00 p.m. if it is large. In such a case it will invite discount houses and clearing banks to bid for Treasury bills of one or more specified maturities. The Bank does not rediscount eligible bank bills back to the market in such instances. To do so would suggest that the Bank were in effect guaranteeing their payment at maturity.

Liquidity surpluses have become quite common and this accounts for the increased issue of Treasury bills of late. Maturities are designed to take out anticipated shortages at a later date and therefore maturities differ from the standard 91 days.

If a discount house finds itself short of funds after the final round of assistance at 2.00 p.m. then money may be borrowed from the Bank on a secured basis within its agreed facilities. A director of the discount house needs to attend personally to effect this, traditionally complete with top hat. The total amount of such late assistance is published on the financial news screen. The rates are not. Further telephone borrowing is possible at the discretion of the Bank and usually at an increased rate of interest. Such late borrowing is necessary because only when Town Clearing has been completed will the final position for the day become known and the final position of the clearing banks in relation to their operational balances at the Bank.

Very exceptionally the Bank may alter the above arrangements. It may announce that 2.00 p.m. lending to discount houses is to be put back to 2.30 p.m., when the rate at which loans are made will be published. Lending limits are often suspended to the discount houses and do not count against their agreed lending facility with the Bank.

9.12   MONEY MARKET INTEREST RATES AND BASE RATE

Having seen the function of the Bank of England in the sterling money markets carrying out its role as lender of last resort, it is now possible to look at the significance of its open market operations in relation to interest rate determination in the money markets and in the wider economy.

When it becomes necessary for a bank to liquidate some of its liquid assets in order that it may then have a desired liquidity position, it will, as has been explained, sell to other banks or discount houses. As has also been seen, for each price of a bill or other market instrument there is a given yield or rate of return. So long as the price is consistent with the current yield then nothing in relation to bank base rates need change.

However, imagine the situation should the Bank of England, when conducting open market operations, alter prices it is prepared to pay to discount houses. Suppose it lowers the prices it is prepared to pay; this will mean a capital loss to the discount house if it has just given a bank a price consistent with current yields. Now the price has fallen and future purchases by discount houses will be at the new, lower rate. This new, lower rate will be consistent with a higher yield on the assets in question as per the inverse relationship demonstrated earlier. It means new funds going into the banks as a result of liquidating assets have cost more. This additional cost, if sufficiently large, will be passed on to bank customers based upon a new, higher base rate.

For administrative reasons it would be undesirable for base rates to change every time money market rates changed, but if the change is large enough, then a base rate change becomes necessary. As a rough guide base rates are usually kept within about a ¼ per cent margin either side of market rates, although it is possible to see base rates outside this 'guide' on occasion.

Thus, when the Bank of England wishes to bring about a change in base rates, which in turn affect all other sterling rates of interest over the whole yield curve, it does so by adjusting its money market intervention rates, in what must be, by definition, the discount market. Rates are altered so that the new price reflects the desired new rate of interest.

Once intervention rates have been altered in this fashion, a change in rates will occur across all sterling money markets. The process of arbitrage would ensure that it occurs although in reality market participants would alter rates immediately, so that arbitrage opportunities did not occur.

In the example given, if prices were to fall in the discount market, and the yield rise, then the process of arbitrage would ensure new rates in the parallel market, should market participants not immediately adjust prices (which in fact they will). If they did not adjust prices immediately then market activity would bring about the changes. If parallel market rates were lower and instrument prices higher, then it would be possible to sell parallel instruments, at a high price, and with the proceeds buy a similar instrument with regard to risk and maturity in the discount market at a low price, and therefore higher yield. In this instance the benefit would be a capital gain between the selling and buying price. The movement of a large number of sellers in the parallel market would drive down the price, and push up the yield until it equalled that in the discount market. Arguably the increased demand to buy in the discount market would push up the price and depress the yield. The only factor which disturbs the markets moving towards each other in this way, as opposed to the parallel market doing all the moving, is the existence of the Bank of England in its lender of the last resort function.

In the above example it is the Bank of England initiating the base rate change. Should a change be initiated in rates downwards, then prices would be adjusted upwards by the Bank of England.

In many instances, however, it is not the Bank of England which initiates the change in rates of interest. Quite often it is the clearing banks which make the first move by announcing a base rate change before the Bank alters its intervention rates. The Bank in this case endorses the change by bringing its intervention rates in line with the new base rate. It must be said, however, that it is extremely unlikely that a clearing bank would announce a change in this way without first getting the view of the Bank as to the desirability of the change at that particular time.

The sequence of events in this latter instance can probably be best explained by 'market expectations' or 'sentiment'.

There may well be an expectation or a sentiment exist that interest rates will change in the near future. Those expectations, sentiments, may well be based upon interpretation of economic data concerning inflation, the balance of payments position, the exchange rate or many other economic variables. If the expectation is held strongly then market participant action may well bring about the event that was expected. In this way events may be a self-fulfilling prophecy.

It may well be that there is a strong market view that interest rates will rise shortly. If this view is held then it makes sense to borrow funds now at low rates to obviate the need for borrowing later, when funds are expected to be more expensive. Equally, if an institution has excess funds at the moment, and expects interest rates to rise, it will be acting rationally if it does not lend those funds out, except very short term. In this way when interest rates do rise it can benefit from these new higher rates. In both instances lenders and borrowers activity will tend to ensure that their expectations become fulfilled.

The increase in demand for borrowing will push up rates. In order to lock into today's low rates potential borrowers will have to agree to marginally higher rates than are really current. But, having agreed these new, marginally higher rates now, they have in fact caused rates to rise. The process will continue upwards until rates rise to meet expectations. Sometimes it can be seen that rates go 'too high' and have to adjust downwards slightly.

On the opposite side of the market there is a reinforcing process at work. At the same time that there is an increase in the demand for borrowing, there is a reduction in the supply of those wishing to lend. In order to 'persuade' lenders to lend, as seen above, fractionally higher rates will be necessary.

It is therefore possible to see movements in interest rates in the money markets as a whole in advance of changes led by the Bank of England. The key market here is the interbank market, as described before the principal source of funds for clearing banks, and where additional funds are obtained. Funds raised in this way represent the marginal cost of funds to the banks involved. It therefore makes sense, as described earlier for banks to keep base rates within ¼ per cent of interbank rates, specifically 1 – 3 months. Shorter maturities are perhaps a little too volatile and respond to day-to-day liquidity conditions too readily to be used as such a guideline. One – three months seems about the right time horizon for raising the majority of deposits. Any longer makes it difficult to easily adjust to market conditions.

It is often possible to see three month interbank outside the ¼ per cent band with regard to base rate. Apart from being a guideline, and not a rigid rule, it is evidence that changes in interest rate expectations are being held, but perhaps behind the scenes approval from the Bank of England has not been forthcoming. The Bank does not hold the view that a change is desireable – yet.

Money markets are therefore a device which has grown up to adjust liquidity principally between financial institutions and at the same time enables a return on deposits to be maximised. Market intervention by the Bank of England enables it to influence market rates of interest and thereby all other sterling interest rates across the complete maturity spectrum.

9.13 MINIMUM LENDING RATE

As a final point of information, the Bank of England still has the facility to re-introduce minimum lending rate (MLR) if it so wishes. It did so for one day on 5 October 1990, on the announcement of the application for UK entry into the exchange rate mechanism (ERM) of the European Monetary System (EMS). The previous example was in January 1985. In both instances the Bank wished to make a very public and positive statement about interest rates. MLR was 'suspended' in August 1981.

CHAPTER 10

EURO-CURRENCY

10.0 DEFINITIONS

There are a number of ways of classifying banking activities.

Domestic banking involves taking and making loans in domestic currency to residents of the country where the bank is located. An example would be a person or company resident in the UK either making a deposit or receiving a loan in sterling to or from a UK bank. It would not matter that the resident were a foreign national or a foreign company, so long as they were resident, were located in the UK and the transaction were in sterling, it would constitute domestic banking.

Traditional foreign banking would involve taking deposits or making loans in domestic currency to non-residents of the country where the bank was located. Here the example might be a UK bank lending sterling to a person or a company living or located in the US. Again it would not matter if the person were a US citizen or not, so long as he or she lived in the US the classification would stand.

Eurocurrency banking activity, the subject of this chapter, has been defined in a number of ways.

Eurocurrency is currency held outside the control of the monetary authorities of the country where the currency originates

or

bank deposits in currency not of the country in which the bank holding them is located

or

currency held on deposit outside its country of origin.

185

If a UK resident had a deposit in a UK bank in any currency other than sterling, this would be an example of Eurocurrency. Thus a company holding US$ on deposit in London would represent a Eurocurrency deposit. The qualification of resident (company or person), coupled with UK bank are the combination which determines the definition of Eurocurrency. By UK bank is meant any bank within the UK – it does not matter whether ownership is foreign or not, it could be an American or Japanese bank, or any other 'nationality', including British. Location in the UK is what counts, in the example cited. Equally, of course a sterling deposit held by a French resident in Paris would also constitute Eurocurrency.

The term 'Euro' does not confine the Eurocurrency market exclusively to Europe. It is now a global market, with the main Eurocurrency centres in London, New York, Paris, Luxembourg, Canada, Singapore, Hong Kong, Tokyo, Bahrain and Nassau. The term derives from the origin of the market in European financial centres, especially that of London. The term 'off-shore' is sometimes used as an alternative, but as this has a meaning in other contexts the term Eurocurrency is the one which has generally stuck and most Eurocurrency transactions continue to be in Europe.

Terms Eurodollar, Eurosterling and so on are also often used, especially Eurodollar. The latter is quite frequently used synonymously with Eurocurrency. So long as the correct conditions are satisfied any currency can be used with the prefix Euro. Occasionally Asian dollars are used to describe US$ held in the Asian financial centres.

The term International Banking Market also appears as a classification in many statistical tables. This market constitutes the Eurocurrency market plus deposits in domestic and foreign currency held by non-residents. Examples would be an American resident holding a deposit in London in sterling or any other currency, including his own US$. Therefore it includes Traditional Foreign banking activity.

It should be appreciated that currencies deposited and lent in Eurocurrency are no different from those deposited and lent via domestic banks – it is the location of the deposit or lending which differs. The Eurodollars which are lent are indistinguishable from domestic dollars which are lent, the source is merely different. If a large sum of Eurodollars is borrowed and then used in a transaction, the recipient of the dollars does not see that they are Eurodollars rather than 'domestic' US$.

Euromarkets are mainly wholesale in that large sums are lent or deposited. The main operators are commercial and central banks, large companies, institutional investors and a few wealthy individuals.

10.1 UNDERSTANDING EUROCURRENCY

It is helpful to understand how money is transferred from one country to another and the bank accounting procedures which accompany such transfers if the concept of Eurocurrency is to be fully understood.

If, as an example, an importer of goods in the UK needs to pay for goods purchased from the USA, the importer will have to send the money to the USA. At one level bank notes could be sent in a parcel to the American exporter. This would be somewhat inefficient and unusual. Imagine that the payment were to be in US dollars. This would mean that a supply of dollar bills would need to be available at UK banks. Where would they come from? – the US is the sole source. A constant stream of US dollar notes would need to be sent from America, only to be sent back a little at a time in individual parcels as above. The same wasted effort and security risk would apply if the UK importer in our example were to pay in sterling. Plenty of sterling notes in the UK! Sterling notes in payment would be sent in a parcel to America, only to be exchanged in US banks for dollars and sent back to the UK again.

Yet a UK importer would still prefer to send the payment for the goods to America, either in US dollars or sterling (or in any other agreed currency for that matter). So how is this achieved? Banks do not aggregate customers' payments and send parcels of bank notes abroad on their behalf either! However, they will still refer to remitting or sending money abroad on behalf of their customers.

A simple insight is to remember that money principally takes the form of bank deposits, without the existence of any other physical form to somehow 'back-up' the deposit. The record of the deposit in the bank is all there is. Money is often telexed or cabled abroad, or nowadays 'sent' via computer systems known as SWIFT. Take the example of telexing money abroad, or receiving it. A telex is only a message sent electronically along a communications cable and translated into type on a piece of paper at the receiving end. Money, in the form of bank notes, does not travel along the cable as well! The telex message is just that – a message, which advises details of the accounting procedures necessary to change bank deposit records and at the same time gives the authorisation to make the changes.

Bank accounts known as NOSTRO and VOSTRO accounts are used along with mirror accounts which record balances in the former. They reflect money balances and just as a mirror image shows everything literally as a mirror image, everything is the opposite way round, so too are the balances in the mirror accounts in relation to the balances in the NOSTRO and VOSTRO accounts. (For example if a UK bank has a credit balance in its NOSTRO account, this will be 'reflected' by a debit balance in the mirror account of the same value).

Given below is a simple worked example of a UK importer sending a payment of $10 000 to the supplier of goods in the USA. The payment will be handled by the importer's and the US exporter's banks on their behalf, using the computerised SWIFT system. This system takes care of both the necessary accounting and authorising messages.

UK importer authorises his bank in UK to pay $10 000 to US exporter as named beneficiary via named US bank.

UK bank debits their customer's account by sterling equivalent of $10 000 (or if the customer has a US$ account this might be debited instead).

At this point it is necessary to know that the UK bank will have a US$ account with their 'correspondent' bank in the US. The money in this account is the property of the bank, it is their money. The UK bank will call this account their NOSTRO account. They will be able to say it is 'our' money. (NOSTRO equals 'ours' in Latin).

Using the SWIFT system a message will be sent to the US bank by the UK bank. It will contain two instructions or authorisations. It will authorise that $10 000 be debited from their NOSTRO account and that this money in turn be credited to the beneficiary, the US exporter.

The US exporter has now been paid, using money from the UK bank's NOSTRO account. It may appear that the UK bank has now given away $10 000 of its own money, the money really is held in the name of the UK bank. It should, however, be remembered that the UK bank had earlier debited the UK importer with an equal amount of value. Profit will be made by charging commission.

Like any prudent business the UK bank will wish to keep a record of what it in turn has on deposit in its account with the US bank. This accounting record is the mirror account.

A summary of the total is as follows:

UK bank: customer account $10 000 dr (or sterling equivalent) mirror account $10 000 cr

US bank: UK bank's NOSTRO account $10 000 dr
             US exporter $10 000 cr

US dollars build up in the UK bank's NOSTRO account when US importers pay UK exporters in US$ (see next example) or when the UK bank buys in US$ in the foreign exchange market.

Example of US importer paying UK exporter $10 000.

US bank: US importer's account
                        $10 000 dr
             UK bank's NOSTRO account
                        $10 000 cr

UK bank: Mirror account $10 000 dr
             UK exporter's account
    (or sterling equivalent) $10 000 cr

In this case the message sent on the SWIFT system from the US bank to the UK bank is that your (NOSTRO) account has been credited by us with $10 000, in return pass on this amount to the named beneficiary, the UK exporter.

(*N.B.* That from the US bank's point of view they will refer to the account as 'your' account when communicating with the UK bank. To the US bank this same account is therefore a VOSTRO = Latin, your account).

On reflection it should be possible to see that all sterling remittances and receipts to and from abroad will be transacted using sterling accounts in UK banks which are the property of banks located abroad. To UK banks they will be VOSTRO accounts, the same accounts to non UK banks will be NOSTRO accounts. (If say something is 'yours' you will say of the same thing that it is 'ours' when you refer to it).

Since the abolition of exchange controls in the UK in October 1979 it has been possible for residents of the UK to hold foreign currency on account if they so wish. This currency could be accumulated by holding, for example, the proceeds of foreign trade sold for foreign currency. It might be held so that this currency in turn could be used at a later date to make foreign purchases of goods or services, a method often used to hedge exchange risk.

If such deposits were aggregated in all UK banks, this would represent the total of Eurocurrency within the UK. If similar deposits were aggregated in all countries then this would represent the total of all Eurocurrency deposits. This corresponds to the second and third of the definitions of eurocurrency given earlier in the chapter:

> bank deposits in currency not of the country in which the bank holding them is located.
> currency held on deposit outside its country of origin.

We will get a sense of the first definition given earlier as the chapter proceeds.

10.2   EUROCURRENCY AND CREDIT CREATION

A further concept concerning Eurocurrency will now be introduced. It is that the sum of currency deposits held outside their country of origin far exceed the sum of the NOSTRO/VOSTRO accounts to which they nominally correspond. That is to say it might be possible, as an example, to find that a particular non–US bank held deposits in a NOSTRO account in the US to the value of

$1m. If in turn the non–US bank aggregated the value of all US$ claims on it, that is the value of all US$ deposits with it, the value of all the US$ claims would far exceed the value of its US$ NOSTRO account in the US. In general terms, Eurodollar deposits in the UK, for example, far exceed the corresponding dollar claims on American banks which UK banks have. That this is possible is due to the process of credit creation outside the country where the currency originates. An example should demonstrate.

The first Eurocurrency deposits were created when, for example, a depositor of US$ in an American bank transferred those funds to a UK bank in London. The depositor now had a claim on the London bank and in turn the London bank had a claim on a bank in America. Both claims were in US$ and were equal. The credit creation process can now begin, creating dollars outside America, exceeding the claims on American banks. That is, Eurodollars can be created as opposed to 'domestic' dollars.

London bank has $1m deposit from customer.
London bank has in turn $1m deposit with US bank.
London bank now lends out dollars.Dollars are spent and re-deposited in London either same or other bank (example uses different bank).
Total deposits in London now exceed the original size of deposits in America.

It may help to follow the process through the relevant NOSTRO accounts.

Bank A in London has customer with $1m deposit
Bank A in turn has $1m on deposit in NOSTRO account in US bank.
Bank A lends $500 000. This $500 000 is spent buying oil from Mexico. Oil supplier re-deposits funds in Bank B in London.
Bank A, via SWIFT network, authorises US bank holding NOSTRO account to debit it $500 000 and credit the NOSTRO account of Bank B $500 000.Bank B credits oil supplier with deposit of $500 000.
Total deposits in London $1.5m
Total deposits in NOSTRO accounts in US $1m.

Eurodollars have been created. Dollars have been used to make purchases outside of America, independent of any aggregate impact on the US money supply. Ownership of the dollars in the US has changed from Bank A to Bank B with regard to the $500 000, but the total remains the same.

The normal process of money creation is taking place within the banking system. Banks outside America do not need to keep in their NOSTRO accounts a sum equal to their deposits. A useful way to understand this is to remember that in a domestic context UK banks do not need to keep operational balances at the Bank of England equal to the total value of their deposits, just in case they are withdrawn. Many deposits end up being re-deposited either in the same bank or another bank in the system. Much inter-bank lending in Eurocurrency takes place and accounts for much of the business. Eurocurrency business is in very substantial sums and also often involves governmental or governmental agency transactions.

A distinction can thus be made between ordinary 'domestic' dollars – those used for transactions with the US – and Eurodollars. Eurodollars have an existence outside the US and can be used to make purchases, denominated in US$, outside the US. They are still US$, the distinction is between Euro and domestic. Eurodollars can be used to cover transactions inside the US, at which point they cease to be Eurodollars and revert to being ordinary, domestic US$ again.

When Eurodollars revert to domestic dollars it is here that the stock of Eurodollars diminishes. Again a view of the NOSTRO accounts should assist understanding:

UK resident has US$ on deposit in UK bank in London and wishes to buy goods in America denominated in US$.

UK bank: customer's account dr
            mirror account cr

UK bank authorises US bank to debit their NOSTRO account with the relevant sum of money and pay American beneficiary who has supplied goods to depositor in London.

US bank: UK bank's NOSTRO account dr
            beneficiary cr

There are two important points to note from this. The first is the one already made and the purpose of the example, it is that the stock of Eurocurrency has now reduced – no dollars have been re-deposited outside the US. The second is that there is now an impact upon the US domestic money supply.

The US money supply has now increased. The beneficiary's account is now larger and there has been no corresponding decrease in another domestic bank account to match it, as would have been the case had the transaction been purely domestic, and thus not created further credit.

It is this which has led some commentators to believe that the Eurocurrency market could create inflation within the US economy should large sums of Eurodollars be spent in the US by transformation, as it were, into domestic dollars.

The fear is unfounded and can be eased by remembering firstly that the existence of sums of US$ in NOSTRO accounts is only possible because there has been a transfer into them from the US money stock. As NOSTRO accounts increase, they do so at the expense of US domestic bank accounts. As the NOSTRO accounts rise they reduce the US domestic money stock. As they fall, as in the example given, they merely replace what was lost in an earlier time period. Thus there is no net loss or gain over the period of time.

It is not possible for all the Eurodollars in existence to be spent within the US. Reference to the first reason given above provides part of the answer. The dollars that could be spent equal the amounts held in NOSTRO accounts which are but a small fraction of total Eurodollars.

Secondly, it must be remembered what would happen in any banking institution should depositors start withdrawing funds which did not end up being re-deposited within the system. This is what is effectively happening in the scenario posed. Loans would be called in or not be renewed when repaid. The whole credit creation process would go into reverse so that the amount of Eurocurrency would drastically reduce and therefore not be totally available for spending within the US. As stated earlier, expenditure could only equal the value of NOSTRO accounts, the size of which only equal withdrawals from the US money supply in earlier time periods in any case.

10.3   EUROCURRENCY STATISTICS

Difficulties in interpreting data on Eurocurrency often lead to problems in assessing the market's economic influence. The main sources of data are the Bank for International Settlements (BIS) and studies published by Morgan Guaranty in 'World Financial Markets'. An examination of the BEQB will show UK bank activity in the Euromarkets from data on currency assets and liabilities. It also reproduces a summary of BIS data.

Much data is published on the wider concept of the International Banking Market in recognition that total external activity of the banking system is important for macro economic concerns and not just that in foreign currency.

10.4   PATTERN OF ACTIVITY IN THE EUROCURRENCY MARKET

An examination of the figures shows that the market began in the late 1950's. During the 1960's there was slow growth with more rapid growth during the early 1970's. From the mid 1970's to the mid 1980's there was very rapid growth. Since the mid-1980's there has been little or no growth.

A number of reasons are often given for the origin and growth of the Euromarket, they include the following:

1. Eastern block deposits
2. Large US current account deficits.
3. US dollar and other currency convertability.
4. Regulation Q of the US banking system.
5. OPEC surpluses on current account.
6. Central Bank regulation of domestic markets.
7. Lack of regulation of Euromarkets by Central banks.

An alteration in circumstances concerning 4–7 of the above reasons has brought about the situation found since the mid 1980's, when there has been a lack of growth.

1.   Eastern block deposits

A view often quoted of the origin of the Eurocurrency market is
that of East European banks, due to the cold war, wishing to have
their dollar balances held in London, rather than in the US. In this
way such balances would be outside the control of the monetary
authorities in the US (see first definition offered of Eurocurrency
earlier in the chapter). The balances in London would of course
have their counterpart in the US, but would be in the name of the
London bank, not that of the East European bank. Therefore,
should cold war tension heighten, it would not be possible for the
US authorities to place a moratorium upon the use of such dollar
balances. Had they been on deposit in US domestic banks, then
naturally such a course of action would be open to them. Since
then there have been instances concerning dollars held in London
by Iran, contrasted with deposits held in the US which illustrate
the point well. Although attempts were made to freeze activity on
accounts in London by the US authorities, these were resisted.

The earliest deposits of Eurodollars seem to have been those in
the Moscow Narodny Bank in London and that of another USSR
owned bank in Paris.

While this may be so, it would be insufficient in itself to explain
the growth of the market. There must have been other factors
present to account for the size of deposits created by the credit
multiplier effect described earlier.

2.   Large US current account deficits

These occurred during the latter part of the 1950's. US current
account deficits meant an outflow of US dollars to pay for the
goods and services purchased abroad that created the deficit. US
dollars thus became owned by the exporters to the US. Foreign
holdings of US dollars increased the role of the US as a vehicle and
reserve currency. In short large sums of US dollars came to be held
on deposit outside the US. That they should be held outside the
US was for reasons which follow.

3. US Dollar and Other Currency Convertibility

In 1957 UK authorities placed restrictions on the use of sterling outside the UK in relation to financing. This reinforced the use of the US dollar described in 2 above, as it filled the vacuum created. UK banks thus began to take dollar deposits to on lend in place of the restricted use of sterling. In 1958 the foreign exchange restrictions left over from the immediate post-war period were eased in many countries in Western Europe. This meant that West European currencies when paid to non-Western Europeans for goods and services imported from them could now be freely converted. This created a more active market in foreign exchange and facilitated the use of the US$ for financing balance of payments purposes. In turn this encouraged dollar lending outside the US, creating further Eurodollars.

To a much lesser extent the process also applied to Deutchmarks, Swiss Francs and sterling itself later on. The dollar still remains the most important Eurocurrency, due to the very large size of the US economy. US dollar deposits also became large as a result of another factor:

4. Large OPEC Surpluses

These dollar deposits became larger as the price of oil, priced in US$, rose during the early and late 1970's. Eurodollar deposits, on lent, became the means by which the OPEC surpluses were re-cycled back to deficit countries to enable such deficits to be financed. The influence of such deposits on Eurocurrency growth should perhaps not be over-stated. Absence of such deposits in the late 1980s has not seen a decline in Eurocurrency.

5. Regulation Q of the US Banking System

This regulation prevented US banks located in the US, but not abroad, from paying interest on deposits above a given rate. When this given rate was below rates in the Euromarket, then funds would flow to the Euromarket. This situation would occur in circumstances as in the late 1960s, when due to a credit squeeze, interest rates rose. Due to the loss of domestic deposits at that time, US banks sourced their deposits from their foreign branches which had 'sufficient' Euro-deposits due to the interest rate effect. In fact this led the US authorities to limit borrowing in this way.

A separate, but similar effect occurred when quantitative controls were introduced on UK domestic lending during 1969 and 1970. In this instance UK firms borrowed unrestricted sterling and other currencies abroad to circumvent the controls. In response the authorities had to place restrictions on capital imports.

6.   Central Bank Regulation of Domestic Markets

Specific examples of such regulation are given in 5 above. As a general point banks in many countries were highly regulated in relation to deposits and lending conducted in their own domestic currency. In relation to US banks they had to hold non-interest bearing reserve balances related to the size of their deposits, as did German banks in the Federal Republic.

UK banks were subject to special and supplementary deposits at the Bank of England during the period of the 'corset'.

These regulations constitute a cost in that they prevent a larger number of deposits than would otherwise be the case, from being on lent. They also mean that lending rates, due to the higher cost must be higher and deposit rates must be lower than they would be in the Euromarkets. In other words, margins were much lower in the Euromarkets than in domestic markets due to:

7.   Lack of Regulation of Euromarkets by Central Banks

Larger proportions of deposits could be on lent, thus the credit creation multiplier could be larger, creating Eurocurrency growth. Naturally deposits would be attracted at higher rates than the equivalent domestic deposit rates and demand for lending would increase at lower rates.

Interest rates in both markets would still, it should be noted, be consistent with one another. If rates were to move up or down they would do so in both markets. Only the margin or spread would be different.

_____	domestic offer
_____	euro offer rate
_____	central rate
_____	euro bid rate
_____	domestic
	bid
	rate

margin or spread = difference between bid/deposit rate and offer/lending rate.

The slow down in the rate of growth in the Eurocurrency market – growth that has been just about static since the early 1980's – can perhaps be attributed to the fact that domestic markets have become increasingly deregulated, while the foreign currency activities of domestic banks have become increasingly regulated by domestic central banks. This has enabled domestic markets to compete on a much more equal footing. If reserve requirements and capital adequacy rules apply equally to domestic and foreign currency deposits and lending then spreads between bid and offer rates will tend to become the same. Indeed the process of arbitrage between the two markets tends to ensure that this is the case.

In this way it can perhaps be argued that the underlying rationale for the existence of the Eurocurrency market has been somewhat undermined, hence the classification by the BIS statistics to encompass the whole International Banking Market, of which the Euromarket is a part. The former of course includes lending or deposits in domestic currency by non-residents and therefore strictly not 'Euro'.

10.5   EUROCURRENCY INTEREST RATES AND FORWARD EXCHANGE RATES

Due to the presence of foreign exchange risk, or simply exchange or currency risk as it is often described, many exporters and importers use the forward market to hedge such risks and a link exists between Eurocurrency interest rates and the forward exchange rate.

Currency risk is the risk that one currency will change its value (rate) in relation to another such that unexpected losses or gains are made. As an example an exporter might decide to quote today a price to a German importer and the price to be quoted is DM100 000 for the consignment of goods in question.

This DM price was arrived at by using the current spot rate of £1=DM 2.75. This gives a sterling value, at this rate of £36,363.64 and is of course the expected return. However, it may take the German buyer say one month to decide to buy; delivery may take a further month and a credit period of a further month may be agreed. Thus between the date of quote and date of actually receiving the Deutschmarks three months will have elapsed.

Now when the exporter exchanges the Deutschmarks for sterling the rate might well be £1=DM 2.95 giving a rate of return of £33 898.31 only, £2465.33 less than expected, or alternatively just below 7 per cent less than expected. This 7 per cent might well represent the whole or a substantial proportion of the expected profit on the transaction.

Naturally, the rate may have moved in the exporter's favour instead of against. The point is, however, that neither the exporter, nor anyone else, can predict movements of exchange rates. Uncertain domestic currency values in instances like this are always going to be present. To charge the German buyer a sterling value is to pass the risk on to him, making a sale less likely, especially under highly competitive conditions.

To cover the 'open' position described above, the position can be 'covered' or 'hedged' by the exporter entering into a forward contract to sell the Deutschmarks at an agreed rate, at a time to coincide with their expected receipt. This agreed rate, the forward rate of exchange, is not someone's guess as to what the spot rate will be in the future. As outlined previously the forward rate is connected to Eurocurrency interest rates.

The bank with which the exporter makes the forward contract must itself hedge its position, otherwise it too will be exposed to currency risk. (It does not do this by entering into a forward contract with another party, the risk would always end up somewhere!) Firstly, the bank can match its position. It will be entering into contracts to both buy and sell specific currencies on or between specific dates. Therefore a certain amount of matching can always take place: contracts to buy can always be matched with contracts to sell. The currency obtained when they buy can be used to sell.

However, there will, always in practice be an unmatched position. Imagine that they have entered into contracts to buy US$1m on September 30th and entered into contracts to sell $1.5m on the same date. Clearly US$0.5m is unmatched – the bank has an obligation to sell US$0.5m more than it will have available. It can ensure that this sum is available when required by exchanging sterling today, when the contracts were entered into, at today's spot rate. These dollars can then be placed on deposit and earn interest. The dollars exchanged at spot plus the accrued interest should equal the sum required in the future, US$0.5m.

The question now arises – has it cost the bank or benefited the bank to do this – that is, would a greater return have been available by placing the sterling sum on deposit instead of the US$? To answer this question reference has to be made to the prevailing interest rates in the Euromarkets, for this is where the deposits would be made. If sterling were at higher interest rates than the US$, then clearly this represents a cost to the bank in that it has foregone a return in sterling better than that available in US$, so that exchange risk can be hedged in the way described. This cost represents the difference between sterling interest rates and US$ interest rates in the Eurocurrency market.

A calculation can be made to pass such costs (or benefits) onto all who enter into the forward contracts by an adjustment to the prevailing spot rate to give a forward rate. In the example quoted, where higher rates of interest were available in sterling, compared with the US$, then the forward rate would be lower than the spot on the day the contracts were entered into. The margins applied to the spot rate would be said to be at a premium, premium because it makes the US$ more expensive in terms of sterling to enable the cost to be passed on. From this it can be seen that the rate of exchange must fall to make the US$ more expensive. Premiums are therefore deducted from the spot rate.

Were matters the other way round, with sterling at lower interest rates than the US$, then the US$ would need to be quoted at a discount.

The basic principle is therefore:

> forward exchange rates are determined by interest rate differentials in the Eurocurrency market.

It should also be possible to visualise matters from the opposite perspective in that forward rates can determine the interest rates. In fact there is a constant interaction between the two in that both are markets where arbitrage ensures that forward rates and Eurocurrency interest rates are kept in alignment.

The following example illustrates this process. Suppose that interest rates in Italy are higher by 2 per cent than in the UK and at the same time the necessary discount applied to the spot rate were only 1 per cent. This would enable investors currently holding sterling to exchange into lire and place the resulting lire on deposit for 2 per cent extra. However, it must be remembered that to do this of itself would incur an exchange risk. If the investor were to return to sterling at some time in the future, the rate of exchange might be such that the extra interest earned would be completely eroded away. The risk that this might occur is why in general terms 'everybody' does not do this when interest rates are positioned in this way.

Knowing that it is possible to hedge by entering into a forward contract therefore seems to be the thing to do, in conjunction with the proposal just outlined. That is, exchange sterling to put lire on deposit. The forward contract would mature at the time when it was proposed to change back into sterling from lire.

If the discount applied to the lire were only 1 per cent as suggested above, then clearly it would be possible to gain over all by earning an extra 2 per cent on the lire deposit and accept that this would be reduced by 1 per cent as the cost of forward cover, making a 1 per cent gain overall in comparison with staying in sterling and importantly be fully hedged.

However, the above situation would tend to move both interest rate differentials and cost of cover together, so that they equalled one another. (This is a further reason why such arbitrage opportunities are available only rarely). In this instance interest rate and cost of forward cover parity would be restored by the following two processes:

1. There would be an increase in demand for lire so that the lire deposit could be made. This would make the spot rate fall and thus adjust the difference between spot rate and forward rate such that the cost of forward cover would increase. This effect would be further reinforced by the increase in demand for forward cover, thus pushing up its

cost. In these two ways the cost of cover would rise to approach that of the interest advantage.
2.   At the same time that the effects in 1. were being experienced, there would also be an interest rate effect.
Increased deposits would push deposit rates down.

The combined effect of the two should ensure that cost of forward cover, as reflected by the rates, fluctuates closely around the interest rate differential of the currencies concerned in the Euromarkets.

REFERENCE

Johnston, R.B. (1983) *The Economics of the Euro-Market* (Macmillan, London).

CHAPTER 11

THE STOCK EXCHANGE

11.0 INTRODUCTION

The Stock Exchange has undergone considerable change in the last decade, and this chapter attempts to analyse those changes with reference to the role of the Stock Exchange and overall efficiency. Topical subjects (particularly for the media) such as the cases of insider dealing uncovered, supervision of the Stock Exchange, and the crash of 1987 are all investigated.

11.1 THE ROLE OF THE STOCK EXCHANGE – PRIMARY AND SECONDARY MARKETS

The London International Stock Exchange (ISE) can, like all stock markets, be divided into two sections, the primary market and the secondary market. The primary market is involved with the raising of new financial claims, whereas the secondary market is involved with the buying and selling of 'second-hand' or already existing financial claims. The secondary market is by far the larger of the two markets.

While the functions of the primary and secondary markets differ it is no accident that the financial institutions participating in them are often the same, because an efficient secondary market, in which existing securities can be bought or sold easily, contributes in several important ways to the strength of the primary market.

The secondary market provides investors with *liquidity*, the ability to turn securities into cash if required, which makes it reasonable for many savers to hold long-term assets. Increased liquidity for investors provided by the Stock Exchange means that investors will accept lower returns for long-term investments than if the exchange did not exist. The Stock Exchange thus reduces the *cost of capital* to companies.

The Stock Exchange is an *information centre*. Companies are constantly being valued by investors and analysts. The Stock Exchange disseminates information, and reflects it in the *share price*. Profitable companies will be valued highly, and this should be reflected in the share price, and in the terms on which the company can raise funds. The cost or price of borrowing or lending is thus set in the capital market. As capital is a scarce resource, it is important that information on a company gives a fair and accurate view of its prospects, such that resources (capital) are *allocated efficiently*.

The secondary market helps new issues get underway in the primary market and therefore provides capital for growing companies. The secondary market helps the primary market in the *pricing of new issues*. The price of a firm's shares will depend upon the prices of *similar securities* at the time the issue is made. An active secondary market in which shareholders who have access to information about the company and are able to deal freely, will lead to share prices *accurately reflecting the companies prospects* and in turn the *accurate pricing of new issues*. This continuous appraisal helps to determine the prices at which securities are traded and makes it much easier for the institutional investors to reach a swift decision when they are invited to subscribe to or underwrite a new issue. In the absence of the secondary market the time required to raise new capital would be prolonged and the costs involved increased.

The secondary market contributes to the primary market by enabling a wide range of institutions to participate in *underwriting* new issues. The underwriter has to take up shares if called upon to do so, and for this has to be able to obtain the necessary funds. While most institutions can rely on borrowing for short periods, the risk associated with underwriting would be greatly increased if institutions were unable to dispose of their existing assets quickly to provide cash (or repay short-term borrowing) should it prove necessary.

The stock market also provides a price guide to the value of a company that can be used for transferral of ownership in the form of a takeover.

Market capitalisation of domestic equities listed throughout the world stood at £6 551 billion in 1989, with European stock exchanges representing 23.1 per cent of the market capitalisation, and the ISE accounting for 30 per cent of European domestic equity capitalisation (the largest proportion of any European country).The ISE is the foremost market in international equities with over 65 per cent of trades. It also has the largest number of overseas companies listed.

The ISE has three tiers, the main market (Official List) of over 2000 domestic companies with a market value of approximately £500 billion; the Unlisted Securities Market (USM) established in 1980 to allow smaller companies that might find the costs of full listing prohibitive the chance to raise capital, with over 450 companies valued at around £9 billion; and around seventy companies on the Third market with capitalisation of £0.6 billion. The Third market closed however at the end of 1990. A variety of EC directives have meant that the listing requirements for the Third market are now very similar to those of the USM and there was no clear rationale for them to be kept separate. Some companies will transfer from the Third market to the USM, some will go to the over-the-counter market (OTC), which is an informal market that consists of trading in small business shares by a group of brokers and licensed dealers to the public.

11.2   BIG BANG

Concern had been voiced for some time by the Office of Fair Trading (OFT) as to the restrictive practices maintained by the Stock Exchange:

1. the operation of the single capacity system,
2. prohibitive membership policies creating barriers to entry to both domestic and foreign companies, and hence reduced competition in the market.
3. minimum commissions offered by brokers which limited price competition.

With the system of single capacity, jobbers were 'principals' and dealt only with brokers, not the general public. They made their profits through the spread between their buying and selling prices. Conversely, brokers could not act as jobbers (and thus had 'single' capacity) and their role was to find the best price from the jobbers for their customers. Single capacity was supposed to reduce conflicts of interest as brokers found the best prices from jobbers for their clients and jobbers competed amongst each other to produce fair prices. It was also thought that jobbers would stabilise prices through their short-term speculative activities.

One of the main problems of the single capacity system was that there were pockets of less actively traded shares that jobbers refused to make a market in. For some shares therefore the deals were often done on a matched basis. One of the problems of some shares being illiquid is that they may be incorrectly priced (i.e. the market may exhibit pockets of inefficiency). Jobbers were supposed to quote buy and sell prices without knowing whether or not the brokers wished to buy or sell (i.e. the direction of the deal). The 1970s and 1980s saw large increases in turnover and in the average size of transaction, which meant greater risks for the jobbers who often wanted to know the direction of the deal before quoting a price.

The 1970s and 1980s also saw the rise of institutional shareholders who often acted on similar information and hence took similar buy or sell decisions. Jobbers often faced one-way markets in which they would either have to buy a greater number of shares than they had sold (go 'long') or they had bought (go 'short'). Both these positions entail a great deal of risk; going long produces the possibility of capital losses on the shares held, going short produces the possibility that the jobber may have to buy in the shares at a future date at expensive prices.

It was felt by many that jobbers were too small and hence under-capitalised in relation to the above risks, and that an injection of capital was needed. The most obvious way of doing this was to allow outside membership.

Under the old Stock Exchange system, membership was through personal partnerships, generally with low capitalisation. Low capitalisation tended to be a factor in stifling competition, as firms were not willing to compete on price terms if they did not have the capital backing. Competition was restricted by member firms by maintaining a minimum commission system.

Some more far-sighted members feared that the restrictive practices of the ISE meant that business was being lost to overseas exchanges, and changes were required. Stock Exchange members were also concerned that their restrictive practices were leading to a loss of business in international equities, with over 60 per cent of business being transacted outside the exchange. Particularly important were American Depository Receipts (ADRs) whereby British shares can be traded by US investors without paying British Stamp Duty, and which completely by-passed the ISE.

In 1976 the ISE was referred to the Restrictive Practices Court. The ISE abolished minimum commissions at the end of 1986 in a deal with the Government in return for withdrawing the referral to the Restrictive Practices Court.

There were three main changes in the ISE in the Big Bang:

1. Corporate members (both domestic and foreign) were admitted to the Stock Exchange.
2. Abolition of minimum commissions.
3. Abolition of single capacity (dual capacity introduced).

Many banks were keen to move into Stock Exchange activities in order to capture some of the business they were losing through disintermediation. By 1985 nearly all the main broking firms and jobbers had linked up with financial institutions, both domestic and foreign.

Under dual capacity a member firm can act as both agent and principal whereas previously jobbers and brokers were separated. Instead of jobbers quoting buy and sell prices verbally on the market floor, quotes are now displayed electronically on screens by 'market makers'. Market makers quote continuous two-way prices for shares in which they deal. There were fears that the advent of dual capacity would produce conflicts of interest, and certain technical changes were made to the mechanics of trading. A trade can only be carried out within one firm if the market maker of that firm offers a price at least as good or better than that offered on the general market. This stops a firm from channelling its business through its own market makers. There is also continuous recording of all deals so that they can be checked if necessary.

Equity inter-dealer brokers provide a service for market makers to deal with each other, largely to keep large transactions between market makers hidden from the market by non-disclosure of the participants names.

Large integrated securities houses were thought to be necessary as an average size broker without a market-maker could feasibly find itself advising on equities, yet the business of transactions could easily be carried out elsewhere. Medium sized firms would thus have difficulty keeping institutional investors' business.

11.3   PERFORMANCE SINCE BIG BANG: ISSUE COSTS

The structure, conduct and performance of the ISE are of importance because they affect the degree of competition in the market, and hence on the costs to investors and borrowers. It must be recognised that if the Stock Exchange is perceived as being an expensive form of raising finance and/or of investing relative to other forms (or relative to overseas stock markets) then the Exchange is likely to lose business. Moreover, any monopoly tendencies in the market will tend to increase transactions costs and lead to an inefficient mechanism of channelling funds from savers to borrowers.

The costs of a new issue provide a good guide to the advantages of the Stock Exchange and to whether or not it is an efficient method of raising funds for firms in terms of costs. The two principal methods of flotation (Initial Public Offer as opposed to a further offer or rights issue) on the ISE are through (i) an offer for sale or (ii) a placing, although within these main methods there are some technical variations.

In an offer for sale a fixed price is set for the shares to be offered to the public by an issuing house for the company concerned. The issuing house will underwrite the issue (i.e. agree to buy up any unsold shares) for a fee, and will generally pass on some of the risk to sub-underwriters, who are usually large institutional investors. In this way the company is guaranteed that its shares will be sold at a certain price, whatever the prevailing market conditions. In an offer for sale *by tender*, there is no fixed issue price, but investors are invited to bid or 'tender' prices for the shares. A final price (striking price) is chosen at which all the shares will be sold (even those tendering higher prices for the shares will only have to pay the striking price).

In a placing the issuing house buys the shares from the issuing company, and 'places' them with investors, mainly institutional investors (although if the placing is for more than £2 million, then a quarter of the issue has to be sold to the public).Privatisations, because of the large size of funds involved, have tended to include elements of both offer for sale and placings.

Table 11.1 shows that £24 billion of equity has been raised (both new equity and to existing shareholders) between 1985 – 1989, the majority in privatisations with £16.6 billion, with the largest single method being offer for sale at £5.8 billion.

Placings were the most popular method of issue over 1985–89, although the average size at £6m was considerably smaller than offers for sale and tenders at £62.3 and £32.8 million respectively, reflecting the fact that smaller companies tend to go for placings as

Table 11.1 *Total Sums [a] raised via Initial Public Offers (£m)*

Year	Offer for Sale	Tenders	Placings	Privatisa-tions	Total
1985	603	103	8	–	714
1986	2375[b]	258	70	5434	8138
1987	1021	–	271	3488	4779
1988	643	–	296	2500	3439
1989	1213[c]	–	80	5239	6532
1985–89	5855	361	725	16661	23603

(a) Includes sums for existing shareholders.
(b) Includes £1.5 billion flotation of TSB which was not strictly a privatisation as the funds were kept by TSB rather than the Government.
(c) Includes Abbey National flotation (£975 million).

Source: Bank of England Quarterly Bulletin (May 1990)

Table 11.2   *Initial Public Offers 1985–9*

Method	No.	Size of Issue (£m) Mean	Median
Offers for Sale	94	62.3	11.4
Tenders	11	32.8	12.2
Placings	120	6.0	5.3
Privatisations	15	1110.7	848.8

Source: Bank of England Quarterly Bulletin, May 1990

they tend to be cheaper (see Table 11.2) and placings have also become more popular as a result of the requirements for the size of company using a placing being relaxed after Big Bang.

For small issues placings tend to be cheaper and faster than offers for sale, (about $11\frac{1}{2}$ per cent of the funds raised for less than £5m as opposed to 14 per cent for offers for sale) largely as a result of savings in advertising and preparing an offer document, and

Table 11.3   *Direct Costs of Initial Public Offers (£m)*

	1985–89 Number	Costs as a % of Funds Raised
Up to £5m raised:		
Offers for sale	13	13.8
Placings	60	11.4
£5–£10m raised:		
Offers for Sale	32	10.1
Placings	42	7.7
More than £10m raised:		
Offers for Sale	56	6.9
Placings	18	5.9

Source: Bank of England Quarterly Bulletin, May 1990
(amended)

because of underwriting costs in offers for sale at about 2 per cent of funds raised.It is also important to recognise that indirect costs of issue exist in terms of the final issue price being below what the market might have been willing to pay for all of the shares (and hence the company receiving less funds than it might otherwise have done). Research has shown that in general, discounts are higher in placings than offers for sale, and that the timing of issue is important, with 1987 being a 'hot' issue period when share prices rose extremely fast and when discounts were high (around 30 per cent at times). Indeed, the large number of placings and the large discounts in that year may have been the reason as to why placings have had higher discounts than offers for sale, on average.

Companies can of course sell their shares directly to the public but this is likely to prove a costly and risky exercise. How are the

Table 11.4 *Admission Requirements to ISE Markets*

	Official List	*U.S.M.*	*Third Market*[a]
Minimum Market Capitalisation (£000)	700	–	–
Minimum Trading Record (yrs)	3	2[b]	1[b]
Minimum Proportion of Shares held Publicly (%)[c]	25	10	–

[a] No companies have been allowed to join the Third Market since January 1990, and it closed at the end of 1990.

[b] Waived for some Greenfield Projects.

[c] The public is defined as excluding directors, connected persons, and larger shareholders (i.e. those holding more than 5 per cent of the company's equity).

Source: *Bank of England Quarterly Bulletin* (May 1990)

shares to be distributed? What if they are not all sold? The responsibility of the issuing house (usually one of the main merchant banks, a member of the Accepting Houses Association) is to ensure *all* the funds are raised, and as cheaply and efficiently as possible, with a minimum degree of risk to the company.

The ISE at the time of writing is attempting to implement changes in the way in which shares are floated. Criticisms have been made that the present system excludes private shareholders. Under the new arrangements there would be an 'intermediaries offer' to increase the distribution of new shares by giving private clients priority when they applied for the 25 per cent of the issue that is not distributed by the sponsor in a placing. These changes are likely to be in place in 1991.

11.4   PERFORMANCE SINCE BIG BANG: BREADTH AND DEPTH

The 'quality' of a stock market can be measured according to 'depth' and 'breadth'. Depth relates to the ability to absorb large buy and sell orders with only small movements in price, i.e. for share prices to fluctuate only marginally as a result of large trades. 'Breadth' relates to the composition of investors and their expectations, and a market is said to have breadth if there is a variety of investors with different expectations as to future prices.

It has recently been recognised that there have been considerable liquidity problems both before and after Big Bang for some of the smaller companies listed on the ISE, prompting some calls for a two-tier market. It is argued that the breadth and depth of the market in small company shares is suffering, particularly as the volume of trading in smaller company shares has dropped since the crash of October 1987 as investors have fled to blue chip shares, and the number of brokers cutting back on their small firms business has increased.

At the present time, the illiquidity of gamma stocks means that it is difficult to make a market in them, and also brokers find that they cannot buy or sell without prices swinging widely in reaction. Improvement in the gamma stocks' liquidity and in the market mechanisms for smaller shares are required, or firms will leave the stock market in disillusion. If gamma shares are not liquid and tradeable, then pricing efficiency will be extremely poor.

Private client broking firms have set up their own trade body in response to fears that the ISE is ignoring small customers in favour of institutional investors and international equities (Association of Private Client Investment Managers and Stockbrokers (AP-CIMS)). David Jones of Sharelink has proposed an order-driven system for small value share transactions which would be displayed on investors' TV screens at home instead of on TOPIC. An order-driven system is one in which prices at which buyers and sellers are prepared to deal are displayed (the existing system is quote driven). John Redwood, the Corporate Affairs Minister, has supported the idea of a new order-driven market for private investors and smaller companies to complement the ISE.

The ISE is sceptical of these developments, although critics of the ISE argue that it is only interested in large companies and particularly in developing the international equity market at the expense of smaller domestic equities. The ISE is aiming at creating a Single European Market in the top 200 international equities in cooperation with European exchanges, with one price mechanism (centred in London, the ISE hopes), although plans are at an early stage.

Rival small company market(s) could develop along the above lines and would provide a considerable degree of competition to the ISE. Any new share market would have to be authorised by the Securities and Investments Board (SIB) as a Recognised Investment Exchange (RIE).

11.5 PERFORMANCE SINCE BIG BANG: SPREADS AND TURNOVER

Operational efficiency within the ISE is reflected in the costs investors incur in carrying out transactions, the main ones being commission to brokers and the spread (the difference between the market makers' buying and selling prices). Any collusion amongst member firms (implicit or explicit) in relation to commissions is likely to produce operational inefficiencies. One of the main arguments for Big Bang was that the abolition of the minimum commission system would result in competition and hence a reduction in commissions and overall transactions costs for investors.

There were some fears however that only a small number of member firms would survive, and the concentration of business amongst a few firms would lead to higher transactions costs and hence lower turnover and liquidity. It was also feared that the market maker system might be by-passed by large powerful institutional investors doing negotiated deals with member firms who carry out the trades in-house rather than through market-makers. If this were to occur the pricing efficiency of the market would worsen. It was also argued that costs for small investors would rise.

The costs of market-making to the investor are reflected in the bid-offer spread (turn), the difference between what the market maker will buy and sell at. The narrower is this spread, the greater will be the operational efficiency of the market. With the increased number of market-makers after Big Bang it would be expected that spreads and commissions would fall,

'In general, a move from oligopoly to competition, from high, cartel-determined charges, commission and rates to fierce competition in rate and price setting should be welcomed'.

Goodhart (1987)

Average rates of commission have tended to fall for all clients, but particularly for institutions (see Figure 11.1). Although average rates of commission continue to fall, the minimum commission has tended to rise to around £20–£30, compared with about £10 before Big Bang, showing the extent to which the small investor has lost out.

From Figure 11.2 it can be seen that touches, the difference between best bid and best offer price, almost doubled after the crash of 1987. The touch in Alphas [1] returned to 1987 levels by the end of 1988, although the touches in Betas and Gammas remained somewhat higher than their previous levels. Touches rose again in response to the mini-crash of October 1989 and are somewhat above touches immediately post Big Bang. At June 1990, the average spread in Alphas was 1.9 per cent, 5.1 per cent in Betas, and 8.5 per cent in Gammas (Table 11.5).

Figure 11.1 *Commission Rates 1980–9*

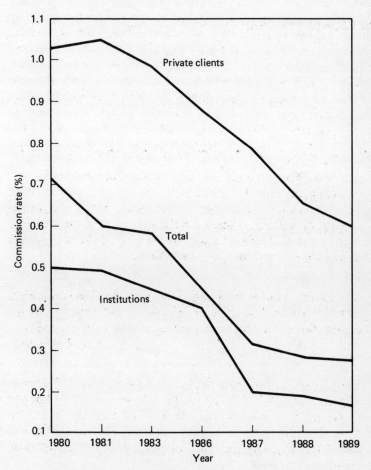

Source: Quality of Markets Quarterly Review, April–June 1990

Turnover rose by about 20–30 per cent p.a. between 1980 and mid 1987 although within this period turnover at times fluctuated by as much as 40 per cent year-on-year. The dramatic fall in turnover can clearly be seen in Figure 11.3, and it is noticeable that turnover had not reached pre-crash levels by the end of 1989.

Table 11.6 shows the entry and exit of market makers in UK equities. The number of participants leaving the market since

Figure 11.2   *Average Best Touch 1987–9*

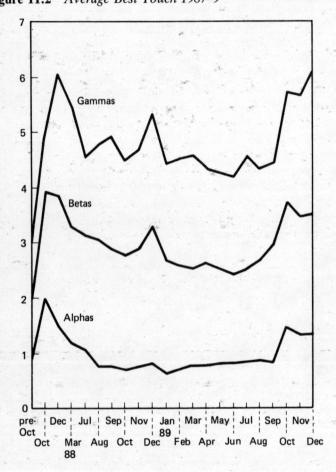

Source: *Quality of Markets Quarterly Review*, April–June 1990

August 1988 (11 firms) with only one firm entering shows the difficult market conditions firms are facing.

Member firms became profitable again in 1989 after heavy losses following the crash of 1987. Pre-tax profits were £503 million in 1989 (see Table 11.7), although at 16 per cent return on capital employed this is an extremely poor performance.

Table 11.5   *Average Spreads*

July	Average	Gammas	5.6%
1988	Spread	Betas	4.0%
		Alphas	1.7%
July	Average	Gammas	5.7%
1989	Spread	Betas	3.5%
		Alphas	1.3%
July	Average	Gammas	8.5%
1990	Spread	Betas	5.1%
		Alphas	1.9%

Source: *Quality of Markets Quarterly Review*, April–June 1990

Table 11.6   *History of UK Equity Market Makers*

Date	New Market Makers	Market Makers Leaving	Balance
27/10/86			32
26/01/87	Guidehouse		33
17/03/87		Greenwell Montagu	32
26/05/87	Morgan Stanley		33
28/07/87	Madoff Securities		34
24/08/87	Nomura Securities		35
20/11/87		Jacobson Townsley	34
08/4/88		Wood Mackenzie	33
20/6/88	SGST Securities		34
01/08/88	Winterflood Sec.		35
14/10/88		Deltec Securities	34
29/11/88		Madoff Securities	33
06/12/88		Morgan Grenfell	32
06/01/89		Chase Manhatten	31
21/04/89		Drexel Burnham Lambert	30
25/05/89		Credit Suisse Buckmaster	29
21/08/89	Prudential-Bache		30
29/09/89		Jenkins (S.) & Son	29
15/11/89		Anstock	28
24/11/89		Laing & Cruickshank	27
08/01/90		Schroder Securities	26
07/06/90		Stock Beech & Co.	25

Source: *Quality of Markets Quarterly Review*, April–June 1990

Figure 11.3   *UK Equity Average Daily Turnover Customer Business 1965–89*

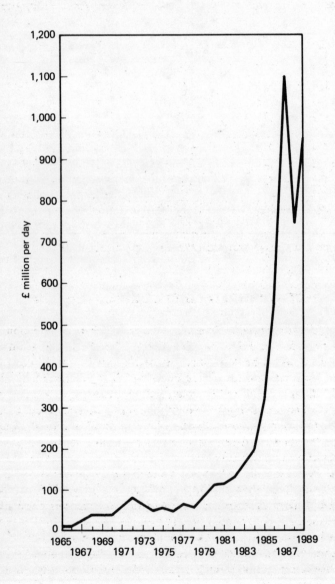

Table 11.7 *Financial Results of all ISE Member Firms (£m)*

	Revenue	Expenditure	Profit Before Tax	Capital Employed
1987 Q1	698	538	160	–
Q2	768	619	149	–
Q3	728	695	33	–
Q4	332	701	(369)	–
1988 Q1	583	524	59	–
Q2	626	606	20	–
Q3	434	582	(148)	3250
Q4	437	633	(196)	3071
1989 Q1	781	639	142	3306
Q2	828	714	114	3808
Q3	923	759	164	3810
Q4	896	813	83	4001

Source: *Quality of Markets Quarterly*, April–June 1990

11.6 RECENT DEVELOPMENTS: DEALING CHANGES

The ISE's Special Committee on Market Development recommended in July 1990 that the Alpha, Beta and Gamma classifications on SEAQ should be replaced with a new measure called Normal Market Size (NMS) which is calculated by the stock's liquidity and trading volume. It also recommended that all equity transactions should be published immediately, except those larger than the value of NMS, whereby publication will occur within 90 minutes. A central limit order system was also proposed (CLOSE).

CLOSE is a limit order system which allows investors to leave orders which are then publicised in the market, e.g. if an investor wanted British Aerospace at £5.00 when the market price was £5.08 the limit order could be left with the investors' broker, and other brokers could see it. CLOSE allows buy and sell orders to be matched at a price which both parties are seeking. An investor can wait for a transaction to match their order by placing it within the limit order system.

The aims of the Committee are to improve the quality of the market by reducing dealing costs in small transactions and by greater 'visibility' or transparency of all deals. The old SEAQ classification did not adequately show the liquidity or quality of the shares, and were a poor guide therefore to marketability. The 90 minute lapse on large trades has been brought in largely because of smaller volumes and because market makers maintained that large trades would be almost impossible with instant publication.

SAEF (SEAQ Automatic Execution Facility) was introduced to speed up small orders in well known shares in 1989. Small orders for main equities are entered into the SAEF terminal by the broker and the transaction is carried out on the best price available on SEAQ.

11.7 SETTLEMENT PROCEDURES

Problems have tended to occur in the settlement of transactions. The ISE still has a paper-based system (in contrast to America and Japan which have electronic systems) that at times (e.g. the 1987 bull market) has been close to collapse. At several times the backlog of unsettled trades has exceeded £5 billion. Figure 11.4 shows the complicated web of paper transfers that go to make up a transaction. A computerised paperless system called TAURUS has been suggested.

The implementation of TAURUS (Transfer and Automated Registration of Uncertified Stock) is a computerised share settlement system that should initially be in place for October 1991, with 'rolling settlement' (a change from the traditional two week account period to a three to five day rolling system) by October 1992. The objective behind TAURUS is to eliminate the need for share certificates and transfer forms, or 'dematerialisation' of the paper-based system. Shares will be electronically transferred from the sellers account to the new investor's account, accounts being kept with an account controller, probably a broker or bank. A disadvantage of moving to a rolling system is that investors will not be able to buy and sell shares within the account period without paying, as happens at present.The rolling system and TAURUS will, however, reduce the settlement delay, and concomitant risks of non-settlement, which were very real in the back-log of unsettled deals after Big Bang. The objectives of TAURUS are to reduce settlement risks, reduce costs, move towards international settlement, and to boost the Government's desire for wider share ownership (Watson 1990).

To enhance the globalisation of securities markets an international body known as the Group of Thirty has made recommendations to improve clearance and settlement of securities transactions on an international scale. The problems identified included incompatibility of systems for matching domestic and international transactions, differences in settlement times, no general requirement for settlement to be made in cash, and excessive amounts of paperwork in settlement procedures.

Recommendations included a trade matching system to which all institutional members should be members by 1992, confirmation and matching of trades one day after the transaction, dematerialisation of share certificates, a delivery-against-payment system by 1992, three-day rolling settlement by 1992, and the ability to borrow and lend securities, which helps in breaking a line of unsettled bargains. These recommendations, if they can be fully implemented, should go some way to increasing the globalisation of securities markets by smoothing out problems in world clearance and settlement systems.

The Stock Exchange has been criticised for anti-competitive practices in relation to market sensitive information. Sir Gordon Borrie, the Director General of Fair Trading, argued that the ISE had used its privileged position as the collector of information for regulatory purposes to dominate the news market through TOPIC. The ISE has plans for a regulatory news service which will sell information to other news services, but Sir Gordon has criticised the high costs of the service to outside competitors.

11.8 THE 1987 CRASH AND MARKET EFFICIENCY

It is important for the economy as a whole that the capital market is allocatively efficient, i.e. that 'scarce' funds are channelled towards the most productive companies. The capital market therefore needs to be efficient in terms of accurately pricing the shares of companies according to their future prospects, i.e. the

Figure 11.4 *Settlement Procedure (stylised)*

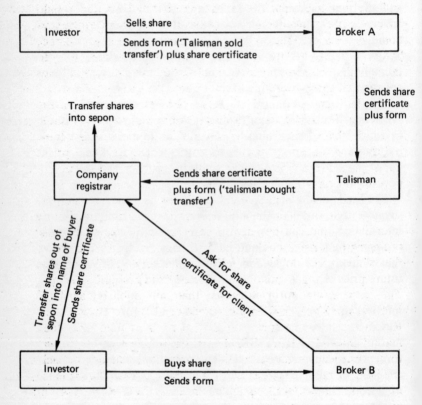

Talisman = Transfer Accounting Lodgement for Investors/Stock Market for Principles
Talisman is the ISE settlement office.
Sepon = Stock Exchange Pool Nominee (an account for holding shares)

present value of the future stream of dividends that the companies will produce. If shares are priced accurately then the market will be allocatively efficient in terms of channelling funds towards those companies that are the most productive. The share price of a company affects its ability to raise further funds, and is therefore an important element in the cost of capital for a company.

Is the Stock Market efficient and what are the implications of the crash of 1987 for market efficiency?

The crash was initially started by fears of trade and fiscal deficits in the USA, apparent disagreement over the Louvre agreement, and the announcement of tax changes in the USA that would adversely affect takeovers. What does this say about efficiency? Some would argue that the real problem lies in the fact that shares had been overvalued for some time, and that prices were likely to fall, and that the above events provided the impetus. It would thus appear that shares were incorrectly priced.

The Efficient Market Hypothesis (EMH) relates to *pricing* efficiency. The EMH states that an efficient capital market is one in which share prices always fully reflect all publicly available information concerning those securities. Therefore share prices adjust instantaneously and in an unbiased manner to any piece of new information released to the market.

The EMH can be analysed at *three* levels. The *'weak'* form test suggests that share price data relating to the past contains no information that can be used to earn profits in excess of those produced by a naïve buy and hold strategy. Research has shown that share prices do indeed follow a *'random walk'*, such that future price changes cannot be predicted from past price changes. The *semi-strong* form suggests that all publicly available information is fully and instantaneously reflected in share prices. Research has shown that over long periods of time, the stock market does tend to exhibit semi-strong efficiency. The *strong* form of efficiency states that *all* information, whether publicly available or not, is taken account of in share prices. The evidence of recent *insider dealer* scandals refutes the strong form of efficiency.

Thus research tends to show that the Stock Exchange exhibits weak and semi-strong forms of efficiency. Under the EMH the price of a share is the present value of expected future dividends (the 'market fundamentals' solution) (Bank of England 1988). The greater the return to shareholders the more attractive it will be to invest in the company and hence the higher the valuation of the company in the view of the Stock Exchange. Maximisation of shareholder wealth is synonymous with maximising the market (Stock market) value of the company.

An extreme view opposing the 'market fundamentals' or 'true-value' approach is that which argues that it makes no sense to talk about an inherent value of a share. Share prices are determined by supply and demand and anticipatory and speculative factors, and the expected earnings of a company are only one of a number of factors which influence investors.

Stock prices may be subject to '*speculative bubbles*' whereby the actual price drifts away from the price warranted on fundamental grounds. It has been suggested that such a speculative bubble may have been responsible for the rapid rise in equity prices in 1987. This suggests that the fall in equity prices in October 1987 may have been no more than a *correction* to the market. It could be argued that the sharp fall in share prices, perhaps as a result of a 'speculative bubble' suggests that, at times, the Stock Exchange is *not* efficient. This may represent an *anomaly* in what is otherwise an efficient market. It does *not* suggest that the EMH is invalid, but that the market shows long-run efficiency, combined with short-run anomalous indicators of temporary inefficiency, that tend to be self-correcting. In other words, the fact that the 'speculative bubble' existed at all suggests possible short-term inefficiency, but the '*correction*' could suggest that markets are, in the long term, efficient.

The markets' valuation of the future dividend flow will also depend upon the relative attractiveness of *alternative investments*. If it is assumed that the alternative to investing in equity is to invest in bonds, then, in the long run, it would be expected that the returns to these two investments would be equal after allowing for risk differentials. There has been a reasonably stable relationship between equity earnings yields and real bond yields in the UK for much of the 1980's. Given the higher risk associated with equity, a *positive yield gap* (i.e. with earnings yield greater than the bond yield) would be expected. However, in the period before 19th October the yield gap had become significantly *negative* and for the earnings yield to rise back to parity with the bond yield a significant fall in equity prices was needed.

The advent of Modern Portfolio Theory (see Chapter 7) may be beneficial to the efficient working of the stock market. Core holdings in large blue-chip companies that are infrequently traded provide them with a solid investor base and reduces share price volatility, whilst active trading and analysis of smaller company shares adds to the liquidity and marketability of these securities, and ensures accurate pricing.

The question as to whether or not the market has become more volatile (and if it has, why?) since the Big Bang and the crash has not been entirely answered. It appears that Big Bang had no effect on volatility prior to 'Black Monday', but that volatility has increased since then (Pope et al 1990). In other words, Big Bang was not responsible for the increase in volatility since the crash.

There is widespread concern about the effects of the financial futures market on the equity market. At times arbitrage across the markets has caused extreme volatility on the Stock Exchange, and there has also been accusations of manipulation of equity prices to enable arbitrageurs to sort out their arbitrage positions. In July 1990, for example, many arbitrageurs who had written futures contracts to buy FTSE 100 Index futures found that they were short of the FTSE contract close to the expiry deadline, and so attempted to reduce share prices to reduce the value of the index. Some market makers quoted offer prices of shares in the index lower than bid prices, the opposite of normal market practice, and there were accusations that some market makers did not answer their phones, so that quotes were not accurate. An investigation by the Stock Exchange found that no malpractice occurred, however. With the increasing growth of the futures market though, it is likely that such problems will occur again.

There has been some suggestion that computer trading techniques have been partly responsible for the crash (or what is called programme trading). There are two types of programme trading – index arbitrage and portfolio insurance. Index arbitrage is used to gain risk-free profits from short-term differences in the price of the index futures and the underlying shares. If, for example, the stock-index futures fall below the prices of the underlying securities, a sample of shares repesenting the index are sold, and relatively cheap stock-index futures are bought. The position can be unwound once the two prices move together (which they will, given this type of arbitrage) by buying the shares and selling the futures, the profit coming from the discount at which the futures were originally bought (minus transactions costs).

With portfolio insurance the objective of the institutional investor or fund manager is to maintain the value of a portfolio. When the market is falling, futures are sold, and if the market continues to fall, the position can be unwound by buying in the futures contracts and making profits on them, which are used to offset losses on the value of the share portfolio.

The problem with the stock market crash was that index arbitrage and portfolio insurance had the effect of feeding off each other and driving down share prices. With prices falling, the stock index futures were below underlying share prices so index arbitrageurs sold shares and bought futures. As shares were being sold this drove their price down, so portfolio insurers sold futures to protect the value of their portfolios. This set up the next cycle by index arbitrageurs, and so on.

The importance of computers is that these arbitrage opportunities can be quickly spotted and capitalised upon. A fund manager could carry out all of the above deals without a computer programme needed, although it would be much slower. The problem thus does not lie with computers and computer trading but in the link between the futures and equity markets.

11.9   STOCK MARKET REGULATION

The Self-Regulatory Organisation (SRO) for the International Stock Exchange is The Securities Association (TSA). The International Stock Exchange is a Recognised Investment Exchange (RIE) which means it is authorised by the Securities and Investments Board (SIB) as an exchange for the trading of securities. The TSA authorises firms to deal in gilts, domestic and foreign equities, fixed interest stocks, international bonds and Eurobonds, financial futures, options and private client advice and management of investments.

The three main problems that affect investors' confidence in the stock market are market manipulation (as in the Guinness affair), insider dealing (Geoffrey Collier, Ivan Boesky), and investment fraud (Barlow Clowes, Dunsdale), all of which are supposed to be eliminated (or at least limited) under the investor protection rules of the Financial Services Act 1986.

One aim of securities market regulation is to ensure that operations in the markets are conducted under transparent rules relating to information on fees, commissions and prices.

11.10 INSIDER DEALING

Insider dealing has been a criminal offence since 1980 under the Companies Act 1980. The Company Securities (Insider Dealing) Act 1985 re-enacts the earlier legislation and specifically defines insider dealing which is when an individual knowingly transacts in a security whilst in possession of unpublished price sensitive information relating to that security. The FSA 1986 gives wide powers to the Secretary of State to investigate insider trading, including seizing of documents, inspection of bank accounts, and the ability to demand witnesses to appear.

At the time of writing the Stock Exchange has passed on 185 cases of suspected insider trading to the Department of Trade and Industry since 1980, of which there have been only twenty-two prosecutions and twelve convictions. This hardly inspires confidence in the system, and emphasises the problem of actually proving that inside information was used, or showing when information stops being 'unpublished' and is widely known about. Contrary to popular belief, it is reported that over half of suspected insider traders are members of the public, which places some doubt on the common perception of city fraudsters being involved in the majority of cases (Quality of Markets Quarterly Review April-June 1990).

Insider dealing can be viewed as a tax on dealing in equities (King and Roell 1988). Market makers are often faced with losses because of insider dealing, and will tend to widen bid-ask spreads for fear of being 'hit'. The costs will thus tend to be passed on to investors. Insider trading may also lead to a significant loss of confidence in the Stock Exchange, particularly amongst small investors. Also, some of the profits of companies attempting a takeover may be captured by insiders, and the acquiring company may find it more difficult to buy up shares in the target company as a result of insider dealing.

One of the most common forms of insider dealing, and probably one of the most difficult to detect and bring to court is the share dealing ring. This is an agreement amongst staff at securities houses who have access to price sensitive information to pool their resources and information in order to profit from insider trading. They are difficult to investigate as the ones carrying out the dealing are obviously not the ones who have access to the inside information. A further technique is known as front-running. This is where shares are bought in advance of a large transaction that is known about and that will push up the price. It is thought that there has been some element of a share dealing ring in the Dunsdale case.

It must be noted, however, that the Exchange deals in thousands of transactions each hour, and instances of malpractice must be viewed against both this high-volume background and the importance of the Exchange to the funding of industry. In general, investors have not been subject to particularly extensive instances where malpractice has damaged the value of their investments.

The detection of insider dealing has increased (although the conviction rate is still poor), and this is likely to be a reflection of better channels of detection rather than any upsurge in the problem as previously it was not a criminal offence (and in some circles was regarded as a perk of the job).

Insider dealing legislation was strenthened by the FSA, with it being illegal from 1980. Inspectors are empowered by the Secretary of State to question people and demand to inspect documents. Non-cooperation is treated as contempt of court. There is a considerable amount of cooperation by regulators internationally on insider dealing (which is a necessity, given the often international aspect of the insider activity), and particularly between the UK and USA.

One controversial practice that the TSA has allowed to continue is 'softing' or soft commissions.

Soft commissions are payments in the form of portfolio valuation, computer hardware and software, to fund managers by brokers in return for a certain amount of business each year. Cash payments are not allowed. Warburg, for example, refunds 83 per cent of its commission to fund managers in the form of soft commissions (August 1990). There is an argument however that soft commissions may increase the practice of 'churning' (see Chapter 13).

11.11 PRUDENTIAL REGULATION

Like any financial business, Stock Exchange members are subject to prudential regulation. Adequate capital has to be maintained, of which there are three main types. The risks of a fall in profitability are covered by base capital (25 per cent of a firm's annual costs), whilst position capital is held to protect against large falls in share prices in those shares held. The more volatile the shares, the greater the capital requirement which has a corollary with risk weighted assets for banks – the greater the riskiness of the assets, the greater the capital requirement and counterparty capital is used to cover any problems that might occur during settlement procedures.

'Bought deals' are becoming increasingly popular amongst large securities houses. This is the practice of buying a long line of stock from one seller and then selling the shares through the market. The risk is that the shares may fall in value leaving the securities house with a huge loss. Bought deals have only been possible with Big Bang and the advent of large well capitalised securities firms, but the risks being taken on are extremely large.

The Stock Exchange is party to the central compensation fund set up under the Financial Services Act, in which losses due to fraud or the collapse of an institution of 100 per cent up to £30 000 and 90 per cent of losses up to £20 000 are recompensed, and then nothing after that.

11.12 TAKEOVER REGULATION

Regulation of takeovers comes under three forms – monopolies and mergers policy, operated by the Monopolies and Mergers Commission and the Office of Fair Trading, company law overseen by the Department of Trade and Industry, and the conduct of companies during bids under the City Code of the Takeover Panel. The main emphasis here will be on the City Code as it relates directly to the conduct of companies in relation to the Stock Exchange.

The Takeover Panel is largely concerned with the interests of shareholders during takeovers. The City Code is not backed up by law, but anybody involved in the securities market must abide by it (removal of authorisation under the FSA being the biggest sanction). The Code sets out a timetable for takeovers and certain standards of conduct, in order that all shareholders receive the same information and time enough to act on that information.

A predator company (the offerer) can buy up to 15 per cent of a company's shares without restrictions, but above that level must then wait seven days before being allowed to buy up to another ten per cent. Then there is another seven day wait. Shares can then be bought again, but care must be taken because once 30 per cent of the shares are held a 'mandatory offer' must be made – a full offer for the company. The purpose of course is to obtain more than 50 per cent, when the offer becomes 'unconditional as to acceptances'. the basic timetable for a bid is 60 days from the date of the formal offer to the shareholders of the company to be taken over. Shareholders must have a fortnight to consider an offer, so that the final offer must come before the 46th day. The purpose of having a timetable is so that all relevant information can be digested and acted upon, and so that bids do not carry on for an unreasonable length of time. The basic timetable can be extended if a new bidder emerges, if the target company board agrees (rare) or if the target company announces significant trading information after the 39th day.

Nicholson (1989) argues that hostile takeovers tend to undermine the public's confidence in the operation of the stock market, particularly in terms of dishonest practices (a point of view endorsed by the Guinness case – see Chapter 12).

11.13   OVERSEAS/EUROPEAN COMPETITION

Stock exchanges vary greatly across the EEC in terms of differences in volume, framework and trading mechanics. The UK exchange is a quote driven market-maker system with electronic trading, whereas many foreign exchanges are order driven and still maintain trading 'floors', although again this is rapidly changing as a result of competition.

At present, stock exchange membership in many EC countries is not open to outside interests.In Germany Universal banks are the only institutions allowed to conduct securities business, whereas in France only stock exchange members are able to, and the UK is somewhere in between, with both banks and non-bank institutions able to compete for security business. Competition is however forcing most EC members to adopt the UK model, and most have, or are going to have their own versions of the U.K's Big Bang.

There has been a great deal of change in European Securities Exchanges, much of it on the lines of London's Big Bang (abolition of fixed commissions in Paris, for example), and much of it with a view to maintaining or gaining business.

Overseas securities markets, particularly those that are at present relatively expensive and illiquid should grow rapidly in the future with convergence of regulations, possibly at the expense of the London International Stock Exchange, as foreign shares traditionally traded in London move to their increasingly sophisticated domestic markets.

Paris and Frankfurt are growing particularly fast (capitalisation increases of 83 per cent and 64 per cent respectively during 1989), with turnover of domestic equities on German Exchanges being larger than the ISE's for the first time ever in 1989. The ISE holds nearly 8 per cent of world domestic equity capitalisation however (Table 11.8).

Table 11.8 *International Market Statistics*

	Market Capitalisation (March 1990 £m)	No. of Companies Listed (March 1990)		Turnover Domestic & overseas (1st Qtr. 1990 £m)	Money Raised by Domestic Companies (Public Offers) (Jan–Mar 1990 £m)
		Domestic	Foreign		
Amsterdam	93387	253	231	6518	73
London ISE	486551	1484	551	85615	2090
Frankfurt	231728	378	351	104291	585
Paris	203978	456	226	19259	na
Zurich	101682	177	232	na	na
Australia	76236	1312	31	5758	1215
Hong Kong	50317	278	15	4531	na
NASDAQ	229323	3983	281	67566	na
NYSE	1763749	1650	91	211279	na
Tokyo	1899480	1610	120	227256	9399
Toronto	161102	1145	69	10243	na

Source: *Quality of Markets Quarterly Review*, April–June 1990

The following aspects of Securities Market Regulation have already been put into place by the EC.

   (i) Collective investments for transferable securities (UCITS) including unit trusts and open-ended mutual funds. Freedom to deal in these securities has been completed, but mutual recognition of licences is needed.
  (ii) Mutual recognition of listing particulars (including prospectuses).
 (iii) Information on the disposal or acquisition of major holdings in the capital of listed companies.
  (iv) Insider trading.

11.14 THE GILT EDGED MARKET

The gilt-edged market was changed in a very similar way to the stock market in Big Bang, with single capacity jobbers and brokers being replaced by dual capacity gilt-edged market makers (GEMMs). The changes brought an inflow of new firms, with twenty seven initially at the time of Big Bang, as opposed to eight jobbers previously, and capitalisation was increased. Three new Stock Exchange money brokers (SEMBs) joined the original six SEMBs to lend stocks and finance to GEMMs, and six inter-dealer brokers (IDBs) were set up to maintain an anonymous transactions service between GEMMs.

In common with the main exchange, the market changed from dealing on the floor to dealing through telecommunications networks. A computerised transfer system was set up – the Central Gilts Office (CGO).

At the time of writing there are twenty-two Gilt-Edged market makers (GEMMs), compared with twenty-seven when Big Bang began. The Bank of England (1990) has concluded that the withdrawal of market participants has not led to a reduction in the quality of service or reduced liquidity or competitiveness in the market.

During 1987 and 1988 GEMMs made heavy losses, but have tended to break even in 1989 and early 1990. With the authorities buying in gilt-edged stock the size of the market has declined – from £142 billion at the end of 1988 to £129 billion at the end of

1989. The improved financial performance of GEMMS in 1989 and 1990 is largely the result of improvements in the efficiency of operations and better management control.

Turnover has increased since Big Bang, although has tended to fall in 1988 and 1989 relative to 1987 (but it is still above Big Bang levels), and dealing spreads and dealing costs have tended to fall.

GEMMs, IDBs and SEMBs are all under the regulations of The Securities Association (TSA) (see Chapter 12). In addition, the GEMMs, IDBs and SEMBs report their positions at the close of each day to the Bank of England, which analyses them and provides a risk assessment by the next day, although the Bank also takes other broad factors into consideration for its supervisory functions. As the gilt market has shrunk, several GEMMs have expressed an interest in making a market in non-gilt fixed-interest sterling securities.

NOTES: [1] Alpha, Beta and Gamma are share classifications. To be classified in a particular category a share has to meet the following requirements:

Table 11.9 *Share Classifications*

Minimum requirements	Alpha	Beta	Gamma
Number of Market Makers	10	4 – 6	2
Turnover/Quarter (£m)	100	–	–
Market Capitalisation (£m)	625	–	–

Source: Quality of Markets Quarterly Review, Jan–March 1990

Alpha shares must pass the market-maker requirement plus either the turnover or market capitalisation limits. For Betas and Gammas only the number of market makers are taken into account. Alphas, Betas and Gammas are to be replaced by Normal Market Size (NMS).

REFERENCES

Bank of England (1988) 'The Equity Market Crash' February, BEQB.

Bank of England (1990) 'The Gilt-Edged Market: Developments in Market-Making in 1989' February, BEQB.

Bank of England (1990) 'New Equity issues in the United Kingdom' May, BEQB.

Copeland, L. (1989) 'Market Efficiency Before and After the Crash' *Fiscal Studies*, August.

Goodhart, C.A.E. (1987) 'Structural Change in the British Capital Markets' in *The Operation and Regulation of Financial Markets* by Goodhart, C., Currie, D and Llewellyn, D. (Macmillan London).

King, M. and Roell, A. (1988) 'The Regulation of Takeovers and the Stock Market'. *National Westminster Bank Quarterly Review*, February.

Pope, P., Peel, D and Yadar, P. (1990) 'Volatility and the Big Bang Factor'. *Professional Investor*, May.

Nicholson, T. (1989) 'This House Believes that Contested Takeovers Tend to be Bad for Industry'. *The Treasurer*, April.

Thomas, W.A. (1989). *The Securities Market* (Philip Allan, London).

Watson, J. (1990) 'The Latest Developments in Taurus' *Interchange*, Spring.

CHAPTER 12

THE REGULATORY FRAMEWORK

12.0 INTRODUCTION

An analysis is made in this chapter of the type of regulation adopted in the UK and Europe and of its effectiveness. The need for the regulation of financial institutions is recognised, particularly given recent cases of fraud. Emphasis is placed however on the need for fairness in applying regulations to groups of institutions, given the need to stimulate neutral competitive conditions. An examination of whether or not financial institutions and markets are over-regulated is made, and the core rules of regulation are set out.

12.1 THE NEED FOR REGULATION

Regulation can best be divided into structural regulation, prudential regulation and investor protection, although there are significant linkages between the three. Structural regulation refers to the type of activities that different categories of financial institution are permitted to carry out, and prudential regulation refers to supervison in terms of, *inter alia*, liquidity, capital adequacy and solvency of financial institutions. The term 'supervision' is used here to mean the monitoring of financial institutions for investor protection, prudential regulation, and structural regulation purposes combined. Investor protection legislation overlaps with both prudential and structural regulation in that the investor is in theory protected from financial institutions becoming insolvent through excessive risk-taking and protected from conflicts of interest by separation of types of business, but also extends much further into the manner in which investment business is carried out – the size of commissions, advertising regulations, cold calling etc.

These three types of regulation can all be carried out through formal legal rules, through self-imposed rules or self-regulation, or some combination of all of these. Regulation has both a micro and a macro aspect (Llewellyn 1986). The former relates to the interests of the consumer and producer, whilst the latter relates to the interest of the system as a whole – systemic interest. A further form of regulation is the operation of monetary policy, which may affect financial institutions, either through direct portfolio controls, as with the corset placed on the banks in the 1970s, or through interest rates which affect the environment in which financial institutions operate. High interest rates are a form of regulation to the extent that they reduce the demand for credit and hence credit granted by institutions.

In standard economic theory it is argued that regulation is required if market failures occur. In the case of financial services, problems occur through inadequate information, the unique character of financial services (there is no opportunity to 'try out' a financial service), ignorance on the part of consumers, and the fear of financial collapse.

Care needs to be taken to ensure that regulation does not impair the efficiency of the financial system. In other words, it must not damage allocative, operational or dynamic efficiency as described in Chapter 2. All forms of regulation have come under intense scrutiny in recent years. Structural regulations have generally been relaxed in order to allow greater competition for financial services, whilst prudential and investor protection regulations have tended to be tightened up and formalised. The main difficulty is to get the right balance between regulation and competition. Structural de-regulation has increased competition in the building society industry and the Stock Exchange, but at the same time investor protection has been tightened.

Notice that the regulations do not intend to stop financial institutions taking on risk, as this is a fundamental part of their activities. Risk taking is fundamental to the efficient operation of financial markets and the economy as a whole. It is necessary, however, for regulators to deter exceptional risk taking. The difficulty here of course is to determine what is excessive and what is not. It may be that in attempting to stamp out over-risky practices the regulators can become over-zealous and adversely affect risk taking activities that are fundamental to the workings of the financial system. Any regulatory framework must be judged against the effect it has on the cost of financial intermediation and the allocative efficiency of the financial system.

Prudential regulation is necessary to protect customers and to provide stability to the financial system, and one of its major functions is to deter financial institutions from taking on excessive levels of risk. Risks can be broadly categorised for financial institutions into a number of areas.

1. Liquidity risk – problems may come about through changes in asset prices, a badly matched balance sheet, or withdrawal of credit lines by other financial institutions.
2. Investment risk – sometimes called 'position' risk, where changes in foreign exchange rates, interest rates or asset prices cause losses on investments.
3. Credit risk – bad debts or delays in payment when due.
4. Earnings risk – increases in operating costs can reduce earnings, provisions for bad debt, changes in interest rates, and changes in asset prices can cause problems.
5. Operating risk – losses arising from inefficiency and poor management control.

The list above is only meant to be indicative, and to it could be added those that are difficult to categorise because of their broad nature – loss of confidence, which could occur because of any of the above risks, but is also a risk in itself, and fraud. Loss of confidence will hasten the insolvency of the institution if a 'run' occurs, and fraud can occur in any and every function of a financial institution, and the risks involved can often be counted in millions, particularly in cases of computer fraud.

The problem of quantifying risk is an extremely large one:

'A fundamental task of financial intermediaries is to appraise and assume risk and to charge for it appropriately. As a result of regulatory change, the growth of derivative product markets, and technological innovation, competitive pressure appears to be increasing the general level of risk assumed by intermediaries, while only partially providing the tools needed to manage that risk.'

IMF (1989)

Credit risk is undoubtedly the most important to banks. With the move towards disintermediation, it could be argued that many banks are driven to taking on less credit-worthy customers, with associated increases in credit risk. With liquidity risk, it should be recognised that diversification into new areas of business may reduce the ability of institutions to obtain liquid funds. The move of the banks into securities business raises the question of how liquid the securities markets are, particularly in a crash. Most UK institutions charge loans on a floating rate basis such that they match floating rate liabilities, but this merely increases credit risk, as interest rate risk is passed on to the customer, with subsequent greater probability of defaults occurring.

Hedging instruments such as swaps, options and financial futures can of course be used by financial institutions to limit risk, but these also contain (often unknown and unlimited) risks of their own – witness the losses of Midland Bank in its interest rate risk hedging in 1990.

Figure 12.1 outlines the major regulatory responsibilities and enactments relating to financial regulation.

Figure 12.1 *Regulation (Simplified)*

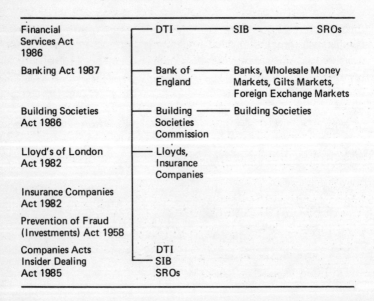

Financial Services Act 1986	DTI	SIB	SROs
Banking Act 1987	Bank of England	Banks, Wholesale Money Markets, Gilts Markets, Foreign Exchange Markets	
Building Societies Act 1986	Building Societies Commission	Building Societies	
Lloyd's of London Act 1982	Lloyds, Insurance Companies		
Insurance Companies Act 1982			
Prevention of Fraud (Investments) Act 1958			
Companies Acts Insider Dealing Act 1985	DTI SIB SROs		

12.2   INVESTOR PROTECTION

With greater levels of competition as a result of structural re-regulation, it was felt that a tightening up of investor protection was required. Figure 12.2 shows in chronological order the various recent studies of investor protection carried out and the subsequent system of regulation as embodied in the Financial Services Act, 1986.

The traditional style of regulation involved members 'clubs' and the ability of this system to work depended largely on maintaining a relatively small grouping of members through maintaining effective barriers to entry – the Stock Exchange being a prime example here. As soon as the barriers to entry in this type of regulatory regime are broken down and outside membership is allowed, the effectiveness of self-regulation and the ability to police members on the old club principle tends to be eroded.

Regulation prior to the FSA also tended to be fragmented, and largely on an institutional rather than functional basis – Insurance Company Act 1982, Banking Act 1979, Lloyds of London 1982. Regulators tended to take an informal stance – particularly the Bank of England and the DTI.

Regulation can also be categorised as formal or informal in that it can be set according to statutes and rules, or set informally through self regulation or some form of implicit agreement. Implicit agreements or what might be called self-imposed regulation (as in the Building Society sector and the Stock Exchange in the past) have tended to be eroded by competition or the need to compete.

Figure 12.2   *Evolution of the Financial Services Act*

1984	J. Gower 'Review of Investor Protection', CMND 9125
1985	White Paper 'Financial Services in the United Kingdom: A New Framework for Investor Protection'
1985	Financial Services Bill (First Reading)
1986	Financial Services Act

In general, regulation has become formal with more specific guidelines and rules than in the past, coupled with the abolition of many informal agreements such as the minimum commission system and single capacity of the stock exchange, and the interest rate cartel of the building societies. With the passing of the FSA 1986 regulation has been placed on a far more formal rule-orientated basis than previously. A more precise regulatory framework was required, it is argued, to cope with the increasingly competitive markets unleashed through structural deregulation (i.e. through the deregulation of the types of business that categories of firms are permitted to engage in).

Self regulation relies heavily upon the expertise and experience of market practitioners who can formulate rules and regulations that are acceptable to both players and regulators. The SROs are self-regulators who formulate rules that are acceptable to the SIB (or authorisation could be lost) and that (in theory) are acceptable to members. It should be recognised that it is in the interests of all firms involved in the provision of financial services that regulation is adequate and seen to be adequate by investors, or custom will be lost for all concerned. Certainly for honest practitioners, there is a desire for fraudulent firms and individuals to be weeded out, lest they taint the reputation of all firms.

Rules governing investor protection seek to ensure that the investing public is not subjected to fraudulent or manipulative practices and, moreover, that they are given sound advice by competent professionals. The Financial Services Act 1986 attempted to standardise investor protection through a more formal 'rule-book' approach rather than through the previously adopted 'club' arrangements. At the same time, the intention was to liberate financial markets through structural de-regulation to allow a greater degree of competition. Financial institutions have thus been encouraged to move into new areas of business, but at the same time have been regulated on a more formal basis than before. Indeed, it could be argued that it would not have been possible to allow greater competition without changes in regulation to counteract the increased levels of risk that comes with more intense competition.

Prior to the Financial Services Act regulation was largely aimed at ensuring the honesty of providers of financial services, and to stop fraudulent malpractice. Ensuring the honesty of those supplying services and advice has been the main *raison d'être* for regulation. The Gower Report extended the concept of regulation further to encompass the *competence* of suppliers of financial services, as well as their honesty.

The Gower Report and the FSA were also stimulated by instances of the failure of small investment firms, in which investors lost funds (often through fraud or incompetence), such as Norton Warburg in 1981.

The basic concepts in the Gower Report were accepted in the White Paper, and the Financial Services Bill, and were later enshrined in the Financial Services Act 1986.

A system of self-regulatory organisations (SROs) was set up under the auspices of the DTI and the Securities and Investments Board, the latter set up to authorise the SROs and oversee their operations. The SROs are responsible for the regulation and authorisation of their members, and are required to devise rules that are at least as stringent as those of the SIB itself.

A separate tier of authorisation is through Recognised Professional Bodies (RPBs) for professional organisations which applied to the SIB to be able to authorise their members to give investment advice which is incidental to their main area of business.

It is also possible for financial institutions to be directly authorised by the SIB, and there are also channels through which non-financial companies that carry out investment business that is incidental to their main activity (e.g. Treasury departments of large companies) to be directly authorised by the SIB. The final area of regulation is through Recognised Investment Exchanges (RIEs) and Recognised Clearing Houses (RCHs), through which securities transactions are carried out in order to be able to monitor investor protection more effectively.

Lloyd's of London and the Bank of England are specifically exempt from authorisation requirements.

Any business that operates within the investment arena that is not authorised can be punished by imprisonment or fines.

Investments are defined as (Part I Schedule 1 FSA 1986):

(1)   Stocks and shares (both UK and foreign).
(2)   Debentures, which includes debenture stock, loan stock, bonds and certificates of deposit.

(3) Government and public securities, which includes gilts, local authority bonds, bonds issued by foreign governments and international organisations.
(4) Warrants.
(5) Depository receipts for shares, bonds and warrants.
(6) Units in collective investment schemes, which includes unit trust schemes and shares in investment trusts.
(7) Options on currency, gold and silver or any investment within the schedule.
(8) Futures contracts for commodities and property.
(9) Contracts linked to the value of property or linked to indices.
(10) Insurance policies which act as investments which includes endowment and unit linked policies – but not policies which merely protect against risk or pure term assurance policies.

Investment business constitutes (Part II Schedule 1 FSA 1986):

(1) Dealing – buying, selling, subscribing for or underwriting investments, either as a principal or as an agent.
(2) Arranging Deals – making or offering to make arrangements to a person buying, selling, subscribing or underwriting investments.
(3) Managing – managing or offering to manage assets of another person which include investments.
(4) Advising – giving or offering advice on the buying, selling, subscription for or underwriting of investments.
(5) Collective Investment Schemes – establishing, operating, or closing down collective investment schemes, which includes acting as a trustee of an authorised unit trust scheme.

Some activities have been specifically excluded: (Parts III and IV Schedule 1 FSA 1986).

(1) A person buying and selling investments for their own account.
(2) Transactions within a company or a company group.

(3) Trustees and personal representatives who manage investments (unless they hold themselves out as providing professional investment services).

(4) Those who give investment advice as a consequence of advice on non-investment matters – e.g. an accountant advising the sale of shares for tax purposes.

(5) Newspapers (but not 'tipsheets').

(6) Employee share schemes and any facility for employees to exchange shares.

(7) A person without a permanent place of business in the UK. Also certain wholesale transactions are excluded (as they are deemed for professional investors rather than personal investors) and are regulated by the Bank of England. It is generally agreed that retail investors need a far higher level of supervision because of their lack of knowledge and because of the severe consequences of loss. Wholesale markets, by contrast, are operated by large institutions that are well aware of the risks involved.

The SIB only authorises 'fit and proper' persons and can withdraw or refuse authorisation if it deems this is not the case. The SIB has wide powers granted to it by the Secretary of State under the FSA, and has a broad authority in enforcing the Act (and can override the decisions of the SROs). The SROs regulate particular areas of investment business (see Figure 12.3) and its members are only authorised to carry out that particular business, unless authorised by another SRO.

The SIB is financed by levies on the SROs and firms that are registered with it, and does not receive any funds from the Government. Those regulations *not* carried out under the auspices of the SIB include insider dealing, takeovers and mergers, and the listing of new issues.

The framework for investor protection is shown in Figure 12.3, and outlines the channels of authority.

12.3   OVER-REGULATION?

Figure 12.4 shows the links between supervisors and institutions, and emphasises the complexity of the regulatory framework.

Figure 12.3   *Investor Protection Framework*

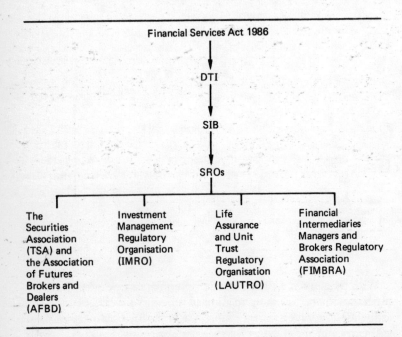

The system of self-regulatory organisations is fundamentally different from the Securities and Exchange Commission (SEC) in the USA. The SEC is centralised whereas SROs are decentralised and rulemaking is spread out amongst the various SROs. Such a decentralised system is open to the criticism that there is a large degree of overlap in regulation, and hence an overburden of costs. The degree of overlap of supervision is a problem, with for example, the Bank of England responsible for the supervision of the banking system as a whole, whilst the SROs are responsible for their various investment activities. The Bank of England tends to be more concerned with systemic risk whereas the SIB and SROs are more involved with investor protection in relation to different areas of activity, although as mentioned earlier there are significant linkages and overlaps between the two. The Bank of England has special responsibility for regulation of the markets that are in any way involved in the operation of the payments mechanism and that might affect monetary policy.

Figure 12.4   *Regulatory Framework (Simplified)*

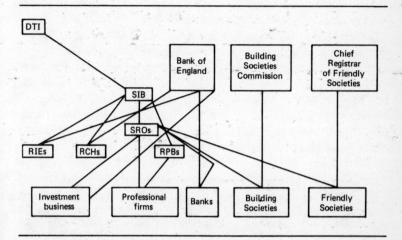

With financial conglomerates, a supervisor is nominated as lead regulator to oversee the exchange of information and data by the individual supervisors involved. The individual supervisors will still carry out their duties, but the lead supervisor will ultimately be responsible for the regulation of conglomerates.

It is probably better to start off with too many regulators which can then merge, rather than starting off with too few and attempting to build on them. Indeed, there has already been some degree of rationalisation of SROs. The Association of Futures Brokers and Dealers (AFBD) has merged with The Securities Association (TSA) in order to reduce bureaucracy and to decrease costs to member firms, many of whom were members of both SROs. The merger of the TSA with the AFBD is also rationalised in terms of the increasing linkages between the securities and futures markets and the desire for both markets to set up a system for trading futures and options on a Euroindex of stocks. This would be in competition with the European Option Exchange and the Matif Futures Exchange in France. IMRO (Investment Managers Regulatory Organisation) has a degree of commonality with the TSA and AFDB and may be the subject of further consolidation of SROs in the future.

The four SROs have evolved largely through the choice of the financial institutions and intermediaries themselves, and there is no suggestion that these were arbitrarily placed on the financial system. Some would argue that only two SROs are necessary (Mortimer 1988). There has, however, been considerable unease amongst institutions as to the complexity of the rule books, the cost of regulation, and the wide range of regulators involved within the system.

The complexity of the regulatory framework and the issue of overlapping responsibility is shown in various frauds. At times there has been no less than five organisations conducting investigations into cases: the Department of Trade and Industry, the Securities and Investments Board, the Financial Intermediaries Managers and Brokers Regulatory Association, the Serious Fraud Office and the Metropolitan Police fraud squad. Such a situation appears to face problems of cooperation amongst the relevant authorities, questions of who is ultimately responsible, and concern as to the cost of regulation.

The DTI has three main investigation wings. One carries out investigations under the Companies Acts, one under the Financial Services Acts, and there is a team of lawyers that carry out the prosecutions and advise the investigators.

The Serious Fraud Office (SFO) was set up under the 1987 Criminal Justice Act in response to a report by the Fraud Trials Committee formed in 1983 as a result of dissatisfaction with the ability of the City of London Fraud Squad to get convictions. Its main objectives are:

    (i)   to gain expertise in specialist financial areas,
  (ii)   to carry out a coherent approach to investigating fraud,
 (iii)   to speed up investigations and criminal proceedings,
 (iv)   to present evidence in laymans terms,
  (v)   to increase successful prosecutions.

The SFO only becomes involved in cases where more than £1 million is involved, and most cases tend to come from the DTI. The SFO has very wide powers to examine personal bank accounts, examine documents and demand interviews, and call for fines in the courts if necessary.

One of the main criticisms of the recommendations of the Gower Report is largely one of methodology, in that no formal (or even informal) approach was taken to attempt to find out how much the self-regulatory framework proposal would cost. In particular, cost benefit analysis was not used, largely because Gower professed that as a lawyer he was not competent to carry out such an appraisal (Gower Report paragraph 1.16). Gower also doubted the usefulness of cost benefit analysis, and although it should be recognised that there are indeed limitations to such a technique, as Veljanovski (1988) points out, this is not a valid excuse for the total disregard of the appraisal of the cost of alternative systems.

Gower argued that the evidence from the United States shows that regulation does not affect market efficiency either beneficially or adversely. In the UK, as the new system of regulation is being put in place at a time of considerable liberalisation in financial markets it is difficult to separate the different factors that impinge on market efficiency. Increased competition should certainly lead to greater levels of efficiency, so long as the competition does not destabilise the financial system, and the new regulatory system is designed to allow competition to increase whilst improving on investor protection. Indeed, many of the new rules ought to increase efficiency as they sweep away examples of market failure or cartels that distort competition.

In analysing the regulatory system it is probably useful to divide the concept of investor protection into the two broad categorisations as used by Gower – honesty and competence. It is important to discuss whether the self-regulatory regime has increased the level of either. With regard to honesty, it could be argued that no system of regulation can ever deter the truly criminally minded from attempting to defraud the investing public. Whatever rules and regulations are enforced, no matter how comprehensive, there will always be unscrupulous people who attempt to pervert the rules for their own gains.

The important factors in a regulatory system are the degree to which such practices can be limited (with the proviso that no system can totally eliminate fraud), and secondly, when a fraud does occur or is occurring, the speed with which the regulatory system can detect it and put a stop to it. Anecdotal evidence suggests that the current system of regulation has failed on both counts. Fraud appears to have increased rather than decreased, and it cannot be argued that this is merely a matter of greater success in detection, as many of the frauds only come to light when investors find that they are unable to obtain their funds (or the directors of the institution are found to be in sunny climes abroad, with little intention of returning to the UK). It appears that the regulatory authorities are *extremely* slow at detecting fraud.

One of the recent cases – Dunsdale Securities, is worryingly similar to that of an earlier case of fraud at Barlow Clowes. At Barlow Clowes approximately £190m was lost by investors who thought they were investing in safe gilts, whereas in fact very few gilts were bought. At Dunsdale, around £17m of investors funds have gone missing, and again the investors thought they were investing in gilts. It appears that regulation has not been tightened after the Barlow Clowes affair, nor have the lessons been learned.

The number of frauds has led to calls for tightening up of audits of investment businesses, and particularly a reduction in the number of many thousands of auditors who examine investment firms so that the ones left can develop greater expertise. A further improvement could be an approved panel of investment business auditors, although this would mean potential members of the panel would be excluded because of lack of experience, and they would not be provided with the chance of obtaining it.

The failure of the authorities to stop such occurrences can be interpreted in at least two ways. Firstly, that the regulatory system is already too costly and still cannot adequately carry out its responsibilities and ought to be scrapped for some other (unspecified) scheme. Secondly, that the framework of current investor protection is adequate but that the self-regulatory organisations are not sufficiently funded and hence lack the resources to fully police the financial system. This latter implicitly calls for more funding and hence an even more costly burden of regulation.

The Building Societies Act was a response to structural changes in the financial services market, whereas the Banking Act and the Financial Services Act were responses to cases of fraud and bad practice, and as such are 'defensive' forms of regulation that might have been expected to be overdetailed and expensive to implement (Goodhart 1988).

Barclay (1978) argues that the existence of surplus profits in the financial services industry will attract new entrants, and that it is the influx of new entrants that tend to cause problems for regulators. Certainly the fringe banking crisis of 1973–74 occurred at a time of a large inflow of new institutions into the market as a result of the perceived liberal market conditions brought about through competition and credit control. With the liberalisation of financial markets in the 1980s and 1990s, and the growth of new entrants (many of them from overseas) there again seems to have been an increase in institutional failures and frauds.

There is some debate as to the actual role of SROs. Should they be seen as the overall enforcers of the regulations, or should they merely be ombudsmen or watchdogs that only act on customer complaints? This is a fundamental point because if they are merely to be ombudsmen then the emphasis of ensuring regulations have been adhered to and best advice proferred rests in the first instance heavily upon the customer, and it is up to the customer to complain. Responsibility lies with the SROs, but it could be argued that they have insufficient resources to carry out this role, and should merely be ombudsmen (although there is also some doubt as to their ability to act in this limited capacity given their degree of underfunding).

The SROs may in fact be subject to 'regulatory capture', where an initially independent body set up to police a particular form of business is 'captured' by the very institutions it is trying to regulate, and becomes a lobby or mouthpiece working on behalf of the industry. It could be argued that this is far more likely to occur to a self-regulatory body than to a statutory body. It should also be remembered that if an SRO is thought to be acting inappropriately, i.e. if it is subject to regulatory capture, then the SIB can simply revoke its status.

An extreme area of concern is the extent to which the regulatory system will stifle financial innovation. The more rules that exist, then the more likely it is that a new product or service will impinge upon or be prohibited in some way by those rules. If innovation is stifled then efficiency of the markets may be impaired. Excessive regulation may also be an effective barrier to entry, thus reducing competition and providing large profits for the incumbents. Moreover those institutions excluded will be tempted to take their business elsewhere and the UK could lose business to overseas markets.

Lloyd's provides an example of a self-regulatory 'club' and the extent to which Lloyd's carries out its self-regulatory role is questionable. Marine Syndicate 317/661 underwritten by Outh-waite underwriting agency experienced problems when writing a number of runoff contracts. In these (legitimate) deals syndicates transferred their liabilities in particular areas to Outhwaite, allowing the syndicates to close their three-year account period. The premiums charged by Outhwaite should have been sufficient to cover future claims, but in fact were not because of a heavy spate of asbestos and professional liability claims after 1982. The question is whether or not the syndicates running off their future liabilities did so in utmost good faith by revealing all pertinent facts about the contract. Suspicions have arisen as to the volume of such contracts transferred over 1979–1982, and the sudden huge claims after that period. If the syndicates running off their contracts were aware of the problems that were going to occur and did not inform Outhwaite, then they were not acting in utmost good faith.

There is some debate as to the omission of Lloyd's of London from the FSA, given the nature of such recent scandals at Lloyd's (and the fact that to some extent these scandals prompted the FSA).

The Neill Report (1987) recommended that:
(1)   An ombudsman and arbitration procedure be set up for disputes between names and Lloyd's, and between names and agents
(2)   Compensation of names for losses should be equal to that of the SIB
(3)   Registration for underwriting agents should be the same as the SIB 'fit and proper' test.

Lloyd's is self-regulated and aims to protect the 'members' or suppliers of funds, protect policy holders, and the reputation of Lloyd's as a whole. To ensure this, minimum standards of competence are set, proper records have to be kept, limits to risk exposure, disclosure rules, and a disciplinary system. Checks are made as to the size of members' deposits in relation to their underwriting activities, and ensuring directors and partners are 'fit and proper' persons.

Concern has been raised about the costs of regulation. Hall (1987) argues that most regulation is simply added on to existing frameworks (often as the result of specific frauds or crises) rather than building up new systems, and that the efficiency of regulation suffers as a result and costs escalate.

The direct costs of financial regulation are estimated at over £100 million per year in running costs (Lomax 1987), and some (e.g. Goodhart 1987) would regard this as a conservative estimate. It is often argued that the costs of regulation are front-end loaded, with the majority of costs being met with the startup of the SROs, subsequent running costs being minimal compared with the turnover of most financial institutions. It would seem however that the costs hit small financial firms far harder than larger ones, and may create a powerful barrier to entry to new firms. Independent advisers regulated under FIMBRA probably feel the costs of regulation the hardest, as they are generally small in size.

Concerning costs, it has been reported in the financial press that FIMBRA merely had to take the word of Dunsdale that it was investing in gilts, as the SRO had too few staff to adequately deal with each individual firm. It is likely that for regulation to be tightened, more funds are needed for the SROs to improve staffing levels, which inevitably means an increase in the costs of regulation.

The combination of a new regulatory system and increased competition ought to lead to an increase in efficiency in the provision of financial services, although this still ignores the cost of the overall regulatory framework. The prime question is whether the gains in efficiency from having a more competitive financial system that involves a degree of consumer protection are outweighed by the costs of setting up and maintaining that regulatory system. A further question is whether or not a less costly form of regulation could be devised that still allows the same degree of competition in the markets with the same level of investor protection.

Some of the above criticisms have been recognised by the SIB, and a restructuring of the rule books is occurring with the aim of simplifying the rules and setting out a set of core rules. David Walker, the Chairman of the SIB, has argued that the regulatory system is overcomplicated:

'We do have a problem with regulatory fatigue at the moment. The fact is, transition to the simpler rules will involve costs, though at the end of the day it will make for more cost effective regulation than the present encyclopedias.'

Financial Times, August 1990.

12.4   THE CORE RULES

The proposed core rules contain a common core of conduct of business rules (SIB 1990). The simplified rules run to 40 in all. Some of the rules which have caused considerable debate are reproduced below:

Polarisation

(1)   A firm which is not a tied firm and which provides investment services in respect of packaged products must act as an independent adviser in respect of those products.

(2)   A tied firm must ensure that:
  (a)   a private customer to whom it or anyone acting on its behalf provides an investment service is informed of its and that persons status; and
  (b)   neither it nor anyone acting on its behalf promotes a packaged product of (or arranged by) a person outside the marketing group of that tied firm.

The FSA has made a distinction between those who are independent intermediaries and those who are tied to a particular company. The distinction, termed 'polarisation' was deemed necessary to make more transparent to customers the possible ties of their advisers, and to eliminate the ability of an intermediary to pass off as an independent adviser yet suggest the policies of the advisers own company (or those which provide the highest commission).

Polarisation means there will be an end to the practice of claiming to be an independent financial intermediary when in fact 80–90 per cent of a firms policies are set up with a parent organisation. Such a change in the rules should be beneficial for intermediaries that are really independent.

Suitability

A firm must take all reasonable steps to ensure that it does not give investment advice to, nor effect, a discretionary transaction with or for, a private customer, unless that advice or transaction is suitable for him having regard to the facts disclosed by that customer or other relevant facts about the customer of which the firm is or ought reasonably to be aware. [Notice that 'best advice' has now been downgraded to 'suitability'].

Customer's Understanding

A firm must not:-

(a)   recommend a transaction to a private customer, or effect a discretionary transaction with or for him, unless it has taken all reasonable steps to enable the customer to understand the risks involved; or

(b)   mislead a private customer as to any advantages or disadvantages of a contemplated transaction.

Standards of Advice on Packaged Products

(1)   A firm which is an independent adviser must take all reasonable steps to inform itself, and all others acting on its behalf fully about what packaged products are available on the market and:

(a)   must not proceed for a private customer with any one packaged product if it is aware of another packaged product on the market which will meet the customer's requirements better; and

(b)   must not proceed for a private customer with a packaged product of, or arranged by, any person with whom the firm has a connection unless the firm believes on reasonable grounds that the product will meet the customer's requirements better than any other packaged product on the market.

(2)   A firm which is a tied firm must take all reasonable steps to inform itself and others acting on its behalf fully about what packaged products are available from the marketing group to which it belongs, and must not proceed with a packaged product for a private customer if it is aware of another packaged product from the marketing group's product range which would meet the customer's requirements better.

Best Execution

Where a firm deals with or for a customer it must take all reasonable steps to deal on the terms which are the best available for the customer in the circumstances.

The SIB established an Investors Compensation Scheme in 1988. Investors would be compensated in the event of the failure of an authorised investment firm of 100 per cent on the first £30 000 invested, 90 per cent the next £20 000 and nothing on the excess, providing a maximum cover of £48 000 on £50 000 or more invested.

12.5   PRUDENTIAL REGULATION

Prudential regulations have the objective of improving financial stability, consumer protection and allocative efficiency. Financial stability should be encouraged through the supervision of the strength of financial institutions' capital and liquidity positions, and through regulations relating to large loans and shareholdings in institutions. The investor confidence that ensues should improve allocative efficiency in terms of the channelling of funds from surplus to deficit units.

Some would argue (Gardener 1978) that the theoretically optimal form of prudential regulation is that of 'vicarious participation' whereby no specific requirements are set with regard to liquidity, capital adequacy, etc, but the authorities assess each individual financial institution on a case-by-case basis, and use some form of risk management technique to assess the strength of the bank.

Perhaps all forms of specific regulations ought to be abolished and more in-depth supervision carried out instead. It is feasible to imagine a system whereby there are no particular rules laid down, with the security and stability of each institution judged on its merits. Given the different nature of assets and liabilities held by each institution this could be a theoretically preferable system. In practice however, a number of problems could occur. There would be no uniformity of the standard of supervision across nations, which would lead to some countries being more heavily supervised (to their detriment) than others. Some regulators might be persuaded to supervise overseas institutions more closely, or if home supervision is in place, home supervisors could apply only a minimum form of supervision to their domestic institutions operating overseas in order to allow them a competitive advantage.

Present day prudential regulations are a mix of prescribed rules and vicarious participation. The Bank of England monitors banks' liquidity levels on an individual basis for example, but has set rules for capital adequacy. Supervisors generally consider a variety of indicators in assessing institutions:

(1) Composition of loan portfolios. (2) Diversification of loan portfolios. (3) Volume of 'large' loans. (4) Quality of earnings. (5) Dividend payout ratios. (6) Liquidity. (7) Structure of liabilities. (8) Currency matching/mismatching. (9) Maturity matching/mismatching. (10) Interest Rate matching/mismatching. (11) Quality of Management. (11) Bad Debts. (12) Provisioning.

The above list is by no means comprehensive (and some items overlap) but gives some idea of the areas where supervision is required.

The off-balance-sheet activities of the commercial banks such as swaps, options and futures provide problems for supervision in that it is difficult to assess the associated adequacy of liquidity and capital. Financial innovation and institutions moving into markets in which they are relatively inexperienced increases individual institutional risk and combined with increasing joint ventures and mergers increases the degree of systemic risk. Financial innovations such as MOFs, NIFs and RUFs (see Chapter 13) may in fact increase systemic risk because, by their very nature, these facilities will tend to be heavily used in an economic down-turn, at the very time when banks may find their profit levels being squeezed.

Fears have been expressed over the high degree of financial 'layering' or the interdependence of financial institutions with regard to lending within the financial sector. The greater is the level of 'layering' the greater will be the domino effect from any initial shock of a financial institution that is experiencing problems.

In the United States, supervisors are keen for banks to separate themselves from their securities business through setting up risk barriers, often called 'firewalls' to ensure that problems that may occur with the securities arm are not transferred to the bank through contagion. 'Firewalls' include separate subsidiaries, and separate capital funds, although the extent to which these firewalls will remain intact in a crisis is questionable.

Although it was stated earlier that regulation could stifle financial innovation, it is also the case that regulation can act as the catalyst for innovation. Off-balance-sheet business is a form of innovation in order to earn fees whilst not damaging capital adequacy ratios (although OBS business is now included). Requirements for capital backing for off-balance-sheet business has meant that many of these products have been re-priced to take account of their greater cost.

12.6 SYSTEMIC RISK

A main objective of prudential regulation and supervision is stability of the financial system as a whole, or the control of 'systemic risks'. The Bank of England has ultimate responsibility for the choice of whether or not to bail out a troubled bank. If there is no likelihood of systemic risk, then the bank will generally be allowed to fail. The desire to ensure the stability of the financial system may lead to an inefficient allocation of resources if institutions are 'saved' from becoming insolvent in terms of the associated costs of administering a lifeboat package. The problem for the central bank is to decide which institutions require assistance in order to avoid systemic risk and which should be allowed to fail.

The problems of systemic risk need to be weighed against the possibility of moral hazard and the costs of maintaining a 'failed' institution. There is a moral hazard in the sense that banks may act imprudently if they are aware that they will be bailed out of a difficult situation by the Bank of England. In the case of JMB it was feared that the reputation of London as an international financial centre (and international gold centre in terms of the risk of contagion to Johnson Matthey PLC, involved in bullion) would be damaged, and international funds would be placed elsewhere.

With British and Commonwealth Bank there was no real evidence that any systemic risk would result. B and C was in an unusual situation in that it was actually brought down by a subsidiary that collapsed, Atlantic Computers. Many UK banks have had to write off debts owed by B and C. Although these debts have proved to be relatively small, they demonstrate the degree to which institutions are linked, and the case demonstrates the problems that can occur when financial institutions are linked closely with commercial companies.

On an international scale, it is highly desirable that Central Banks move towards agreements on setting up international 'lifeboat' style operations given the increasingly multinational nature of many financial conglomerates.

Hall (1987) argues that current prudential regulations are not sufficient to guarantee that bank failures on the scale of JMB would not occur again, and the case of B and C seems to vindicate his view. Moreover it is likely that bank failures will occur again in the future.

One method of ensuring depositor confidence and hence stopping bank 'runs' is through a deposit protection system. The objective of such a scheme is to maintain confidence in the financial system and ensure stability. The Deposit Protection Scheme was set up under the 1979 Banking Act, under which 75 per cent of the first £20 000 of a depositor's sterling deposits with any one member institution are guaranteed to be repaid. Authorised institutions fund the scheme in proportion to the size of their deposit bases. Only 75 per cent is paid in order to reduce problems of moral hazard, although the extent to which this works is probably negligible. The success of deposit insurance should really be measured against its ability to *prevent* bank failures, rather than the payment to deposit holders after failure has occurred (Gardener 1978).

Deposit Protection Schemes may unfortunately give rise to problems of 'moral hazard' whereby financial institutions take on unduly risky business in the knowledge that depositors are protected. Indeed, if irresponsible financial institutions can temporarily earn high interest rates on risky loans and hence pay high deposit rates, they are rewarded by an inflow of deposits, the investors disregarding possible risks because of the safety net of deposit insurance.

Deposit Schemes can be criticised because larger more safe financial institutions are seen to be subsidising the risks of smaller less prudent institutions. It may be that a deposit scheme should be funded by the small, more risky institutions, that can graduate into leaving the scheme once they are deemed large enough and prudent enough (and this may act as an incentive for institutions to run their businesses prudently). In practice however, this means an extra cost on smaller financial institutions and will inhibit their ability to compete, and should be ruled out on these grounds alone.

The working of market discipline, whereby depositors would withdraw funds from unsound banks has declined, as depositors know they are insured against loss. A market mechanism for preventing banks lending too much in risky areas has largely been lost. There could be an argument for actually lowering deposit insurance. The collapse of British and Commonwealth merchant bank will cost at least £60m in compensation to depositors from the Deposit Protection Scheme, the largest amount paid by the scheme since it was set up in 1979. The fund only maintains about £6m, so the banks will have to make additional contributions.

There is a valid case for banks paying premiums to the deposit scheme according to the riskiness of their loan portfolios. Critics argue that risk is difficult to quantify, yet capital adequacy ratios are risk-weighted, so there is no reason why the same principles cannot be applied to deposit protection schemes.

A problem not often raised in relation to deposit schemes is that they can affect the competitiveness of banks on an international scale. Banks in a country that has a large deposit scheme with heavy premiums will be at a disadvantage to banks in countries that pay less to deposit insurance pools (or none at all – although in the UK at least overseas banks have to pay in to the Deposit Protection Scheme unless they can demonstrate that they contribute to an equivalent scheme in their home country).

It has been suggested (Litan 1988) that the deposit taking and lending functions of banking should be separated in order to insulate insured deposits from risky assets. This could be carried out by the securitisation of the risky loans, and there would be no need to apply risk-weights to the asset portfolio for the purpose of calculating premiums to be paid to the Deposit Protection Scheme. Securitising a large proportion of assets may not be easy to do however, and if a lot of banks attempted it there could be a surplus of securitised assets, driving their prices down.

12.7 HARMONISATION OF EUROPEAN REGULATION

One of the aims of the single market is to encourage the growth of financial intermediation across borders, in order to direct surplus funds within Europe more efficiently and at less cost to deficit units within Europe. Both savers and borrowers in the community ought to benefit, the former through a greater variety of choice, and the latter through greater access to funds.

A more liberalised European financial market was needed to effectively compete against other markets, particularly the USA and Japan. Without the changes that have occurred and are occurring, substantial amounts of business may have been lost because of uncompetitive EC markets. It has been widely agreed for some time that for true European integration in financial services then prudential regulation and supervision and investor protection between EEC member states would need to be harmonised to some degree. In fact, competition between countries would tend eventually to create pressure on those countries that have too strict regulatory controls to reform them, or face substantial loss of business. This is particularly the case with conduct of business regulations adopted in each host country (which are not being made uniform), whereby a country with over-strict rules will tend to find an outflow of business to other European countries.

The FSA and the role of SROs in the UK is unique in Europe, where regulation is carried out by government organisations. Mutual recognition of regulatory organisations is a start, but some degree of harmonisation of regulatory frameworks (whether along the lines of the UK system or not – and doubts have already been expressed about it earlier) is needed to simplify the whole regulatory process across Europe.

It has been argued that as SROs have been expensive to set up in the UK and that self regulation has been the norm, then European countries should recognise the value of such a form of regulation, and not seek to reform or dismantle it. It remains to be seen, however, whether SROs have been able to adequately regulate the UK financial system, given the problems outlined. There would tend to be competition induced adjustments that eliminate any major regulatory variations amongst countries. Such competitive processes can take a considerable time to evolve however, and a move towards agreement on regulation is a far faster and more preferable stance. There is also a problem that the standards might be set by the most poorly regulated countries thus dragging down the regulations to the least common denominator, endangering standards and consumer protection. The response to 1992 by individual countries has generally involved reactions from domestic governments and regulators to ensure that market positions in financial services are not lost to overseas financial markets (and indeed to improve on market shares).

Initial aims were for full harmonisation of Europe's financial markets. It became clear however that this was a massive task, with a great diversity in the financial systems of Europe. In 1985 the single market initiative was started, but with a move away from full harmonisation that was simply too ambitious, towards a framework for liberalisation. Full harmonisation would have required a high degree of centralisation of regulation, which may have resulted in more bureaucracy, and greater costs of compliance and authorisation for financial institutions. This framework is built around four main principles:

(i) home (parent) country regulation by the appropriate supervisory authority

(ii) recognition by each country of EC members' regulations

(iii) harmonisation of essential minimum standards of supervision

(iv) single European 'licences' that authorise financial institutions to operate across Europe.

The main hope is to achieve liberalisation and consumer protection at the same time through the main elements of regulation.

The home control principle means that there has to be accepted minimum standards of regulation, in order to stop financial institutions from registering for business in countries where regulations are weak. The principle of home country regulation still faces a number of barriers however. Countries still tend to maintain restrictive internal regulation if it is deemed to be in the public good. Budd (1989) points out that a branch of a German bank would not need to be authorised under the Financial Services Act to carry out banking business in the UK , but it would be governed by the conduct of business rules made under the Act, until an EC directive is issued to harmonise the rules. In the meantime, it is difficult to distinguish between those national rules that have been maintained for the public good, and those that have been kept to protect the national interest and keep barriers to entry intact.

Fears have been expressed as to the effects of the reciprocity rules on the future growth of London as the leading European financial market, if reciprocity leads to 'fortress Europe'. The reciprocity clause means that a bank from a non-EC country would not be able to establish itself in the EC if EC banks did not have similar rights of establishment in that institution's home country. An American bank wanting to set up a subsidiary in London would not be allowed to do so if, say, a Spanish bank did not have reciprocal rights of establishment in the US.

The fear of many UK financial institutions is that as London has the most liberalised financial regime, it would be involved in many reciprocity arguments, and may lose out as an international financial centre. Some EC countries may, it is thought, invoke the reciprocity clause to stop non-EC banks establishing in London, even if the EC countries have no desire to set up in the non-EC country concerned, merely to stop the growth of London and limit competition within the Community. Non-EC institutions may only set up a subsidiary or require a subsidiary under the reciprocity rules, setting up a branch will still require authorisation from each country.

REFERENCES

Barclay, C.R. (1978) 'Competition and Financial Crises – Past and Present' in *Competition and Regulation of Banks* (University of Wales Press).

Budd, A. (1989) 'Financial Services: Banking' in *Planning for Europe* by W.M. Clarke 1989 (Waterlow Publishers, London).

Gardener, E.P.M. (1978) 'The Philosophy of Bank Capital Adequacy' in *Competition and Regulation of Banks*, (University of Wales Press).

Goodhart, C.A.E. (1987) 'The Economics of Big Bang' *Midland Bank Review*, Summer.

Goodhart, C.A.E. (1987) Introduction in Lomax (1987) London. *Markets after the Financial Services Act* (Butterworths, London).

Goodhart, C.A.E. (ed.) (1988) *Financial Regulation or Over-Regulation?* (I.E.A. London).

Gower, J. (1982) 'Review of Investor Protection – A Discussion Document' *CMND 9125* (HMSO London).

Hall, M.J.B. (1987) 'UK Banking Supervision after the Johnson Matthey Case' in *The Operation and Regulation of Financial Markets* by Goodhart (ed.) (Macmillan, London).

IMF (1989) *International Capital Markets*, April. Washington D.C.

Litan, R. (1988) in *Breaking up the Bank: Rethinking an Industry under Seige* by L. Bryan (Dow-Jones, Irwin).

Llewellyn, D.T. (1986) *The Regulation and Supervision of Financial Institutions* (Institute of Bankers).

Lomax, D. (1987) *London Markets after the Financial Services Act* (Butterworths, London).

Mortimer, K. (1988) 'The Securities and Investments Board' in *Financial Regulation or Over-Regulation?* by Goodhart (ed.) (I.E.A).

Neil Report (1987) *Regulatory Arrangements at Lloyds*, CND 59 (HMSO London).

SIB (1990) 'The Proposed Core Rules on the Conduct of Business'. *Consultative Paper 42* July.

White Paper (1985) *Financial Services in the United Kingdom: A New Framework for Investor Protection* CND 9432 (HMSO London).

Veljanovski, C. (1988) Introduction in *Financial Regulation or Over-Regulation?* by Goodhart (ed.) (I.E.A).

CHAPTER 13

CURRENT ISSUES/TRENDS

13.0 INTRODUCTION

As will be appreciated from earlier chapters, UK financial institutions and markets have undergone a number of structural changes in recent years, and this chapter attempts to bring together some of the major trends that have occurred and are still occurring. The effects of mergers amongst financial institutions on the level of competition are analysed, as are the effects of deregulation and liberalisation on the degree of competition.

The increase in off-balance-sheet business and securitisation is discussed and the final section examines the threats and opportunities of 1992 for UK financial institutions.

13.1 CONGLOMERATION

The last decade has seen the growth of many financial institutions into large, integrated financial services groups, or conglomerates. The existence of these conglomerates raises important questions in relation to the efficiency of the financial system, the effective supervision and regulation of conglomerates, possible conflicts of interest and implications for the stability of the system.

One of the main purported aims of diversification into several areas of financial services is the ability to cross-sell financial products to customers in one-stop financial institutions or so-called 'financial supermarkets'. If a customer enters a branch of a bank or building society for a mortgage, the opportunity exists to sell them insurance, equities, a personal pension and any other services available.

Some diversification activities have been a defensive response, such as the banks' move into securities business to counteract the fact that disintermediation was occurring (companies moving away from traditional bank finance to issuing paper).

A further main reason for the growth of conglomerates has been the desire to spread risk through diversification. Many institutions have become wary of being too dependent on a particular market and have sought to insulate themselves from a downturn in that market by moving into others. If one particular area of business is suffering, at least others may be profitable. The results of the clearing banks for 1990 suggest however that in a general economic downturn all areas of business will be affected and produce poor results.

Finally, many financial institutions appear to believe in the 'critical mass' concept, whereby only those firms that achieve a certain size will be able to effectively compete in the highly competitive market place of the 1990s. Coupled with this suggestion is the belief that many medium-sized financial institutions will be in an invidious position because they will be too small to compete through market share, but too large to adopt specialist niche strategies, which smaller institutions will be able to profit from.

Whilst many financial institutions have had the desire to diversify into conglomerates, there has also been a number of catalysts to diversification. One of the most important has been the breaking down of barriers through deregulation. Big Bang at the Stock Exchange allowed outside ownership of member firms and opened the way for the banks to move into the securities business, the Building Societies Act 1986 allowed building societies to offer unsecured loans, cheque books, wholesale funding and a range of banking facilities (see Chapter 5). A change in the operation of monetary controls from direct portfolio controls on the banks to operating through interest rates, allowed the banks to move into the mortgage market on a large scale and compete with the building societies.

Deregulation has led to a great increase in competition amongst similar types of institution, and amongst different groups of financial institution, and the need to compete has in turn been met by diversification and financial innovation. The building societies, for example, faced with intensified competition from the banks in what was traditionally their preserve – the mortgage market – lobbied for the ability to compete on a level playing field and will be able to move into banking business.

The globalisation of markets and the need to compete against foreign competitors, particularly with the advent of 1992, has resulted in the need for global or at least international financial institutions that can effectively compete overseas. Diversification on an international scale needs strong capital backing, and it is argued that only large, heavily capitalised financial institutions will be able to provide this.

More sophisticated technology has undoubtedly increased the ability of financial institutions to move into new markets and has made conglomeration easier. Automatic teller machines (ATMs) reduce the entry costs for new competitors compared with the costs of retail branches, for example, and on-line terminals allow institutions to make quick decisions relating to a transaction. The ability to hold detailed customer profiles on disc helps in cross-selling financial services and increases the effectiveness of marketing.

Ultimately the move towards conglomeration has been to achieve both stability and long term profitability for individual financial institutions, but in some instances, as discussed below, the very nature of the conglomerate firm has led to problems for these institutions themselves, and may also impinge upon broader issues of regulation and stability of the financial system as a whole.

The growth of financial conglomerates has raised fears that conflicts of interest may result. Many of the fears expressed relate to the combination of banking and securities business within the same institution. With a conglomerate the broking arm may be advising a client as to the buying and selling of a particular stock, and could receive information from the mergers and acquisitions arm or corporate finance department as to a takeover bid on that company. The investor would of course benefit from the information, but it would be through the use of information that should not be available. A further example is that the broking department may pressure the fund managers to increase the turnover in their portfolios in order to increase commission income ('churning').

Conglomerates can thus use their own structural form to benefit clients by providing them with inside information, or can inflate their own profits through dubious practices. Conflicts of interest can also disadvantage conglomerates however. One example of a conflict of interest for a conglomerate occurred in 1989 when Storehouse, a UK retail group, replaced Barclays as its lead bank and moved its business to Midland, because Barclays de Zoete Wedd (BZW), the investment banking part of Barclays was acting as adviser to an American arbitrageur who was considering bidding for Storehouse. Barclays maintain that the main clearing bank and BZW are independent sections within the same parent, and both have a duty to their customers. This does not of course stop it (or other conglomerates) from losing business through perceived conflicts of interest. Other examples have occurred. Midland Bank's merchant banking arm, Samuel Montagu, was involved in advising Goodman Felder Wattie in launching a takeover bid against RHM, a Midland client, and received considerable complaints from RHM.

The existence of 'Chinese walls' is supposed to stop flows of sensitive information from one department to another, but many are sceptical as to the strength of these walls,

> 'The Government is not convinced that total reliance can be placed on Chinese walls because they restrict flows of information and not the conflicts of interest themselves.'
>
> White Paper on Financial Services.

The SIB defines a Chinese Wall as:

> 'arrangements within the organisation of the firm, or between a firm and any associate of that firm, for ensuring that certain information obtained by individuals engaged in one part of the firm's or associate's business will be withheld from other individuals engaged in another part of it.'
>
> SIB (1990)

Most conglomerates strengthen their Chinese walls by physically separating their departments, sometimes placing them in a different building. Concern has been expressed however that the concept has been stretched too far by S.G. Warburg which has attempted to build a Chinese wall *within* one department – its corporate finance department – because of two separate dealings with Powergen. The corporate finance arm advised on both the possible flotation of Powergen and possible management buy-out, and attempted to prevent sensitive information leaking from one team to another, within the same department. Some observers argued at the time (August 1990) that such an undertaking would be extremely difficult if not impossible to police. In fact, the supposed advantages of conglomeration may have been exaggerated.

The need for Chinese walls negates to some extent the rationale of forming a conglomerate. Chinese walls have the disadvantage that they inhibit economies of scale in that they reduce the value of pooled information and expertise, one of the supposed benefits of conglomeration. Moreover, the costs of maintaining Chinese walls and compliance can be significant.

Financial conglomerates may also face problems in the internal running of the business. Management control tends to be difficult in any large organisation, but may be especially so in finance, where it is rarely acknowledged prior to takeovers/mergers that create conglomerates that different areas of the financial services industry have very different cultures.

Stockbroking is very different from merchant banking which is very different from retail banking, yet some institutions have bundled them all together with seemingly little regard to the differences in culture and attitude of the staff (not to mention salary differences between the areas of business, which quickly breed discontent). A large conglomerate may suffer in management control terms simply through becoming too bureaucratic and suffering from diseconomies of scale.

Moreover, with a conglomerate taking on different areas of business and innovating, staff need to be fully trained (or re-trained) in the new skills that are required, and this may take considerable time and expense. Somebody who has spent ten years as a teller will not find it easy to sell life assurance, for example (a trite example, but one that serves to make the point).

The advantages of one-stop financial institutions and the need for critical mass to compete are belied to some extent by the success of niche players. James Capel is a prime example of the way in which it is possible to maintain independence in the face of conglomeration. It remained the only main agency broker, and probably benefited from the adverse publicity of the effects of diversified securities houses – problems of Chinese walls, conflicts of interest etc. Similarly, small regional brokers have done well in recent years, many of them having lower overheads and costs than London firms, and have tended to attract personal customers that are drifting away from the large securities houses that are increasingly concentrating on institutional business to the detriment of the personal client.

Conglomerates also raise the question of market distortion in the form of monopoly. Large integrated financial services institutions may raise fears by controlling a significant proportion of the market share of a particular service, or may raise fears through simply restricting the number of outlets that a whole variety of services are supplied from (although many tend to be branded under a subsidiary name, they can be traced back to the parent organisation). This raises the question as to the efficiency of the financial system and the range of consumer choice.

Conglomerates may cause problems for supervision and for financial stability. It can be argued that the supervision and regulatory roles become much more problematic when a financial conglomerate undertakes many different activities. A major question in relation to this is whether regulation should relate to institutions or to functions. If regulation is related to particular groups of institutions, then the regulator will have to have expertise in a number of financial services areas, whereas if it is functional the conglomerate will be responsible to a number of different regulatory authorities.

Functional rather than institutional criteria need to be applied, but it may be difficult to identify the different services provided and hence determine which SRO has responsibility, or determine the status of a subsidiary for supervisory purposes. There is a very real danger that some activities may not be regulated due to the complex nature of interlocking business within a conglomerate.

A financial conglomerate that operates through several subsidiaries, through several countries, and through a variety of products and services has the ability to hide activities from host supervisors if necessary. This may be particularly attractive to conglomerates if a competitive advantage can be gained through non-disclosure of certain deals or areas of business.

Financial stability of individual institutions and of the financial system as a whole (systemic risk) could be weakened by the growth of conglomerates. Conglomeration, by its very nature, means that there is an increase in the interdependency of financial institutions. If one institution should experience solvency problems, the danger of this having a knock-on or 'domino' effect to other financial institutions is heightened with the existence of conglomerates. Large conglomerates can also suffer greatly from 'contagion', whereby a (perhaps) relatively minor subsidiary experiencing solvency problems or fraud or insider dealing might taint the reputation of the parent.

The risk of cross-infection between a conglomerates' activities has already come to the fore. Midland Bank suffered through buying Croker National Bank in the United States whilst National Westminster Bank was tainted by allegations of insider dealing at its securities arm, County Nat West.

13.2   SECURITISATION

Somewhat confusingly, the term 'securitisation' is used by financial commentators to describe two activities. The straightforward definition merely involves the issuing of securities rather than borrowing through bank loans. The more sophisticated type of securitisation is the bundling up of assets into securities which can then be sold to investors.

A prime example of the second form of securitisation is mortgage-backed securities, of which over six billion pounds worth have been issued 1987–1990 (Cox 1990). The normal situation is for a special company to be set up which buys the assets with finance provided by investors, who in turn receive debt securities. The advantage of securitisation to financial institutions is that assets can be taken off the balance sheet which improves capital adequacy ratios.

Growth in the first type of securitisation stems from the fact that many large companies are now more credit worthy than the banks, and can raise funds on better terms, through Sterling Commercial Paper or the Eurobond markets for example.

Banks have changed to such a degree that they can be viewed as a bundle of separate contracts, rather than the usual deposit taker/loan provider (Lewis 1987). Figure 13.1 shows how securitisation, new instruments and hedging techniques have changed the traditional manner in which banks carry out their operations, and

Figure 13.1 *Off- and On-Balance Sheet Banking*

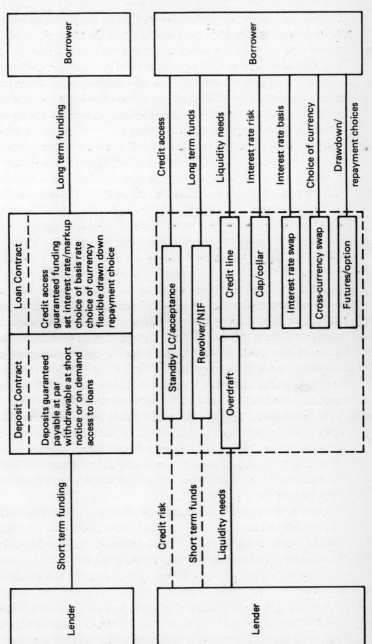

Source: Lewis 1987

emphasises the shift towards transactional banking and away from relationship banking.

The UK financial system is now moving into the third stage in the evoluntionary process as outlined by Rybczynski (1985). The stages are (1) bank orientated, where banks are the major intermediaries, (2) market orientated, where capital markets channel a large proportion of funds amongst sectors (disintermediation), (3) strongly market orientated system, where securitisation and hedging instruments are highly developed. With the UK in the third stage, there is the presumption that the financial system has a powerful ability to take on risk and hence encourage economic growth. At the same time, however, it is argued here that the attendant supervisory problems are also increased.

Securitisation poses problems for prudential regulation, because although the assets are taken off the balance sheet, in most cases some form of guarantee or contingent responsibility still exists (and indeed this is a selling point to investors) for the bank, and the degree of risk involved is difficult to quantify, probably more so than other risks. The BIS capital adequacy ratios do however take account of these guarantees in the risk-asset-ratio approach.

Securitisation means that there are more linkages between financial institutions and the complexity of deals tends to be increased, making the job of supervision more difficult. It may also be the case that as interdependencies amongst financial institutions are increased the possibility of systemic risk is enhanced.

Securitisation means that the business of corporate banking is in decline somewhat, and the Single EC Market is likely to speed up the process of securitisation further. As mentioned earlier however, banks have generally pre-empted this loss of business through becoming integrated securities houses, and heavily involved in securitisation.

Securitisation means that risk is shifted from banks to investors. One problem from the banks' point of view is that more and more lending will be provided to less and less credit-worthy customers, if the credit-worthy ones are attracted away from banks and towards the securities markets. Credit-worthy customers tend to be the larger corporations, many of whom are now setting up their own corporate finance departments, which again represents a loss of business to the banks. Scottish and Newcastle Breweries, for example, has treasury and finance departments that it argues are as knowledgeable about raising finance as any merchant bank, and the company is therefore deal orientated rather than having a special relationship with any particular bank.

13.3   GLOBALISATION

Capital markets are becoming more and more interlinked on a world-wide basis. Wholesale markets that deal in large transactions for companies are becoming increasingly globalised, particularly in the area of raising funds. Figure 13.2 shows the main elements of the move towards globalised markets.

The first step towards the internationalisation of financial markets was the introduction of the Eurodollar markets in the 1960's and 1970's. A further impetus to internationalisation has been the development and growth of the Eurobond market, which has increased with the development of swaps.

Figure 13.2   *Globalisation of Financial Markets*

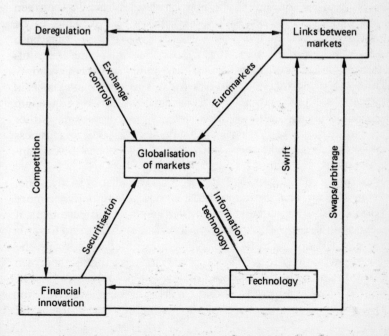

The Euro-Commercial Paper market is already international, with British investors buying, for example, the paper of a German company, although at present this form of financing is only available to large credit-worthy companies that have well-known names in international markets.

Undoubtedly the major push to global financial markets has come from deregulation, particularly in the form of the removal of exchange controls in many countries in the 1980's, and in the removal of barriers to entry to foreign firms.

International deregulation has its antecedents in the writings of Adam Smith over two hundred years ago,

'To give the monopoly of the home-market to the produce of domestic industry... must in almost all cases, be either a useless or hurtful regulation.'

Adam Smith, *Wealth of Nations*, p.456.

Elementary economic theory shows that the notion of comparative advantage applies to trade in both manufactured goods and services. There should thus be gains on all sides from the growth in internationalisation of financial markets.

The globalisation of financial markets has to a large extent been on the back of growth in international companies (multi-national corporations – MNCs). As companies grow and become international in scope they tend to look for finance on an international scale. This may be done for convenience in terms of raising a specific currency in the country of operation, for cost reasons, or because the domestic market is inadequate in some repect. For investors, there exists the opportunity to diversify inter-country.

Markets are thus becoming increasingly worldwide for both borrowers and lenders.

It is now relatively commonplace for large corporations to sell shares through a new issue in several countries simultaneously. The flotation of British Telecom for example was carried out in over five countries in 1984.

The more that financial markets become deregulated and globalised, the more likely it is that London will lose out as an international financial centre, as funds are increasingly repatriated back to their domestic markets that have become more liberalised.

The volatility of exchange rates and interest rates in the 1980s and 1990s has increased the need for innovatory techniques to hedge currency and interest rate risk. Financial innovation has also been a major factor, particularly with the advent of currency and interest rate swaps.

One of the major stimuli to increased competition in all financial markets is the greater availability of access to information that is a fundamental requirement of efficient markets. This increased access to information has largely come about through advances in technology and the ability to transmit information quickly and relatively cheaply around the world. With global markets and state of the art communications systems, information from one market is quickly assimilated by another, such that markets tend to move closely together.

It should be remembered that many financial markets are global or becoming globalised, and competition for UK financial institutions in the European market is merely an element of world-wide competition. Barclays, for example, argues that it needs a strong home base to succeed globally, and as the UK market is becoming saturated it must move into Europe (Norrington 1989).

As the above remarks imply, wholesale markets are the most globalised of financial markets, largely because of the global nature of many multinational corporations. Retail financial services, by contrast, are still to a large extent nationally based, although the 1992 changes being implemented for financial services in Europe will increase the international dimension of many retail products.

13.4 1992

The Cecchini Report for the European Commission examined the economic consequences of a liberalised financial market within the EC, and argued that gains would be around ECU 22 000 million for the community of countries as a whole in the areas of banking, insurance, brokerage and securities. It showed that substantial price differences exist for the same financial products across EC countries (differences of over 50 per cent being common). Table 13.1 shows that France, Belgium, Italy and Spain have extremely expensive insurance and brokerage services in general (although

Table 13.1 Percentage Differences in Prices of Standard Final Products in Eight Community Member States compared with the Average of the Four Lowest National Prices

	Germany	Belgium	Spain	France	Italy	Luxembourg	Netherlands	UK
Banking Services								
1. Consumer credit	136	−41	39	n.a.	121	−26	31	121
2. Credit cards	60	79	26	−30	89	−12	43	16
3. Mortgages	57	31	118	78	−4	n.a.	−6	−20
4. Letters of credit	−10	22	59	−7	9	27	17	8
5. Foreign exchange drafts	31	6	196	56	23	33	−46	16
6. Travellers cheques	−7	35	30	39	22	−7	33	−7
7. Commercial loans	6	−5	19	−7	9	6	43	46
Insurance services								
1. Life insurance	5	78	37	33	83	66	−9	−30

2. Home insurance	3	−16	−4	39	81	57	17	90
3. Motor insurance	15	30	100	9	148	77	−7	−17
4. Commercial fire and theft	43	−9	24	153	245	−15	−1	27
5. Public liability	47	13	60	117	77	9	−16	−7
Brokerage services							
1. Private equity transactions	7	36	65	−13	−3	7	114	123
2. Private gilts transactions	90	14	217	21	−63	27	161	36
3. Institutional equity transactions	69	26	153	−5	47	68	26	−47
4. Institutional gilt transactions	−4	284	60	57	92	−36	21	n.a.

Source: 'The Economics of 1992' in *European Economy*, No. 35, March 1988 (Cecchini Report).

none of these countries has costs of private equity transactions as high as the UK) and prices are likely to fall substantially as a result of competition. The UK and Germany are notable in having much higher consumer credit prices than the rest of the EC.

At the present time the majority of financial intermediation activities are intra-country, i.e. surplus funds of a country are mainly lent to deficit units in the same country, although there are opportunities for inter-country financial intermediation and inter country financial disintermediation (as represented by the Euro-currency markets) and the intention of the 1992 changes (see Chapter 11) is to increase cross-border financial intermediation.

Higher prices in one country would normally be subjected to increases in overseas competition and a reduction in price, although in the past barriers to competition in the form of exchange controls, demarcation of business and restrictions on overseas competitors have tended to restrict the level of competition. Other restrictions include cartels and other forms of restrictive trade agreements, and limitations as to the purchase of domestic financial institutions by foreign competitors.

The regulations in community countries tend to affect the competitiveness and efficiency of their respective financial institutions and markets, and these factors, in turn, influence the type of services offered and their price.

Once barriers to entry have been removed, competition from foreign institutions tends to erode implicit agreements amongst domestic intermediaries. In Spain the agreement not to pay interest on current accounts has recently been breached, and it is likely that France will soon follow suit.

The aim is thus to remove restrictive practices and barriers to entry in order to increase competition, reduce prices, and improve customer choice.

The effects of 1992 are likely to be far greater in retail financial markets than wholesale, largely because wholesale markets are already organised on an international scale.

Alongside the liberalisation of EC financial markets, it has been recognised that a unified framework of regulation is necessary. The main elements are to be similar for banking, insurance, and securities business (see Chapter 11).

There is some debate as to the best method of diversifying into Europe. Individual financial institutions can and have followed a

number of strategies for diversifying geographically
into Europe:

(i)   cross border takeovers
(ii)   cross border joint ventures
(iii)   cross border mergers
(iv)   starting up of new business from scratch.

Cross-border takeovers can be extremely expensive as the market capitalisation of European banks is around 35 per cent greater than net asset value. In other words, European banks cost a great deal more than they are worth, and takeovers represent an expensive form of diversification. When National Australia bank bought Yorkshire Bank, it paid almost £1 billion, three times its book value. On the other hand, this makes agreements, joint ventures and mergers far more attractive.

There is some contention that branch networks are a pre-requisite for competing effectively. Some have argued that these retail networks, that are undoubtedly costly to maintain, can only be sustained in a non-competitive highly regulated environment, with internal cross subsidies amongst products. Those institutions that have large branch networks may find themselves with extremely costly dinosaurs on their hands, and may become increasingly uncompetitive. New methods of delivery (home banking, more sophisticated Automatic Teller Machines) coupled with sophisticated rather than standardised retail services will mean that branch networks could become increasingly cumbersome. Takeovers of foreign institutions in order to gain a distribution network may not therefore be as popular as setting up joint ventures. Mergers that are designed to create pan-European conglomerates could be questioned for this reason too.

The main UK clearing banks have already developed European links. Most strategies do not appear to be 'pan-European', but carefully designed segmentation of markets for specific products, and the tailoring of existing products for those markets, as there are significant differences between markets.

The advantages of joint ventures are that overseas institutions already have retail networks through which services can be sold, and hence are far cheaper than setting up a distribution outlet from scratch or taking over an institution with a network.

The Royal Bank of Scotland has been involved with Banco Santander of Spain that involves cross-shareholdings and access by the Royal Bank of Scotland to serve British people in Spain through Santander's branches. At present these services are fairly limited, and more joint ventures are being sought to offer services in other European countries. The link up with Santander only contributed £1.7m out of the Royal Bank of Scotland's £337m pre tax profits for the year end 1989, although of course the link is at a relatively early stage of development. Joint ventures may thus take some time before they significantly add to profits.

It should be recognised that strategic alliances and joint ventures can easily disintegrate, with problems of conflict of managerial objectives between the two companies, over-bureaucratic structures, unclear hierarchy and chain of decision making.

There are many proponents of the view that the larger the financial institution (and the wider the product base) the more likely it is to be successful in competing in Europe. Such a contention appears to be based on the advantages of economies of scale, the ability to cross-sell financial services and an adequate capital base to allow expansion of business, all of which imply that takeovers and mergers will be beneficial. Large European banks such as Deutsche and Banque Nationale de Paris have taken the pan-European conglomerate route, and hope to offer a whole range of retail services.

Niche strategies are likely to be extremely powerful, and according to at least one consultant, banks should set up their subsidiaries as separate companies under an umbrella holding organisation. Compagnie Bancaire of France is already carrying out this policy, and seems to be doing extremely well from it. National Westminster Bank is trying a niche approach by attempting to capture the lucrative private banking market. To that end it owns Coutts in the UK , L'Européenne de Banque in France, and F. Van Lanschot in Holland, all private banks with wealthy customers. This type of niche strategy is likely to be a crucial area of profitability in the 1990s.

Although it is highly likely that the degree of concentration in European financial markets will increase dramatically over the next decade, it is possible that there will be an eventual reverse trend of breaking up of financial conglomerates and a move towards core business. It thus appears that financial institutions should try to stay in areas of business where they already have strengths, and develop those strengths in Europe through joint ventures or niche strategies, rather than attempting a pan-European approach through takeovers and mergers.

What services then, are the most amenable to development on a European scale? Many wholesale services are already international, and are not likely to be greatly affected by 1992.

Ugeux (1989) points out that 'mainframe products' such as life assurance and credit cards will be dominant, although they will need to be adapted to some extent for different markets. The profitability of credit cards in Europe can be questioned however, in the light of the market in the UK. The UK clearers used to make extremely good profits from credit cards, but it is estimated that the return on capital in this business has fallen from around 40 per cent in 1985 to approximately 25 per cent now, and will probably fall to 10–15 per cent over the next five years. (*Economist* July 21st 1990). The reason this has occurred is that new entrants have entered the market, in many cases offering lower interest rates than the clearers, and no charges for the use of the cards (which Barclays and Lloyds started to do in 1990, although with reductions in interest rates). A further factor affecting profitability is that about half of credit card users pay off their spending in full rather than incur charges.

With increased competition for credit card business in Europe and a flood of new entrants, it is possible that the market will follow the UK example, driving down profitability and reducing the attractiveness of what many think will be one of the few pan-European products.

Many industrial and commercial companies are becoming increasingly pan-European, and as they do their requirements tend to change. Insurance for example is needed to cover companies' EC–wide activities, and hence there is a growing market to be tapped. On the other hand, personal insurance business is likely to grow relatively slowly over the next five years at least, for a variety of reasons after which growth could be fast.

There are significant cultural differences, taxation differences, and incompatibility of insurance policies across member states that make liberalisation of the markets an extremely slow and arduous process. Very good potential for growth does exist though, e.g. pensions and life assurance in Spain where the financial institutions are relatively small in size and life assurance in France, where the market is competitive but still in the early growth stage of the product life cycle, and life assurance in Italy where the market is at present small but quickly expanding.

With insurance a major need is to establish local distribution networks which are essential to compete effectively. Setting up a sales force *de novo* would be costly and time consuming however, and independent financial intermediaries in the continent with which agency agreements could be made are rare as they tend to be tied to domestic insurance companies.

Although liberalisation of the European insurance market is slow, there is growing recognition that a truly single financial market cannot come about without more freedom in the insurance area, given the very size of insurance companies, and the savings and investments that they command. Initial plans have been set out for a single insurance passport along the lines of the single banking licence, although it is not likely to be in place until at least 1996.

The traditional business of the Finance Houses in the UK – (see Chapter 7) is likely to be a product that will be relatively homogeneous across Europe, and is potentially a huge growth area. It is therefore somewhat surprising that Midland and Barclays are contemplating selling their finance houses (July 1990). Finance houses have had poor results in 1990 because of high interest rates, but the expertise they possess could be vital for competing in Europe – although of course both banks could be contemplating buying the equivalent of finance houses in Europe, or setting them up.

Providing bank services to large commercial companies is already international, and is unlikely to be changed a great deal by 1992. For medium sized companies, distribution channels are relatively strong in most countries, and entry by foreign banks is extremely difficult. UK banks are unlikely to try to move into this area of business overseas. Similar arrangments apply to lending to small businesses. The personal mass market for banking products suffers from the fact that the 'critical mass' argument is very powerful – institutions need to capture a large portion of market share for it to be profitable. Some argue that the 'quality' personal sector banking market is likely to be a growth area,

'If there is blood to be spilt in the post 1992 market for financial services, this is the sector where some of the biggest battles will be fought'.

(Norrington 1989)

Personal pensions are likely to be a large market, once regulations are harmonised to a greater extent.

Figures 13.3 and 13.4 show some of the main areas of financial services business within Europe, and the degree of competition, capacity, competitive advantage and level of prices in a matrix format. The most important quadrant on the first matrix is the one with weak domestic competition and high capacity. Markets in this area include Spanish and Portuguese insurance (particularly life assurance). It is also noticeable that these markets are in the most important quadrant of the second matrix, where the competitive advantage of UK firms is high, and prices are high. By contrast, the West German insurance market is heavily regulated and suffers from overcapacity, and offers few prospects for UK institutions, even though the prices are on the high side. (See second matrix).

Figure 13.3 *Competitive Matrix 1992*

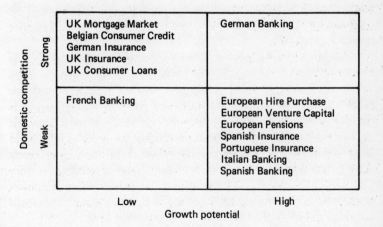

Figure 13.4   *Competitive Matrix 1992*

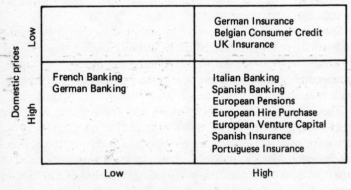

Competitive advantage of UK firms

The UK insurance market is already extremely competitive and relatively free from barriers to entry, such that 1992 will not bring any great surge of competition, although it is thought some of the large German insurers may be looking for organisation targets in the UK in order to set up distribution channels.

UK insurers ought to be seeking to gain a greater presence in Europe, particularly as they seem over-exposed to the American market, which has a problem of being cyclical in nature. The greatest benefits will be in life assurance, which UK insurers have expertise in (UK has the highest premium for life assurance business in the UK), although as mentioned earlier, initial growth in the market is likely to be slow. Once the concept of life assurance has taken hold in many of the extremely under-insured European countries however, growth is likely to be fast. Distribution networks must be built up now in order to benefit.

Those countries that are moving away from state social security type systems with collective insurance towards more market orientated private systems such as Spain, Italy, France, Portugal and Greece are likely to be growth markets for life assurance and pensions (see both matrices).

The UK banking market is the most liberalised in the EEC, with foreign banks already well established (there are more foreign banks in London than any other city), so that freedom of financial services in the community is unlikely to provide a major threat to UK banks (and at least one major UK bank – Lloyds – has concentrated on the domestic market).

Spanish banking is relatively fragmented, with over 100 banks, and widely regarded as inefficient, although prices and profitability are high. It is a market that UK banks are likely to expand into. Italian and Spanish banking are in the bottom right quadrants of both matrices, and could be profitable areas for expansion.

The West German banking market is fairly conservative, and tightly regulated (present capital adequacy requirements are very strict, for example), and is unlikely to be a fast growing market for UK banks to enter. Similarly, France is not a very good market to enter, with over 99 per cent of French adults already holding some form of bank or savings account. Belgian banks are relatively small, and will find it difficult to compete. Mergers and takeovers are occurring e.g. Generale de Banque of Belgium and AMRO of the Netherlands.

The mortgage market across Europe is extremely diverse (Boleat 1985) and harmonisation of legislation is extremely unlikely. West Germany is against allowing foreign mortgage institutions into their market, the Belgians do not allow variable rate mortgages, and around half of the French mortgage market is supplied by governmental institutions.

An area infrequently mentioned is that of venture capital, which the UK has expertise in, and which is relatively poorly developed in most EC countries, and will be a major growth area in the 1990's.

13.5 FINANCIAL INNOVATION

Llewellyn (1985a), (1985b) categorises *financial innovation* as the *types* of financial instruments introduced, the growth of new financial markets and the methods by which financial services are provided. *Financial change* is related to the *area* of business activity financial institutions are prepared to move into and hence is a factor in laying down both the demarcation lines between different groups of financial institutions, and the degree of competition involved.

There have been numerous attempts to specify the *underlying causal factors* affecting the nature and degree of financial innovation. Technological, market, and regulatory factors are maintained to be the major determinants of financial change and financial innovation (see Figure 13.5), although the emphasis placed on each tends to differ somewhat between authors (and there is no precise standardisation of terminology). Bain (1986) classifies the factors influencing the changing variety of financial instruments available as structural, legislative, and market. The first includes the location of surplus and deficit units in the economy, portfolio preferences of the users of financial services, and the economic and political environment. Legislative influences include taxation

Figure 13.5   *Financial Innovation*

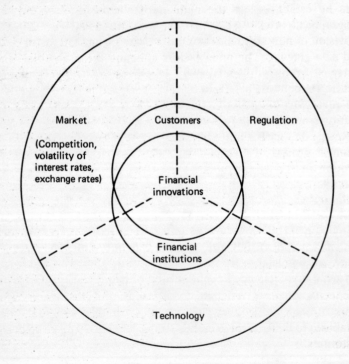

considerations, and monetary and supervisory controls, whilst market factors involve the stage of development of financial institutions and markets in the economy, particularly in the form of the competitive relationships between different financial institutions.

Smithin (1984) categorises financial innovations by distinguishing those that are *caused* by technological, institutional, and regulatory factors.

A slightly different approach is taken by Rybczynski, (1986). Changes in financial markets are differentiated by Rybczynski according to whether they are changes in 'internal' or 'external' frontiers. The former refers to the elimination of traditional demarcation lines as to the activities carried out by financial institutions. These he outlines as the payments mechanism (preserve of the banks), the collection of savings, (provided by non-bank financial intermediaries), and the underwriting of securities and fund management (investment banking). The external frontiers he establishes as the number of clients for services, the geographical area over which services are available, and the provision of new financial services both by incumbent institutions and new entrants. The main factors affecting these 'internal' and 'external' frontiers, according to Rybczynski, include economic factors (under which technological innovation is subsumed) and the regulatory framework, the latter cited as the main cause of shifting frontiers.

Re-regulation has been responsible for increasing competition amongst groups of financial institutions, which have competed through financial innovation. Banks and building societies, for example, have been prime innovators since re-regulation of the building society sector has intensified competition with the banks.

Monetary regulations have also been responsible for financial innovation, in the form of the commercial paper markets which evolved when the banks were restrained from lending by monetary controls (see Chapter 9).

Technology has also been a major factor, particularly for financial change, in reducing the costs of entry for new competitors through cheap computer facilities, and allowing customer databases to be used for accurate selling of innovations to relevant customers.

Interest rates and exchange rates have been far more volatile in the 1980s and start of the 1990s than in the 1970s and have led to the need for sophisticated techniques to hedge these risks. On the personal sector side low start mortgages and fixed rate mortgages have evolved, whilst on the corporate side currency and interest rate swaps and options have become increasingly popular, as have financial futures.

Innovations

In the explanations below it is only possible to give brief outlines of some of the financial innovations that have become popular over the last decade or so.

MOFS

A multiple option facility (MOF) is a situation in which a firm's banks are tied into one agreement to supply funds. Two groups of banks are involved, uncommitted lenders (the 'tender panel') and the 'committed banks', who provide funds if the first group for some reason cannot provide sufficient funding. The advantage to the company is that it is an extremely cheap form of finance (but of course not very profitable for the banks).

SWAPS

Swaps started in 1981 and initially exploited differentials between bond markets and the short-term credit market. Swaps can work when one of the companies involved has an advantage in both markets, or when the two companies have advantages in separate markets.

For example, assume company B can borrow from banks at LIBOR $+ \frac{1}{2}$, whereas company A would pay LIBOR $+ \frac{1}{4}$. In the bond market, company B can raise funds at 13 per cent, but company A can raise at 12 per cent because of a higher credit rating.

If company A wants to pay floating and company B wants to pay fixed rates, then it is beneficial to swap (even though A has the advantage in both markets).

Company A raises funds at LIBOR (13 per cent) instead of LIBOR $+ \frac{1}{4}$ ($13\frac{1}{4}$ per cent) and company B pays 12.75 per cent

Figure 13.6 *A 'Classical' Swap*

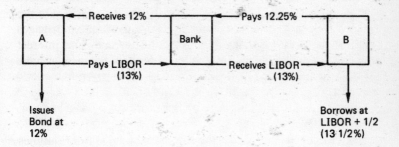

whatever LIBOR is ($\frac{1}{4}$ per cent cheaper than it could have got in the bond market). The bank receives $\frac{1}{4}$ per cent for the deal (12.25 per cent minus 12 per cent).

This is known as a 'plain vanilla' or 'classical' swap. When swaps were first introduced, banks used to wait for two suitable counter-parties. Now, 'warehousing' is common, whereby the bank agrees to one side of the swap and then waits for the counterparty.

Financial Futures

The London International Financial Futures Exchange (LIFFE) started in 1982. Futures contracts exist on currencies, interest rates, and Stock Exchange Indices. An example is given below of how a company might use interest rate futures to hedge interest rate risk. Given the space available it is only possible to give the flavour of a typical transaction.

A Simplified Hedge using Sterling Futures

An interest rate financial future can be used, for example, to hedge against interest rates rising. Suppose a company has a £2 million three month loan which costs 12 per cent p.a. The loan has to be rolled-over on August 1st (the date is now May 1st) and the company is worried that interest rates may rise. The company can hedge this risk by selling LIFFE's short sterling contract. These contracts are for three month deposits of £500 000, and the price of a futures contract is derived by subtracting the interest rate from 100 (i.e. an 11 per cent interest rate means a contract will be priced at 89).

The company sells four September £500,000 futures contracts at 88.00 (12 per cent, assuming the rate on the contract is the same as present spot rates). If, in September, interest rates do rise to 14 per cent as feared, the loan will be rolled-over at 14 per cent and will cost an extra £10 000 (2 per cent of £2 million for three months), but this will be offset by the profit on buying back the futures contract at 86.00 (14 per cent interest rate), which also equals £10 000. The profit on the futures contract is worked out as follows: The smallest price fluctuation (a 'tick') on a short-term sterling futures contract is 1/100 of one percentage point (a 'basis' point), i.e. 88.01 to 88.02 for example. One tick is worth £12.50 (.01 per cent x £500 000 x three months).

The profit on the hedge is thus 200 ticks (2 per cent) at £12.50 per tick = £2 500 for four contracts = £10 000.

If interest rates had dropped instead of risen, the company's loss on the futures would have been offset by the gain on the cheaper loan. Of course, protection is provided against a rise in rates, but the company cannot benefit from a fall in interest rates.

13.6 SHORT TERMISM

A major trend has been the growing importance of institutional shareholders such as insurance companies, pension funds, unit trusts and investment trusts over the past 20 years. Individual investors have been moving away from direct holdings of equities towards indirect methods through financial institutions. The majority of shares are owned by institutional shareholders (even though private ownership has risen from 3m to 11m from 1980–1990, only approximately 20 per cent of shares are owned by individuals).

A major question with regard to the capital market is whether or not institutional investors take too short term a view of firms' prospects.

The 'short-termism' view rests on a variety of allegations – that institutional investors invariably sell out in a takeover bid, that they do not take enough active participation in the management of companies, that share turnover is too high, that not enough credit is given to research and development expenditure by companies, and that they are only interested in short term profitability at the expense of long-term growth. A related criticism is that banks also take too short-term a view, and do not provide sufficient funds for industry, or when they do, it is at too high a price.

It could possibly be argued that the growth of large institutional shareholders has been to the detriment of the efficient management of UK commercial companies. Some critics argue that institutional investors do not exercise enough control over the management of companies, preferring to sell their shares if performance is not adequate rather than getting involved in management strategy and change. Selling the shares of a company, of course, reduces the share price and leaves the company in a vulnerable position as a possible takeover candidate, which is the market method of ensuring that inefficient and poorly run companies are changed around through a change in ownership. The main rationale is that the threat of takeover makes management less complacent and _may_ lead to companies being managed more effectively. Relying heavily on takeovers to oust poor incumbent management teams may be an inefficient and costly method of improving the performance of companies however. Fighting off a hostile takeover bid can be extremely expensive and take up a great deal of management time.

The existence of institutional shareholders has probably exacerbated the practice of 'dawn-raids', whereby it is far easier to contact a dozen large investors to buy large blocks of shares than it is to get in touch with many thousands of small investors, each of whom may only hold a small number of shares. Moreover the 1980s bull market meant that those companies with highly valued equity (some would say overvalued) could over-indulge in takeovers. Indeed, much of the bull market was fuelled on speculative takeover activity, providing a vicious circle.

Many have argued that it has in fact been too easy to carry out takeovers in the UK, and that takeovers have resulted in companies with no logical rationale for being in so many different areas of business. The move back to 'core' business may be a reflection that the takeover boom was taken too far. There is some sense in arguing that institutional shareholders could play a much greater role in the affairs of company management, thus limiting the need for takeovers. It is argued that institutional shareholders should take more direct responsibility in the way companies are run, rather than simply sell the shares if they are dissatisfied. Critics point to Germany and Japan, where merchant banks take a far more involved part in the running of business, and where companies have in general been more successful. In West Germany, for example, Deutsche Bank has a 25 per cent stake in Daimler Benz.

It is not often recognised however the extent to which *banks* have control over industry (or at least *could* have control over industry, were it to be exercised) because of the large proportion of shares owned by pension funds and insurance companies, which are in turn managed by the banks (Minns 1980).

Companies are in fact partly indirectly responsible for any short-termism that may exist. Fund managers are obviously encouraged to get the best possible investment yield from their portfolio by the trustees of company pension funds, some of whom are likely to be directors of companies. Directors are thus encouraging a short term approach on one hand, but decrying it on the other.

It is also argued that short-termism of institutional investors reduces the amount of Research and Development expenditure by UK companies, which is vital for long-term expansion. It is maintained that fund managers do not adequately take account of R & D expenditure in their valuations, and that management cannot divert enough funds to R & D for fear of losing out on short-term performance. One problem in relation to this is the preoccupation with annual growth in earnings per share (EPS) to the detriment of long term investment. A complement to the EPS measure might be an investment per share (IPS) measure that emphasises capital investment for long term growth (Collison 1990).

It is also argued that dividend payments, higher in the UK than overseas, deter firms from investment. If dividend payments were reduced and a greater proportion of earnings retained then investment would increase, the argument goes. This presupposes of course that UK firms have adequate investment opportunities. A theoretical (albeit costly) model would be for companies to pay out 100 per cent of earnings as dividends and then compete for the return of those funds from shareholders, ensuring that capital flows to the most successful businesses and ensuring efficient allocation of scarce resources.

The Innovation Advisory Board in the UK which advises the Department of Industry has argued for changes in the UK taxation system to encourage long-term investment and particularly R & D. Possibilities would be to place a tax on transactions in shares, or perhaps changing the capital gains rules such that those holding shares for a short period time are taxed heavier than those that are kept for longer. Both proposals would cause substantial liquidity problems for the markets (and a subsequent need for a higher return for loss of liquidity – see Chapter 3), and would discourage arbitrageurs, who help to stabilise markets.

It is sometimes argued that funds have been channelled from the UK to overseas firms to the detriment of UK companies in that a smaller pool of funds is available for investment domestically, but this really only looks at one aspect of flows of capital. True, UK capital investment overseas has increased since the abolition of exchange controls in 1979 (See particularly Chapters 7 and 11), but there has also been a considerable inflow of funds to the UK capital markets from abroad. Capital markets are truly global and there appears no reason to suggest that UK companies are worse off as a result of investment overseas.

High share turnover is an inadequate proxy for short-termism, as Tokyo has a higher turnover than London, yet Japan does not appear to have suffered in terms of industrial performance.

The evidence for and against short-termism tends to be somewhat anecdotal. Proponents of the city point to massive long term projects financed through the Stock Exchange, such as Eurotunnel, to counteract criticisms of short-term interests. Also, the move by companies away from relationship banking where the vast majority of financial services are obtained from a single institution towards transactions banking where a variety of institutions and different financing methods are used has to some extent left them in difficult positions when business conditions take a downturn.

Many financial innovations such as MOFS and NIFS mean that industrial and commercial companies move further away from relationship banking, and this may not necessarily be beneficial to the long-term growth of the economy. It should be recognised that whilst companies complain of short-termism and lack of funding, at the same time they are exacerbating the problem by taking up innovatory services that drive a wedge between institutions and the company. With MOFS, for example, there are usually more than ten 'committed' banks and often as many 'tender-panel' banks. As mentioned earlier, the profits to these banks are relatively small, and many argue that the return does not equate with the risk, so that they tend to feel justified in pulling out of the deal at even the slightest breach of a covenant. Such problems would not occur with traditional bank loans.

Where the blame lies is a moot point – with the banks for identifying and satisfying a demand with a specific service, or with companies for taking up that service when in the long run it may not be in the firms' best interest. Laura Ashley, for example, an extremely well-run company, was threatened with insolvency when a MOF went wrong in 1990, with some banks withdrawing because of the breaking of a covenant (even though it related to permissible gearing – debt/equity – levels, and breaking the covenant did not mean that Laura Ashley was in trouble).

REFERENCES

Ayling, D. (1986) *The Internationalisation of Stockmarkets*, (Gower, Aldershot).

Bain, A.D. (1986) 'Causes of change and Innovation in the Mix of Financial Instruments: The UK Experience' in *Shifting Frontiers in Financial Markets* by Fair, D. (Ed.) (Martinus Nijhoff, Netherlands).

Boleat, M. (1985) *National Housing Finance Systems: A Comparative Study* (Croom Helm).

Cecchini (1988) 'The Economics of 1992, European Economy, No. 35, March (*Cecchini Report*).

Chorafas, D. (1989) *Bank Profitability* (Butterworths, London).

Collison, D.J. (1990) Letter to the Financial Times, 18th July.

Cox, K (1990) 'Securitisation in the 1990s', *CBSI Journal* May.

Goodhart, C.A.E. (1986) 'Financial Innovation and Monetary Control' *Oxford Review of Economic Policy* 2 (4) (Oxford).

Lewis (1987) 'Off-Balance sheet Banking in J.S.G. Wilson (ed) *Asset and Liability Management* (Euromoney Publications, London).

Llewellyn, D.T. (1985a) *The Evolution of the British Financial System*, Gilbart Lectures on Banking, (Institute of Bankers).
——(1985b) 'The Changing Structure of the UK Financial System'. *Three Banks Review*, March.

Mayer, C. (1986). 'The Assessment: Financial Innovation, Curse or Blessing?' *Oxford Review of Economic Policy* 2 (4) (Oxford).

Minns, R. (1980). *Pension Funds and British Capitalism* (Heinemann, London).

Norrington, H.T. (1989) 'A UK Bank Planning for the Internal Market in 1992', in *Planning for Insurance and the Financial Services Sector* (Butterworths, London).

Podolski, T. (1986) *Financial Innovation and the Money Supply* (Blackwell, London).

Rose, H. (1986) 'Change in Financial Intermediation in the UK' *Oxford Review of Economic Policy* 2 (4) (Oxford).

Rybcynski, T.M. (1985) 'Financial Systems, Risk and Public Policy'. *Royal Bank of Scotland Review*, December.

Rybcynski, T.M. (1986) 'Shifting Financial Frontiers: Implications for Financial Markets (Martinus Nijhoff, Netherlands).

Securities and Investments Board (1990) 'The Proposed Core Rules on Conduct of Business'. July.

Smith, A. (1776) *The Wealth of Nations*, Glasgow Edition (1976).

Smithin, J.N. (1984) 'Financial Innovation and Monetary Theory'. *Three Banks Review*, December.

Ugeux, G. (1989) 'Europe Sans Frontiers: The Integration of Financial Markets'. *Royal Bank of Scotland Review*, June.

White Paper (1985) 'Financial Services in the United Kingdom: A New Framework for Investor Protection'. *Cmnd 9432* (HMSO London).

INDEX

Litan, R., 259
Llewellyn, D. T., 8, 285
  on building societies, 53, 56, 57,
    62
  on regulation, 145, 236
Lloyd's Act (1982), 76–7, 238, 239
Lloyd's of London, 76–7, 84–8
  Central Fund, 100–1
  computerisation, 86–7
  Council of, 76–7, 100
  Members' Agents Pooling
    Arrangements, 86
  names at, 86
  open years, 84–6
  profitability, 84–9
  regulation of, 100, 241, 249–50
  syndicates, 86
  see also insurance
Lloyds Bank, 32, 33, 281, 285
Loan Guarantee Scheme (LGS),
  134
loanable funds theory, 23–5
loan
  commercial, 129
  personal, 128–9
  unsecured, 62, 68, 128–9, 265
Local Authority Bills, 160,
  169–70, 177
Local Authority Bonds, 170
Local Government Act (1972),
  169
Local Government Act (1985),
  169
Lomax, D., 251
London Discount Market
  Association (LDMA), 39
London Inter Bank Deposit
  (LIBID), 151
London Inter Bank Offer Rate
  (LIBOR), 20, 151, 171, 288–9
London International Financial
  Futures Exchange (LIFFE),
  289

long tail risks, 86
long-term insurance, *see* insurance
Louvre agreement, 223
Luxembourg, 186, 276–7

Madoff Securities, 217
Major, John (as Chancellor), 147
managed pension funds, 118
marine insurance, 86, 87–8
market makers (GEMMs),
  gilt-edged, 232–3
market makers, equity, 207–8
Matif Futures Exchange, France,
  245
maturity transformation, 9–10, 48
Medium Term Financial Strategy,
  142–4
  see also monetary policy
Members' Agent Pooling
  Arrangments, Lloyd's, 86
Mercantile and General
  Reinsurance, 97
merchant banks, 39–40
Metropolitan Police, 246
Midland Bank, 32, 33, 238, 267,
  270, 282
Minimum Lending Rate, 184
Minns, R., 292
Modern Portfolio Theory, 121,
  224
MOF (multiple-option facility),
  255–6, 288
monetary policy, 140, 141, 142–4,
  151, 244
money
  control of supply, *see* monetary
    policy
  definition of, 143–4
  see also interest rates
money market instruments, 151,
  152, 153–60, 160, 177–8
  see also Bills of Exchange;
    Certificates of Deposit;